Microsoft®

S0-BYN-343

MOBILIZE YOURSELF!
The Microsoft® Guide to Mobile Technology

Robert L. Bogue

PUBLISHED BY
Microsoft Press
A Division of Microsoft Corporation
One Microsoft Way
Redmond, Washington 98052-6399

Copyright © 2002 by Robert L. Bogue

All rights reserved. No part of the contents of this book may be reproduced or transmitted in any form or by any means without the written permission of the publisher.

Library of Congress Cataloging-in-Publication Data
Bogue, Robert.
     Mobilize Yourself! : The Microsoft Guide to Mobile Technology / Robert L. Bogue.
        p. cm.
     Includes index.
     ISBN 0-7356-1502-0
     1. Mobile communication systems.   2. Cellular telephones.   3. Pocket computers.   I.
Title.

TK6570.M6 B65   2002
384.5'3--dc21   2001056255

Printed and bound in the United States of America.

1 2 3 4 5 6 7 8 9   QWT   7 6 5 4 3 2

Distributed in Canada by Penguin Books Canada Limited.

A CIP catalogue record for this book is available from the British Library.

Microsoft Press books are available through booksellers and distributors worldwide. For further information about international editions, contact your local Microsoft Corporation office or contact Microsoft Press International directly at fax (425) 936-7329. Visit our Web site at www.microsoft.com/mspress. Send comments to *mspinput@microsoft.com*.

ActiveSync, ActiveX, Bookdings, Hotmail, InkWriter, Microsoft, Microsoft Press, Mobile Explorer, MSN, Outlook, PivotChart, PivotTable, PowerPoint, Visual Basic, Windows, Windows logo, Windows Media, and Windows NT are either registered trademarks or trademarks of Microsoft Corporation in the United States and/or other countries. Other product and company names mentioned herein may be the trademarks of their respective owners.

The example companies, organizations, products, domain names, e-mail addresses, logos, people, places, and events depicted herein are fictitious. No association with any real company, organization, product, domain name, e-mail address, logo, person, place, or event is intended or should be inferred.

Acquisitions Editor: Alex Blanton
Project Editor: Jean Cockburn

Body Part No. X08-41931

I dedicate this book to the past, the present, and the future:

The past, which has allowed me to become who I am through the numerous contributions of my friends and colleagues, including the support of my long-lost friend Ronald Peyton. I miss you, my friend.

The present, which is the essence of being. My wife, Shelley, who reminds me to stay in the present and supports all that I do, no matter how insane.

The future, with all its possibilities, not the least of which is my unborn son, Alexander Nathaniel, whom I have waited such a very long time to meet.

Contents at a Glance

Table of Contents

Acknowledgments

You are now reading what is perhaps the hardest part of the book to write. It is difficult not because of some complicated technology or confusing technique, but because this is the part of the book that the author knows won't be carefully scrutinized by the rest of the team that is so crucial to the book's development. This is a small place in the book where I am not supported as I have been privileged to be throughout the rest of the work.

Without the help and assistance of all the people acknowledged here, this project would quite simply never have happened. The list of people who were an integral part of the development of this title starts with Alex Blanton, my acquisitions editor, who was instrumental in both providing perspective and refining a vision for the book during the early development phases.

Wendy Zucker, who was for a brief time my production editor, put up with my demands upon her time, which was so precious and lacking. I appreciate her care in selecting a custodian for this project who had more time to nurture it.

Jean Cockburn, my project editor for most of the project, took care of all of the issues that I couldn't wrap my mind around. She's the one who can be credited with making my writing consistent and having the critical eye to ensure that I never forgot any essential parts of the puzzle.

Jason Dunn, my technical editor, provided insight on the market, and his knowledge of the industry has substantially helped to balance the book you are about to read. I feel honored that Jason agreed to help with this project. I encourage every reader to visit his Web site at *http://www.pocketpcthoughts.com*.

The team who put together this book is rounded out by the fantastic group at Online Training Solutions, Inc.: Joyce Cox, Nancy Depper, Nealy White, Lisa Van Every, Liz Clark, and R.J. Cadranell. These people not only executed the tasks of putting the book together, but also provided support and alternatives when things didn't work out just right.

In addition to those who had a direct hand in the production process, there are others who were kind enough to spend their time with me and share their perspectives on the mobile technology industry. I particularly want to thank Barry Issberner of Symbol and Jonas Hasselberg of Microsoft. They were immensely helpful in making me able to provide you with a balanced and hopeful set of solutions.

I also want to thank all of the vendors who supported me by providing evaluation units to allow me to explore a variety of products and show you what works best. Rather than attempting to list all of these organizations here, I've provided links to their Web sites and details about some of the most promising products in the chapters themselves.

Finally, I thank you for picking up this book and reading these acknowledgments.

Introduction

Even before I sat down to start writing this book, I was reminded of a situation I experienced when I was traveling to my first information technology (IT) conference. I had never traveled much for business, so everything I was experiencing was relatively new to me.

I was on my way to Vail, Colorado. It was summer, so there wasn't going to be any skiing, but it would a memorable trip to the mountains. I was traveling to a conference on IBM's Midrange AS/400 systems, which I had only limited experience with, so I knew I would have a chance to do some serious learning.

At the airport, I ran into a salesperson from the company I worked for. He was on his way to visit customers on the West coast. I remember running into him, because in the space of about 10 minutes, he taught me a handful of tricks for traveling that I use even today.

He told me that gate agents could upgrade you from coach to business class if you asked, and they were in a good mood. From then on, I made a point of being nice to gate agents, and always asked if there was "room up front." My colleague also taught me that joining a frequent flier program is advantageous even for people who don't fly that often. Joining the frequent flier program makes it easier for other people who are part of the frequent flier program to upgrade your tickets for you.

Finally he taught me about the airline clubs. You can get free sodas at these. (I've never been much of an alcohol-drinking person.) More importantly, however, you get a quiet place to work—often with a phone line that enables you to send and receive e-mail.

These tips were very helpful to me when I began to travel more and more for my company, and for companies I worked for after that. Of course, you can find helpful tips on almost every travel Web site, but my colleague's advice was particularly valuable to me, because I received it before the Internet was popular.

The reason this experience comes to mind is that what the kind salesperson from my company did so many years ago, is what I intend to do for you through this book. I'll spend a fair amount of time explaining the mobile technology options available to you as a mobile worker, but exploring all of the technology options isn't my ultimate goal.

My ultimate goal is to make the mobile technology that you do have, or the technology that you decide to get, useful to you. This means pointing out the tips, tricks, and shortcuts you'll need to actually use mobile technology. It also means pointing out potential pitfalls, such as how to avoid running out of battery life on your notebook while traveling.

I hope that while reading the book, you will feel as if you're being led by someone who's already climbed the mountain of mobile technology. Because I know the ropes, I can steer you clear of problems that don't yet have solutions. I would be misleading you if I told you I will be able to steer you clear of every obstacle, but hopefully I can help you avoid most of the major ones.

Are You Frustrated?

One of the biggest challenges for mobile technology is that it has been very frustrating to use. Mobility devices always have some component—or several components—that doesn't quite fit your needs or doesn't work quite as advertised. As a result, users of mobile technology have often spent their time trying to overcome the limitations of the technology.

I count myself among the people who get frustrated by mobile devices. A few years ago, I was doing a consulting job in northeastern Ohio. I had two mobile devices that I kept with me all the time: my cellular phone and my nationwide pager. The devices were serviced by two different providers. Because of this, I felt assured that I would have coverage almost anywhere I wanted to go.

Neither of the devices worked at this consulting engagement. I had previously had times when one or the other of the devices wouldn't work, which was why I had both devices. However, I hadn't yet run across a situation where neither worked.

The point of this story is that it was one of the most technologically frustrating times in my professional career. I thought I had already worked through the problems of one device by having a backup. The problem was that I had found a situation where both devices failed at the same time.

That was years ago, when the infrastructure for mobile devices was still being built; however, the memory has stayed with me, because I was used to the idea that I could work away from my office and remain completely productive. I felt that the device failures robbed me of that productivity.

Tip If you are away from your office, and you want people to be able to reach you at all times, the phone company can set up a call forwarding service on your office phone line. This service will forward calls to your cellular phone when the line is busy or you don't answer. It provides a great backup for when you're on the line; it handles your need for voice mail; and when you're traveling, you can take your phone off the hook and have calls forwarded to you immediately. Your clients don't have to know that you're not in the office.

Not all of the frustrations are based on wireless connectivity failure. Sometimes the problem with a mobile device is as simple as not having enough battery life. If you've been using a notebook computer while traveling, you've probably run into situations where the notebook's battery ran out of juice. Perhaps it was a long coast-to-coast flight, or perhaps it was just a road trip on which you forgot to bring your power cord.

When the battery fails, and there's no power around, you're suddenly carrying around a seven-pound brick. The technology has failed. Your notebook will be useless if it has a dead battery. Sometimes the solution is simple: Just buy another battery.

This, of course, leads to another problem. Eventually, you end up carrying so much stuff that you're no longer mobile. Most mobile professionals know that carrying less is better. Carrying backup devices for a two-day sales trip won't be high on your list of things to do. In fact, for short trips, most mobile professionals decide it's better to be out of touch for a day or two than to carry an extra twenty pounds of gear.

Although I won't be able to prevent problems from happening or solve every mobile problem, I'll devote much of the first few chapters to the problems you're likely to have with your technologies, and provide options for solving or avoiding them.

What Mobility Means

Sometimes the computer and consumer electronics industries get so wrapped up in the technology that they seem to make outrageous claims about what the technology can do, or will be able to do shortly. Any claims about exciting new technologies are likely to be partly fictional.

If you don't believe me, go back to old issues of computer magazines from ten or twenty years ago, and look for articles about speech recognition. If these were to be believed, we should all have been talking to our computers as our primary means of interface years ago. In most situations, if we talk to our computers, people look at us as if we've watched too much *Star Trek*. Our computers today have speech-recognition capabilities, but we usually don't use them, because the technology requires a lot from the user and the audio capabilities of the computer. (I'll address speech recognition in Chapter 11.)

In the consumer electronics market, we were all supposed to buy laser disc players, because they produced a much better picture than a VHS videotape. We didn't, because they were too expensive and cumbersome. We were also all supposed to have high-definition televisions by now, because the picture is so much better than a regular analog TV. Most of us still don't have high-definition TVs, because we don't want to deal with the expense and the headaches.

If you think back to examples like this where the industries have greatly miscalculated what the impact of a technology will be, it's easy to become skeptical of the latest types of technologies that are getting industry attention: mobility and wireless. You can't accept everything written about mobility and wireless devices with wide-eyed conviction, but you can accept that mobile devices can solve a great number of problems today.

To help you separate the hype from the reality, I must first define what I mean when I say *mobility*. For the purposes of this book, *mobility* means remaining productive while away from your desk. For some people, being away from their desks means being in a meeting room down the hall. For others, it means being in a meeting room across the country. No matter where you are, the goal of a mobility device is to make you as effective as possible at doing your job.

This definition of mobility will give you a lot of choices—choices that I'll address in the first few chapters when I help you understand the differences in the mobility devices you can use. I'll cover a wide array of hardware, software, and services designed to make you mobile, but I'll focus primarily on computer-related mobile technologies. So, for instance, a paper-based day planner might help you to be mobile, but I won't cover it here, because it's not computer related. (Besides, the Pocket PC can do almost anything a paper-based day planner can.)

Another important distinction is that I won't cover mobile telephones as such. I briefly cover Microsoft's new Pocket PC-integrated phones and Microsoft Smart Phone in Chapter 1, and mobile phone Internet connectivity in Chapter 2, but I won't spend much time covering types of phones, cellular service providers, or service plans. Frankly, figuring out which service plan is best for you and what provider to use seems to require a secret decoder ring, and I haven't eaten enough Cracker Jacks to find the decoder ring. I'll get back to you if I find it. With these limitations in mind, most of the remaining topics related to mobility are fair game for this book.

Wireless vs. Mobility

One of the discussions I've often had with people throughout the development of this book has been the difference between *wireless* and *mobility*. Strictly speaking, *wireless* means "connected without wires." *Mobility* is the ability to move freely.

Unfortunately, the industry often uses the two terms interchangeably. In many ways, the use of the term *m-commerce* for mobile commerce is making this situation worse, because what the industry calls mobile commerce is really wireless commerce. You must be connected to a wireless network to start and execute a transaction with another server.

Perhaps in the future—when we can use a mobile phone to get a cola from a vending machine even when we're beyond our normal service area—we will have mobile commerce. For now, things get confusing when we talk about wireless commerce as if it were mobile commerce.

Here, I am careful not to call wireless connectivity a mobility solution. If you hear someone talking about mobility, you might want to find out if he or she is really talking about wireless connectivity, or a service that will truly allow you to be mobile. For the purposes of this book, mobility always implies productivity—which isn't always the case with wireless solutions.

Who Should Read this Book?

This book is intended for mobile knowledge workers who need to become—or remain—productive. A knowledge worker is anyone who processes information, such as a salesperson or manager. (A less flattering term for such a worker is "paper pusher.") Mobile knowledge workers are knowledge workers who are away from their desks more than 20 percent of the time.

Specifically, you should read this book if you:

- Need to decide what devices and services to buy to remain productive while traveling or in the office
- Need to better use the mobile devices and services you already have
- Want to evaluate how your business can use mobile devices and services to enhance your competitive advantage
- Are tired of carrying your notebook computer and want to leave it at home
- Need to be productive even when you're stuck in what seem like endless meetings

There are certainly other readers who will find value in the information in this book, but the book is intended for people solving the problems just listed.

You won't need an extensive background with computers or a special knowledge of information systems to learn from this book. The book is targeted at the mobile knowledge worker—not the information technology department. That doesn't mean you shouldn't read the book if you do have this knowledge, because there are lots of tips and tricks scattered throughout the book that should be helpful to everyone.

How the Book is Laid Out

This book is designed so that you can read it from cover to cover (although probably not in one sitting), but it does not have to be read that way. Occasionally, I'll tell you that you can, or should, skip a chapter if you have knowledge of a subject area, but even if I don't mention it, please feel free to skip ahead. If you later feel you're missing something, you can go back and review.

How to Get the Most from this Book

One of the unique elements of this book is a set of questions, designed to help you take a moment and review the material, at the end of each chapter. It might seem odd for a guidebook such as this one to include review questions, but I feel they are an important part of your experience.

There are no right or wrong answers to these questions, and you won't find an answer key at the back of the book. They are there to help you work through applying what you've learned to your environment. If you feel put off by the questions, or think they are too trivial, skip them. They exist only to help you.

Understanding the Automotive Metaphor

If you've flipped through the table of contents, you might have noticed that the titles of the first five chapters (the first part of the book) have an automotive theme. I did this so that as I laid the groundwork for your understanding in later chapters, you would have a point of reference, or a map, as you're going along.

In many ways, mobile technology is like a car. It gives you some freedom. A car allows you to move around a city; mobile technology allows you to move and remain productive.

Chapter 1 is about choosing the vehicle. The devices you decide to use will dictate most of your remaining mobile technology decisions. Just as you choose what kind of car you want before you start looking into the colors and fabrics, you should choose the devices you want to use first.

Chapter 2 is about choosing the transmission. The connectivity of your devices will control how much of the power of that device you can use, much as a transmission transfers the power from the engine in a car to the road.

Chapter 3 is about choosing your alarm. Just as you must protect a new car, so you should protect the data on your devices. This chapter covers protecting your data.

Chapter 4 is about customizations. When you first get a new vehicle, it's not truly yours. Most people customize their car in some small ways to make it theirs. You might customize your car by installing an upgraded CD player or a sunroof. Others might simply hang a pendant or crystal on the mirror. This chapter reviews the customizations you can make to (or get for) your mobile devices.

Chapter 5 is about parking the vehicle. Synchronizing your devices to each other and to the corporate network backs up your data and protects it from being lost, damaged, or destroyed. This is much like parking your car in the safe haven of a garage.

As with the other elements of the book that I've discussed here, you should feel free to ignore this one if you don't find it to be of value.

In Parting

I hope you find this book useful. I always appreciate feedback, for better or worse. Although I can't guarantee a response to every message, please feel free to let me know what you think of this book at *Rob.Bogue@ThorProjects.com*.

Foundations

In this book, I start off our journey by laying the foundations, the things that you'll need to be at least aware of—or familiar with—to be able to take advantage of the techniques introduced later in the book.

Part I is devoted to the topics that you'll need to know to decide which mobile technology is right for your needs. This is the section of the book that will help you understand the technology you already have, and what the other options are.

Chapter 1 covers the devices and services that you can use to be mobile. This includes everything from laptops to PowerPCs to access points to the Internet (such as cyber cafés and business centers.) This chapter's goal is to show you what you can carry—and when you don't have to carry anything—to remain productive while mobile.

Chapter 2 covers your wired and wireless connectivity options, everything from the cradles that come with handheld devices to wireless LANs and wireless cellular connections. You will learn the differences between the connectivity options in terms of both range and speed. You'll learn the quickest and easiest methods to keep connected.

Chapter 3 focuses on security both to access corporate systems and also to protect the data on your handheld computer from being used by another party. This chapter focuses on keeping your data secure, whether you're sending it across a public network (like the Internet) or keeping it on the device.

Chapter 4 shares the tools and tips that you can use to use your devices effectively, whether you spend your time in the office, or whether you are freely mobile. With everything from compact phone cords to external keyboards for your handheld, this chapter is for the gadget lover, and for those who need that little something to make their device perfect.

Chapter 5 introduces you to the idea of synchronization. Whether you're synchronizing your notebook to the corporate network or your handheld device to your computer, there are some basic skills and understandings that you need to help make things go smoothly. You'll find them here. This chapter is also important because it shows you how to move files to and from your Pocket PC.

Choose Your Vehicle: the Devices

Choosing the mobile communication devices that you want to carry with you is a difficult proposition. No single device is the perfect solution that will fit every person's needs. In fact, most people have a great deal of trouble just deciding what devices to buy. Even if you have devices already, or think you know exactly what device you want to buy, you might want to read this chapter so that you'll know the limitations and benefits of each type of device.

This chapter provides a foundation for the information I will cover throughout this book, so if you're particularly savvy you might get a little bored as we walk through the advantages and disadvantages of each type of device and service. If you find that you're getting bored with the material, I invite you to skim the chapter, reading only the headings, and then move on to the next chapter. You might also want to review the questions at the end of the chapter to make sure you feel you can answer them.

This chapter's goals are to:

- Identify the devices and services that you can use while on the move.

- List the features and drawbacks to each type of device and service.

- Evaluate which devices are appropriate for your needs.

This chapter will cover the five basic types of devices and services you can use to maintain your productivity:

- Notebook computers
- Personal digital assistants (PDAs)
- Phone-integrated PDAs
- Smart Phones
- Internet access points

However, before evaluating these devices and services, let's take a brief (and I mean brief) look at computers and technologies that have led us to this point.

A Brief History of Personal Computers

Most people don't think of their PDAs as computers, but they are. They contain a processor not unlike the one in your desktop computer. They contain memory similar to the memory in your desktop computer. In fact, all the mobile devices we use today share their heritage with the personal computer movement of the 1980s and since.

Shortly after the original IBM PCs were available, Compaq created the first "luggable" PC. These computers contained a small monochrome monitor and a keyboard that snapped in place to form the top of the computer case. They required a power outlet because they didn't have batteries, but they did provide a greater level of mobility for professionals who absolutely had to take their computers with them.

The size of the luggable PCs started to come down, and some of them started using batteries. These devices were incremental improvements over Compaq's initial offering. A little weight was removed, and a smaller size, or footprint, was developed, but these devices were still too bulky to be used by anyone but die-hard professionals who would not let the limitations of the technology stand in their way.

After liquid crystal displays (LCDs) replaced the traditional cathode ray tube (CRT) monitors in the luggable PCs, it was just a matter of time before the process of miniaturization would shrink the luggable PC down to what most of us would consider to be a laptop computer. (The CRTs in the original luggable PCs were essentially smaller versions of what most of us have on our desktops today.) However, to fit the entire unit on a lap, a few of these computers required users who are about 7 feet tall.

Now we enjoy notebook computers that are, as their name implies, notebook sized. The last few years have even seen these devices gain powers that were previously reserved for their desktop cousins. In many organizations, the notebook computers that were once used only when someone needed to do an out-of-town presentation are replacing desktop computers entirely for professionals who travel.

Now that we have a quick foundation to start from, let's look at the mother of all mobile devices, the notebook.

Notebook Computers

Just as cellular phones have become a common part of the business landscape, so too have notebook computers. Most people who travel on business use notebook computers whether that travel is to customer offices or to other company offices.

It might seem strange to review notebook computers when almost every mobile business worker has one. However, the fact that they have them doesn't mean they use them. I'm sure that if you haven't yet left your notebook computer at home because it was too heavy to bring on a short business trip, you eventually will.

I know that is a strong statement. Your notebook is your connection back to the main office. However, even if your 2.5-pound notebook is one of the slickest, thinnest, and lightest on the market, it will still become a burden at some point. This is in part because the 2.5 pounds figure is what the notebook manufacturer's marketing department wants you to believe. The "Disadvantages of Notebooks" section later in this chapter will cover why, no matter what the weight of the notebook, it will eventually get left behind.

Variations in Notebooks

Determining which notebook is the appropriate device for your mobile needs is a big challenge; there are several different classes of notebooks, each one optimized for different purposes and different characteristics. There are essentially three different classes of notebooks available today:

- Ultra-light
- Standard
- Super-user

Before weighing the advantages and disadvantages of notebooks in general, let's look at the differences between the classes of notebook.

Ultra-Light

An ultra-light notebook is optimized for size and weight. Almost every design decision for this class of notebook errs on the side of lighter weight. In this type of notebook, all the input-output sources, such as floppy drives, DVD-ROMs, and even the basic access ports such as serial and video, are often available only through one or more master access ports on the device.

The rub of this is that even though the notebook manufacturers quote the lower weight of the unit itself, that weight doesn't include the additional 4–6 pounds of weight in the power adapter, DVD-ROM, and floppy disk drive. Nor do they mention the octopus of cables that you end up with when every device that you need to use with the notebook is external.

These notebooks, because of their smaller size, often support some of the smallest screen displays of any notebook on the market, and as such aren't suitable for situations in which you're likely to need a great deal of workspace on the computer.

The final concern with ultra-light notebooks is that their power and memory capacity rarely match those of other notebooks. Ultra-light notebooks should be considered an option for replacing the computers of users who need only basic capabilities. Running a word processor, e-mail, spreadsheets, or other standard office applications won't be a problem, but ultra-light notebooks are generally not advisable for developers or other users with advanced processing needs.

Standard

Standard notebooks—the ones that most users will end up running—are notebooks that balance size and weight with power and functionality. These notebooks, although not as powerful as desktop computers or super-user notebooks, have sufficient power to support the needs of most users, and are of a weight that most users can tolerate.

The weight of notebooks in this class is usually between 5–7 pounds. Their LCD displays start at 13 inches and get larger from there. They won't get the looks of amazement you see in TV commercials for some notebooks, but they will get the job done. Most notebooks fall into this category.

Super-User

As the character Tim Taylor on the TV series *Home Improvement* would say, super-user notebooks are all about "more power." (I can't figure out how to put his primal grunts into readable words.) Although no notebook will be able to beat a desktop computer in terms of raw power, the super-user notebooks try. They are optimized for power.

Weight and physical dimensions are secondary to power. These notebooks typically have processors that are only a few hundred megahertz (MHz) slower than the fastest desktop computers. They typically have between 256 megabytes (MB) and 1 gigabyte (GB) of RAM. (Few desktop computers accommodate more than 1 GB of RAM.)

Screen sizes for super-user notebooks are up to 15 inches measured diagonally. Their video cards are sometimes capable of driving external monitors at high resolutions and are suitable for software development and graphic design.

Despite the additional power, the weight of the super-user notebooks is similar to that of the standard notebooks, ranging from 6–8 pounds. In fact, many standard notebooks are just super-user notebooks without the extra memory, larger hard disk capacity, faster processor, and faster video card installed.

Advantages

Now that we've covered the different classes of notebooks and the niche in the market each one is geared to, let's look at the basic advantages that notebooks have over other mobile solutions. The advantages of notebooks fall into the following categories:

- Ability to run any Microsoft Windows–based software
- Superior processing and storage capability
- Availability
- Size of display

The following sections review each of these advantages in turn, and explain why they are important.

Ability to Run Windows-Based Software

No matter how great the device is, it is useless if it doesn't support the software that you need. The software is responsible for controlling all the electrical signals occurring in the hardware and bending them to your will. Perhaps one of the biggest advantages that notebooks have is their ability to run any Windows-based software.

This ability is important because most applications are developed first for Windows. The developers working on projects for Windows far outnumber the developers working for other operating systems. Further, the tools that developers use to create Windows-based software have had many years of refinement, so developing applications for Windows is quicker and easier than for other platforms.

Say, for instance, that you need a sophisticated contact manager. Applications that can perform this task are now available on a variety of platforms with varying features, but they started on the personal computer, and have developed in Windows. When you're evaluating contact management systems, you can use one of the market leaders. Microsoft Outlook, Act!, or Goldmine can all manage your contacts, but only Outlook has a version that will run on the newest Pocket PC platform. (Goldmine provides support for Palm devices.) These kinds of contact management and customer relationship management support applications would be ideal for PDAs; however, PDAs don't support them—yet.

Custom applications, written by consultants or an organization's own programmers, are much more likely to be supported on Windows-based notebooks because writing them to run on a PDA requires more time, and you must pay for every hour that was spent developing the software. Writing the software to run both on a Windows platform and on a PDA can be a time-consuming process that isn't justified for most applications.

If you need to use a corporate application, it will almost assuredly be supported on the version of Microsoft Windows that your notebook can run, even if no other platform supports it.

Superior Processing Capability

Superior processing capabilities, relative to other mobile options, make a notebook a necessity for people who have to analyze large volumes of data, or who need to perform complex analysis on the data.

For instance, a notebook is a good fit for a sales manager who's interested in analyzing sales data while traveling. Microsoft's SQL Server includes On-line Analytical Processing (OLAP) tools that allow an information technology (IT) department to create an interface for browsing huge amounts of raw data, such as the sales of an entire organization. The tools enable the data to be viewed by region, industry, customer, manufacturing location, or any other dimension that the organization feels is appropriate. These tools are beneficial because they use techniques to simplify the data so that browsing the data can be done in minutes, not hours or days. However, even with the tricks for simplifying the data, it's still generally more than a PDA or handheld computer can accommodate and requires more computational power than is available in that platform. So to be able to take advantage of this type of technology to analyze sales data or other organizational information, you'll need a notebook.

Similarly, if you're a chief financial officer (CFO) or senior accountant, you'll find that manipulating your complex Microsoft Excel spreadsheets is faster and easier on a notebook than on a handheld device. The speed difference for complex spreadsheets will certainly make you appreciate a notebook's computational power.

Availability

Putting it simply, notebooks are easier to acquire than other mobile devices because there's usually a corporate procedure for getting them. Most notebooks are ordered through the traditional channels and supported by the IT department. In most cases, you don't have to worry about loading your software onto the notebook, trying to get it to work with the corporate systems, or any of the details that come with a piece of hardware.

Another topic that generally falls under availability is the issue of support. Because notebooks are common devices in the corporate landscape, it's reasonable to assume that your corporate IT department will be able to provide support when problems arise. The same cannot be said of other devices because they are not prevalent enough yet for most IT departments to have built up the experience necessary to support them.

Size of Display

The more information you try to process and, more importantly, to associate, the more screen space you'll want. With more screen space, you can fit more data on the screen and ultimately have more sources of information from which to correlate data.

Screen size is measured in two ways. The first is the size of the screen itself, which has little to do with how much information can be displayed. Essentially the size just describes how big the image will be when it is displayed.

The real measure of a screen is the resolution that it can display. Resolution is the number of dots, or pixels, that make up the image on the screen. In the case of handheld devices, you're limited to a grid of pixels that measures 320 by 240, or in some devices 640 by 480. Contrast that with the typical notebook capable of displaying 1024 by 768 pixels or higher. Figure 1-1 shows you exactly how big a deal this is.

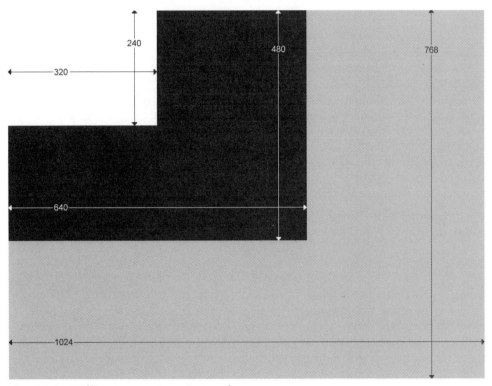

Figure 1-1 *Different screen sizes compared.*

Note The desktop system that I use when writing in my office has two monitors running at 1600 by 1200 pixels and 1280 by 1024 pixels, respectively. These resolutions provide a larger screen space than a notebook computer. I use this extra space to display reference materials, such as the book's outline and vendor Web sites. Even though I do use my notebook for writing, I'm more productive writing from the desktop system because I can quickly glance at the reference materials that I need.

Disadvantages

Now that we've covered the positive aspects of notebooks, let's look at the disadvantages. Notebooks don't have too many drawbacks, but there are some that you should be aware of. They are:

- Size and weight

- Battery life

- Usability

    The following sections review these disadvantages of notebook computers and why they are important.

Size and Weight

Notebooks are much smaller than they used to be, but they are still large and heavy compared with the other mobile devices. Because of their size, most notebooks need their own bags, or bags specifically designed to protect them from the hazards of road travel. Notebook bags add to the weight that you must carry when using these devices.

    Weight is the number one reason why mobile professionals choose to leave their notebooks at home. It's simply a matter of whether they want to carry around another 10 or more pounds in exchange for enhanced productivity. In many cases—particularly on short, regional trips—notebooks get left behind.

Battery Life

Batteries for notebooks have been getting better, but most notebooks cannot last for even four hours of activity. This means that they struggle to keep going for long domestic flights, and just can't make a trans-continental trip without help. You can purchase additional batteries to extend the amount of time you can get from battery power. In the case of trans-continental flights, you can often buy special adapters to enable you to use your notebook, but they increase the amount of weight that you have to carry. Which leads us back to the number one drawback of a notebook.

    To say that battery life is a disadvantage for notebooks might be a bit misleading. In run time, notebooks probably do as well as any device; however, because they are used differently than other mobile devices, people tend to think about their battery life limitations differently. Whereas most mobile devices are used for small amounts of time to access or store small amounts of information, people tend to use notebooks for long stretches of time. A PDA's batteries might not survive six hours of continuous use; however, that's not how most people use PDAs. People turn them on, get information, and turn them off again. This isn't something that is very practical with notebooks because of their third and final disadvantage.

Note As PDAs get more powerful they are starting to be used for longer continuous periods. Tasks that could historically only be done on a notebook, such as playing music or reading an eBook, can now be done from your PDA. This tends to make their use more long-term, and therefore battery life can become a problem.

Usability

Notebooks are great when you need to use them for long periods of time, but there are two reasons why they aren't ideal for performing brief tasks. First they require time to start up. The new "suspend and sleep" options have significantly reduced the amount of time necessary to start a notebook and make it available for use; however, it takes time for the notebook to get going.

The other reason is that notebooks, because of their size and weight, cannot easily be used while you are standing. To use notebooks you need a lap or other horizontal surface. Without a horizontal surface, you end up struggling to control the device. Notebooks are typically used for extended periods of time, but they don't work well as tools to locate phone numbers or to double-check the location of a meeting. That's where PDAs come into the picture.

Tips and Tricks for Notebooks

Here are a few tips for you in case you decide that you want to use a notebook in your struggle to remain productive while traveling.

Plug In When Possible

Although this tip might seem obvious, it bears stating anyway. If you have the opportunity to plug in your notebook, do it. You might later find yourself in a place where you need to use the notebook's batteries. If you don't plug in your notebook when you can, you might run out of battery power when you need it.

Finding power outlets in airports can be difficult; however, you can sometimes find a free one on posts or along the walls. Even if you're not going to be using your notebook, consider setting your notebook bag next to a post and plugging it in. Your notebook's batteries will then be charging while you're waiting for your airplane.

Insist on Lithium Ion Batteries

For notebooks, lithium ion batteries are superior to other types. They provide more power and don't need to be fully discharged before being charged again, the way older batteries do.

Most of today's notebooks come with lithium ion batteries; however, if you're buying your own, you should make sure that they are lithium ion batteries.

Make It Modular

Carry only the devices that you believe you will need. For instance, if you don't anticipate needing to use the floppy disk drive while traveling, don't take it. Carry only what you need so that you don't get tired from all the extra weight.

Tip If you need to move files between your notebook and someone else's while you're traveling, you can use a CompactFlash card and a PC Card adapter. Every Windows operating system since Windows 95 has provided native support for CompactFlash cards. When they are inserted into the computer, they look just like a hard disk. I'll explain CompactFlash storage cards in Chapter 4.

Use Stand-By or Hibernate

If you're working on a document while in the airport, when it's time to board your airplane, save your document and put the notebook in stand-by or hibernation mode rather than shutting it down completely. That way you won't have to wait for it to start back up after you're on the plane and at altitude.

Stand-by mode is the notebook's low power consumption mode, and it is designed to use only enough power to keep the memory and processor functioning. Starting up the computer takes only enough time for the hard disk to spin up after having been shut down.

Note My research into whether or not the airlines consider a notebook in stand-by mode to be "turned off" didn't reveal any documented stance. My suggestion is to ask the airline personnel when you check in if the airline accepts stand-by mode.

Hibernation mode is a special mode of Windows 2000 and Windows XP that enables the system to be completely shut down but return quickly to the point where it was left. It does this by creating an image of the memory and storing it on the hard disk. As a result, you must have at least the same amount of space available on your hard disk as you have memory. For most people this won't be a problem, but it can be a bit awkard if you have 512 MB of RAM installed in your notebook.

To turn on hibernation mode in Windows 2000 or Windows XP:

1. Click the Start button, point to Settings, and then click Control Panel.

2. Double-click the Power Options icon, and then in the Power Options Properties dialog box, click the Hibernate tab.

3. Select the Enable Hibernate Support check box to turn on the Hibernate feature, and then click OK. Hibernate mode will appear as an option when you select Shut Down on the Start menu.

Note You might find that hibernation support is already enabled. On some operating systems, the feature is turned on by default, and on others it is not. If it is, you don't need to do anything.

Eject Cards to Extend Battery Life

Removing any PC Cards from your notebook's card slots will extend battery life. These cards, even when not connected to the outside world, are drawing power from your notebook. Eject them before starting up or after you stop using them—every little bit helps.

Reset the Windows Power Management Settings

You can set Windows to turn off different devices to save battery power. In particular, the monitor, or LCD, and the hard disk can be turned off when not in use. You can control how long the device must be inactive before it is powered down, so it will be turned off only when you're not using it any more.

In the case of the LCD, there's little concern, because it starts up almost instantly. Be careful not to set the period of inactivity so short that the LCD turns off while you're reading a long passage of text. This can be a little annoying even though you only have to press a key to get the LCD turned on again.

Note This setting can be annoying if you've set the period of inactivity too short, because you will have to press the key repeatedly to keep the display running. It can be particularly troublesome during a sales presentation—although it's a great way to save power, you should give some serious thought to what the setting should be.

In the case of the hard disk, power management is a little more inconvenient, because the hard disk must spin up before you can use it. That means there will be a brief (10–30 seconds) pause when you attempt to access the hard disk. Some applications that do automatic backups might trigger hard disk restarts at inconvenient times; you could lose some of your typing if you continued to type while the hard disk was restarting. Because of this, you'll want to give careful consideration to how long the period of inactivity should be before powering down the hard disk.

Configuring Windows Power Management settings in Windows 2000 or Windows XP is a two-step process: turning on Advanced Power Management Support, and configuring the power settings.

To turn on Advanced Power Management Support:

1. On the Start Menu, point to Settings, and then click Control Panel.

2. Double-click the Power Options icon.

3. In the Power Options Properties dialog box, click the Advanced Power Management (APM) tab to display the options shown in Figure 1-2.

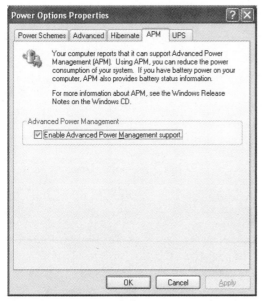

Figure 1-2   *To have different options for plugged-in and battery-powered use, you need the Advanced Power Management feature.*

Note If your computer doesn't have an APM tab, it supports a newer version of power management. You can skip down to the next procedure.

4. Select the Enable Advanced Power Management Support check box, if it's not already selected.

5. Click the Apply button.

To configure the time delays from the power settings:

1. In the Power Options Properties dialog box, click the Power Schemes tab to display the options shown in Figure 1-3.

2. Set the length of time the system must be inactive before turning off the monitor and hard disk when the system is plugged in. I recommend selecting Never, because there is no need to conserve battery power when plugged in.

3. Set the length of inactive time before the system is put into stand-by mode. As with the above options, I suggest Never.

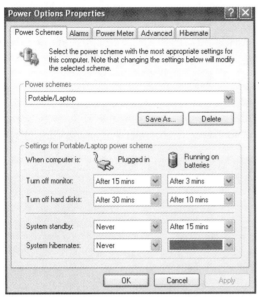

Figure 1-3   *Notebooks have two power schemes—one for when they're plugged in, and another for when they're running on batteries.*

4. Set the length of time that the system must be inactive before turning off the monitor, or in this case the LCD, while running on batteries. The minimum setting is one minute. That might be a bit too short. Find a setting that works for you. Three minutes is an appropriate setting.

5. Set the length of time that the system must be inactive before turning off the hard disk. This setting should be as low as you can tolerate it. Three minutes is the minimum setting allowed.

6. Set the length of time that the system must be inactive before entering a stand-by state when on battery power. This should generally be enough time that you will have walked away from the computer. Because it takes a little more time for the computer to power up from stand-by mode, you might want to set the period of inactivity for as long as 15 minutes before the computer enters stand-by mode. That way you can be certain the computer won't switch to stand-by mode while you are still using it.

Note If you want to save your settings as a new power scheme so that you can rapidly change between settings, click the Save As button, and name your new profile.

---

7. Click OK.

Something to keep in mind when changing these settings is that they might cause a problem when you're trying to give a presentation. When you're giving a presentation, try to have your notebook plugged into a power outlet, but if you can't do that, change these settings back to Never before the presentation.

Tip You might want to use a different set of power settings when you're giving, or about to give, a presentation. You can create your own profile for presentations that will prevent the computer from powering down. This way, there will be no embarrassing moments caused by a laptop that turns off unexpectedly.

Personal Digital Assistants

There was a time when most managers and groups had their own personal assistants to manage their calendars, type their letters, and generally take care of them. Although for most people those days are gone, the idea is still alive. The Personal Digital Assistant, as its name implies, is designed to do some of the things that the assistants of yesteryear used to do.

If you or your group still have an assistant, you can think of your PDA as an extension of that assistant. Because your calendar can be with you all the time, your assistant doesn't need to constantly print out calendars for you. Likewise, he or she doesn't have to look up numbers for you from a Rolodex.

PDAs manage your calendar and your contacts, but there are many more things that they can do today. Before I explain the advantages of a PDA, you should know the differences between types of PDAs.

Palm OS vs. Pocket PC

In the 1980s and 1990s, there were heated discussions about what kind of operating system and platform you should be running. These *flame wars*, as they were called, existed on bulletin board systems (BBSs) and eventually on the Internet. One person would cite the advantages of one operating system, and someone else would point out the limitations.

It seems that everyone has finally grown weary of arguing about the best operating system for personal computers, but a new group of people has taken up the war in the PDA market. You'll hear some people swearing that the Palm platform is the only place to be and others saying that Pocket PCs are the only answer.

But Wait—There's More

The Pocket PC platform is one of four Microsoft mobile device platforms that use the Microsoft Windows Consumer Edition (Windows CE) at their base. Windows CE has a similar user interface to the Microsoft Windows operating system that you run on your desktop computer, but is very different internally.

These four mobile device platforms differ from each other primarily in their screen size and methods of input. The Pocket PC is currently the most popular of these platforms because it can easily fit into a pocket. If a Pocket PC doesn't fit your needs, check out the other Microsoft mobile platforms. The other device platforms are:

- **Handheld PC**   A "clam shell," or flip top, device with a small keyboard and a landscape screen orientation that is similar to a notebook PC, but much lighter.

- **Tablet PC**   A device similar in size to a tablet of paper. It has a landscape screen orientation, and data is input with a stylus.

- **Microsoft Smart Phone**   A mobile phone with a screen slightly smaller than that of a Pocket PC. It is specifically set up to accept one-handed input from buttons or from a stylus.

As with the flame wars, the truth lies somewhere between these two views. Pocket PCs are clearly the focus in this book, but that doesn't mean that the Palm OS doesn't have any value. In fact, Palm has a substantial percentage of the market for PDA devices. However, the tide is turning as individuals and corporations begin to ask more of the PDAs they are using.

Palm OS–based devices do what they do very well. They are small, light, and for the most part, reliable. Historically, they have offered the basic applications most people needed. The calendar and contact management functions built into the Palm OS, while not perfect, are certainly passable, particularly when coupled with a calendar and contact management program such as Microsoft Outlook.

Caution By default, a Palm OS device will only synchronize with Palm's own desktop contact management application. Third party add-ons are required to enable a Palm OS device to synchronize with Microsoft Outlook.

The Palm OS won its market share because it is a relatively low-cost device that provides the standard applications including calendar and contact management, and because it could be programmed to do other things. There are other PDAs on the market that enable people to maintain calendars and contacts, but these devices have limited connectivity with PCs and computer-based management programs. Further, these other devices don't allow programs to be written for them.

As people begin to ask more from their PDAs, the advantages of the Pocket PC become clearer. Pocket PC devices have processors that run in excess of 200 MHz; Palm devices creep along at less than 35 MHz. Additionally, most Palm OS devices come with 8 MB of memory or less. Most Pocket PC devices ship with 32 MB of RAM or more.

The impact of all this is that the Palm devices are more cramped than the Pocket PC devices. Mobile professionals who manage a large number of contacts, appointments, and messages might be concerned about how much information they can keep on a personal digital assistant.

The final challenge with Palm OS–based devices is that there are two different and non-standard expansion options for them. They utilize Handspring's Springboard expansion slot or Palm's new expansion card slots. Both are reasonable platforms to extend PDAs, but there isn't a wide variety of expansion modules that can be used with the Palm OS devices.

In contrast, most Pocket PC devices utilize industry standard CompactFlash expansion slots, or PC Card slots. The PC Card slots utilized by Pocket PC devices are the same slots that have been used on notebooks for years. That means there's a wide variety of hardware that will work with a Pocket PC, although each piece of hardware has to include a driver for the Pocket PC platform.

The CompactFlash support means that the same memory card you use in your digital camera or MP3 music player can be used in your Pocket PC, making it a snap to transfer information between your devices.

If you're interested in more information about Pocket PC devices, you can visit the Microsoft Pocket PC Web site at *http://www.microsoft.com/mobile/pocketpc*.

Windows CE

Up to this point, I've confined this review of the Windows CE platform to Pocket PC devices. There is another type of Windows CE-based device that bears mentioning here: the Handheld PC device (HPC 2000). These devices run the same Windows CE operating system as the Pocket PC, but have a few significant differences.

Handheld PCs use a landscape screen orientation rather than a portrait orientation. This means that the Handheld PC screen is wider than it is tall, whereas the Pocket PC screen is taller than it is wide. Handheld PCs have larger screens—typically 640 by 240 or 640 by 480 pixels, and many Handheld PCs have keyboards, whereas Pocket PCs don't.

Handheld PCs will be addressed again in Chapters 15 and 16. These devices are particularly suited for use in environments where a notebook might not be appropriate, but a full size screen and keyboard might be. For now, though, I'll focus on Pocket PC devices.

How Mobile is Mobile?

The introduction defined *mobility* as remaining productive while away from your desk—not necessarily away from your office. This definition was used for a very specific reason: PDAs are often quite valuable tools to help you remain productive while within your office but away from your desk.

Most non-recurring meetings end with a discussion of when the next meeting should be. Those who still keep their paper calendars with them can chime in about vacations they are taking, or when certain deliverables are due.

Historically, those who used the organization's electronic calendar system were left out. They didn't know what was on their calendar, particularly weeks or months in advance. As a result, meetings would usually end with the coordinator agreeing to look at everyone's calendars and send a message out on proposed times.

If everyone had their calendars available with them, perhaps on PDAs, the group could look at their calendars and make an immediate decision about the time and place for the next meeting. Although the coordinator would probably still be responsible for entering it into the corporate calendar system for eventual propagation down to the PDAs, at least there wouldn't be any need to start an e-mail exchange.

Exchanging contact information is even easier. If your colleagues need contact information for someone you've been dealing with, you can beam it to them. The infrared ports on PDAs enable you to exchange information wirelessly over short distances. (You can learn more about infrared ports in Chapter 2.)

The final advantage of PDAs is the ability to read and respond to e-mail during the parts of meetings, presentations, and so forth in which your attention isn't required. Before a meeting, there are generally a few minutes when you are awaiting the start. Likewise, at the end of the meeting, there are usually a few minutes when housekeeping issues are being addressed that you might need to be present for, but that might not pertain to you. Add that to those meetings where your presence is required, but your input isn't, and it adds up to a great deal of time.

Notebooks are generally not acceptable for these environments because of corporate culture; PDAs, however, are generally acceptable. You can take your PDA into a meeting, read and respond to your e-mails, and then return to your desk to actually transmit the messages you sent in the meeting. Or better yet, if you have wireless connectivity to your local network, you can receive new messages while sitting in the meeting.

Advantages

Now that I've covered the background, let's look at the advantages of Pocket PCs. Like any good tool, the Pocket PC has some nice features that make it a welcome addition to a road warrior's tool kit. The core advantages are:

- Instant access
- No flat surface needed
- Lighter and more portable

Instant Access

When you turn on a Pocket PC, you instantly return to the place where you left off. You don't have to load information from a disk or wait for programs to restart. The Pocket PC "wakes up" and is immediately ready for action. It is ideal for situations in which you need a small piece of information and you don't want to have to wait for your notebook to start.

No Flat Surface Needed

Because Pocket PCs are designed to be held in the palm of your hand, you can use them without having to sit down or set them on a surface. This means they are good for getting information on the go.

If you're charging down the concourse between connecting flights at LaGuardia airport, you can quickly pull out your Pocket PC, get the number of the contact you're meeting, and tell them that you're going to be late because all flights are delayed.

Lighter and More Portable

In the earlier section about the lightest notebooks, I explained the advantages of the light-weight models. An ultra-light notebook weighs 32 ounces or so, not including, of course, all the accessories. Compare that with the 6.3 ounces of a Compaq iPaq Pocket PC and you can see that Pocket PC devices are much lighter than even the lightest notebooks.

In addition to the weight advantages of a Pocket PC, it's also smaller. Although size can be a disadvantage when you need to display more information on the screen, it is quite handy when you want to be able to hold the device in the palm of your hand.

Disadvantages

With the good, there must be some bad. Pocket PC devices are very good at many things, but they do have some challenges as well:

- Screen size
- Data entry

- Applications
- Batteries

You can work around some of these limitations, but they might frustrate you from time to time.

Screen Size

If you refer to Figure 1-1, you'll see that the 320 by 240 pixels offered by most Pocket PCs is much smaller than the size available on a notebook PC. However, because Pocket PCs are often used to retrieve small amounts of information, such as a daily calendar or the phone numbers for a contact, the screen size is workable.

Note There are utilities available that change the orientation—and in some cases, the resolution—of the Pocket PC screen.

You always have the option of selecting a Handheld PC instead of a Pocket PC if screen size is your primary concern, although that larger screen size will limit your ability to use the device whenever you want.

Data Entry

The Pocket PC's handwriting recognition feature is good, but not perfect. You can also display a "soft keyboard" on the screen, which you can tap with the stylus. This is effective for some people, but it will still not be as effective as a regular keyboard. Pocket PCs are good devices for accessing and retrieving information, but their use as a data entry device is limited.

Note In Chapter 4, I introduce you to keyboards that you can use with your Pocket PC when you're stationary to make entering data a little easier.

Using a Handheld PC device instead of a Pocket PC device will address the keyboard issue because most Handheld PCs have integrated keyboards. But you will lose some of the Pocket PC's size advantages to gain a keyboard.

Applications

A notebook can run practically any application that you want it to, but Pocket PCs can run only applications compiled for Windows CE, the Pocket PC and Handheld PC operating system. The number of applications designed for Windows CE, or the Pocket PC specifically, is growing, but there still isn't as wide a variety of applications available for the Pocket PC as there is for the PC.

In general, this means you'll be able to find generic applications, such as a clock that will tell you the time in every city in the world, but you probably won't be able to find an application designed specifically to help you keep an inventory of your Beanie Baby collection. You might be able to manage it with a more generic program written to track the value of collectables. Most of the time you can find a way to solve basic needs by using existing software; however, many business applications have yet to be written for any PDA platform.

Chapter 15 will show you a little trick that will enable you to run Windows applications on your Pocket PC—or at least make it appear that the Windows application is running on your Pocket PC. Despite the fact that they can work on a Pocket PC, they won't always work correctly because Windows applications are optimized for a Windows screen, and everything might not fit on a screen as small as the Pocket PC's.

Batteries

In the previous section on notebooks, you read that batteries are one of the main problems with notebooks. PDAs and other devices have similar battery problems. This is particularly true of Pocket PC devices.

Because they are supposed to be small and lightweight, most Pocket PCs have gone to a lithium ion polymer battery. These batteries are rechargeable, but not always replaceable. This means that when the battery on some Pocket PCs wears out, there is no way to replace the battery and continue on as you can with a notebook.

Most Pocket PCs are just starting to have ways to supplement their internal batteries. Compaq's expansion jackets for the iPaq contain rechargeable batteries, but they aren't capable of fully recharging the main battery. Neither can they be used instead of the main battery. There is a wide variety of options for powering your Pocket PC other than its cradle. I'll introduce you to some of those in Chapter 4.

The battery life of Pocket PCs will vary wildly depending on your usage patterns, but you might be able to get ten hours of use out of a Pocket PC if you're conservative with your configuration and use of the device. Of course, with judicious use of alternative power options like replaceable batteries, car chargers, and other options, you probably won't run out of power on your Pocket PC.

Tips and Tricks for PDAs

Each PDA differs in some regard, but there are some relatively universal things that you can do to improve your PDA experience.

Cover All Connectors

Although it sounds simple, covering the connectors on your PDA can help ensure problem-free operation for a long time. Connectors, if left exposed, pick up contaminants that prevent you from making a solid connection from the PDA to add-ons or the cradle. Dirt and other contaminants that don't conduct electricity can eventually prevent a connector from working altogether. The more conscious you are about the potential problems that connectors can have, the fewer problems you'll have with connections.

A practical example of a PDA that needs its connectors protected is the Compaq iPaq. Its expansion pack connector contains many individual conductors. If any one of these is contaminated, it can be difficult to diagnose problems. It's important to keep the expansion port covered as much as possible. The expansion port will automatically be covered when you use an expansion pack, but you can also protect it by using the plastic jacket that Compaq provides with the device.

Get a Protective Case

The basic protection that ships with most PDAs is often not up to the rigors of daily use. A case is one of the best investments you can make for your PDA. There are two issues to be aware of when selecting a protective case.

The first issue is protecting the screen from accidental damage. This usually requires a hard or thick area of the case that covers the entire face of the device so that it's not possible for a sharp point outside the case to crack the LCD panel on the device.

The second issue is shocks that can occur if you accidentally drop the device. Dropping a PDA from a height of only a few inches can dislodge internal components and lead to failure or instability. By protecting the unit in a case with some padding, you can help minimize the damage that it will take when you accidentally drop it.

Protect the Screen

If you scratch the back of the PDA, there is no great harm done. Cosmetic damage might not be appealing, but it won't inhibit its use. However, if you scratch the screen or mar it with repeated use of the stylus, it will definitely affect your ability to use the device.

Fellowes (*http://www.fellowes.com*) makes a product called WriteRIGHT that covers the face of your PDA with a thin plastic sheet, much like the one you find on the LCD screens of home electronics when they arrive. This thin plastic sheet is removable and disposable, so when you've marred its surface, you can peel it off and replace it. It's easier and less expensive than replacing the screen on your PDA.

Optimize Battery Life

It shouldn't be any surprise that one of the greatest challenges with your PDA will be power management. Here are some quick suggestions for getting the most out of the battery life:

- **Turn the backlight down**   Backlighting the display consumes a huge amount of power. Use the lowest setting that lets you see comfortably. If you happen to walk into bright light and need a brighter backlight, you can turn it up while you're in the bright area and turn it back down afterward.

- **Set low delays for the Backlight Off and Unit Off settings**   Most devices monitor their level of activity; if there's no activity for a certain period of time, they can turn off the backlight, or turn the unit off altogether. In general, the shorter you can make the periods of inactivity through which the device must wait before powering down, the more battery life you'll keep.

- **Use headphones when possible**   Outputting sound through the speaker takes more power than outputting the sound to headphones. If you're going to be listening to music, use a set of headphones to conserve power.

- **Turn off unnecessary sounds**   It takes power to drive the speaker or headphones. If you don't need an audible warning for an event, turn the notification off. This can be done from the Sounds and Reminders applet. Chapter 11 shows you how to control and change your sounds.

Use Sleeves

The Compaq iPaq is most notable for its use of expansion packs, known as sleeves. These sleeves offer additional battery power, access to CompactFlash, or access to PC Cards. If you're going to purchase only one sleeve, I recommend that it be the single-slot PC Card jacket.

There are two good reasons for this. First the PC Card jacket will accommodate a CompactFlash-to-PC Card adapter, which costs only a few dollars, and some CompactFlash cards include the adapter as well.

The second reason is that the PC Card jacket includes an additional battery that can extend the amount of time you can use your iPaq even if you're not using a PC Card. This might eliminate the need to purchase a battery expansion pack, or at the very least can extend the amount of time that you can use the unit.

Selecting a single sleeve, in particular a PC Card sleeve, can help your pocketbook and can keep your Pocket PC portable. With expansion packs costing over $100 at the time of this writing, purchasing two or three jackets can represent more than 30 percent of the total cost of the solution. One jacket, although costly, can solve most needs.

Phone-Integrated PDAs

It's a given that most of us will carry a mobile phone; for those of us who also carry a PDA, it's natural to ask why these two devices can't be combined. Some manufacturers have taken this question to heart and have developed devices that integrate both the features of a telephone and the features of a PDA. One of the most notable organizations developing this technology is Trium (*http://www.trium.com*).

This merging of technologies offers some unique benefits. Perhaps the most interesting benefit is the ability to use the data capabilities of the cellular service provider to provide nearly instant data connectivity. In the next chapter, I will explore connectivity options. For now, you need to know that using a wireless data service often means service concerns in addition to the complication of a separate antenna that doesn't quite fit in.

The integrated nature of these phones means that the cellular phone antenna—which has been designed and refined for reliable communications—is used for both your voice calls and your data calls. This generally provides better data reception no matter where you go.

One of the other advantages is that the PDA portion of the device can control the dialing and other call features of the phone. You don't have to transcribe it from your Pocket PC to your phone; instead, you can press a button or select an option, which dials the number for you. It also means a much larger screen for displaying features such as call waiting, call timers, and others.

Unfortunately, these devices have two rather large drawbacks. First these devices are much larger than a typical cellular phone. They aren't so large that they are unwieldy, but they weigh approximately double what a typical phone weighs. For instance, the Motorola TimePort that I have weighs approximately 110 grams. The Trium Mondo phone weighs 200 grams.

The second issue is that these phones tend to have battery lives that are on the shorter end of the cellular phone scale. Because of their large display and the additional processing power in the phone, it takes more power to keep the device operating. This translates into less talk and stand-by time for the phone.

Microsoft Smart Phones

You can think of the Microsoft Smart Phone as the evolution of the phone-integrated PDA into a device that has many, if not all, the same features, but a smaller size and weight. Of course, there are other important refinements in the user interface of the Microsoft Smart Phone compared to the phone-integrated PDA; however, the reduced size is the most compelling difference between the two types of devices.

Microsoft gave Smart Phones a slightly smaller screen size so that they would not need to be as large as the Pocket PC-integrated devices. The total screen resolution of the Smart Phone is still roughly 75 percent of the screen size of a Pocket PC, but Smart Phones provide this resolution in a much smaller space.

The smaller size of the screen means that the smaller size and weight that most consumers are after in their mobile devices is possible. Microsoft Smart Phones are still larger than some of the smallest mobile phones on the market, but they are small enough to make them comfortable.

The software has been improved to better integrate the PDA features of the device into the phone. This includes a significant retooling of the input mechanisms, including wheels, input pads, and soft buttons, so that the device can be operated with one hand.

Microsoft Smart Phones are not available at the time of this writing, but they should be very soon after the release of this book. If you have not yet purchased a PDA and your mobile phone provider supports Microsoft's Smart Phones, I strongly encourage you to look at these devices as an option for your PDA and mobile phone needs. The integrated features are quite impressive.

Internet Access Points

Up to this point in the chapter, I've described devices that you take with you while you're traveling. This section is about not carrying anything at all. *Internet access points* are locations where you can access the Internet and use the Web-based services with which you have an account.

The idea behind the Internet access point is simple. You set up, rent, or borrow the infrastructure necessary to access the information you need from any computer on the Internet. Then you can go to any location with Internet access and use any computer that is available to access your information. This is typically done for Internet e-mail, but it can be used for any Web-based application.

The Different Kinds of Internet Access Points

Internet access points can be found in most major cities and even in a substantial number of small communities. Internet access points come in three basic varieties:

- Office services locations
- Public facilities
- Cyber cafés

Customer locations could also probably be added to this list, but for reasons I'll elaborate on in the following section, you probably won't want to access your information from your client's office. Let's review the types of Internet access points you can use.

Office Services Locations

The most popular franchise, and thus the one with the most locations where you can gain access to the Internet, is Kinko's. You can rent time on their computers, with Internet access charged in tenths of an hour in most places. The advantage this type of Internet access point has over the others is that they are typically available 24 hours a day, so even if you are getting ready for a red-eye flight back to your home office you can check your e-mail and let everyone know when you'll be in at the office.

Unfortunately, this convenience comes at a price. Kinko's is one of the most expensive ways to gain short-term access to the Internet. Of course, it's all relative; even if you spend an hour online reading your e-mail and getting caught up, you'll spend less than $10.

Note Some facilities allow you to use their high-speed Internet connectivity with your notebook—if you bring it. Kinko's is not one of these places at the time of this writing.

Public Facilities

Thanks to a large number of grants and gifts, cities and counties are beginning to offer free or low-cost Internet connectivity at public locations such as libraries.

Libraries are often good choices for quick Internet access, but they sometimes have limits that might not be conducive to getting a lot of work done. Some libraries limit access to 15-minute intervals, and some require proof that you live in the local area, which presumably you don't. Still, the quiet environment is a good place to go to check a few e-mail messages.

Cyber Cafés

If you have a caffeine addiction that needs to be constantly fed, or you just enjoy the cool groove of cyber cafés, they might be a good way for you to gain access to the Internet. Because these facilities make their money selling beverages, their Internet access charges are generally less than what you might pay at an office services location.

However, there are two distinct disadvantages of cyber cafés. First they are hard to find; most telephone books don't yet have a special category for cyber cafés, so you might have to work to find one. Second, cyber cafés are sometimes hangouts for "gamers," a special class of computer users who love to play computer games. If a cyber café is a popular gamer hangout, you won't exactly have a serene environment where you can concentrate. That is, unless you consider the sound of gunfire serene.

Advantages

If you've ever felt weighed down by your notebook, PDA, cell phone, and their paraphernalia, you'll appreciate the two advantages that Internet access points bring:

- Light weight
- Low or free per-use charges

Light weight

OK, light weight is a bit of an understatement. When you're using an Internet access point, you don't need to carry anything at all. Freedom from having to carry any devices is a wonderful thing. It also helps to have this kind of mobility as a backup plan should you forget your notebook, or more likely, when you forget the power adapter you need to make your notebook work after the battery is drained.

Low or Free Per-Use Charges

This could probably be listed as a disadvantage, but remember that the per-use cost is an alternative to the high cost of buying a device outright. A high end PDA might cost as much as $600, and a super-user notebook can cost in excess of $3,000. So suddenly $5 per hour doesn't seem that expensive.

Disadvantages

Most people initially respond positively to the Internet access point idea, but there are some serious limitations that have to be considered. These include:

- Locations and availability
- Check-in wait time
- Privacy
- Infrastructure costs

Locations and Availability

The biggest problem with Internet access points is that you have to find one, and until you do, you don't really have access to your information. Unless you're carrying a PDA, you won't have access to your calendar or your contacts. You won't know whom you need to contact if you're running late unless you've printed out that information before leaving.

This is particularly true for airline flights from your office to a remote location. If you aren't carrying a device, you might not be able to make productive use of this time.

Locating an Internet access point can be tricky. Although office service locations, libraries, and cyber cafés might seem easy to find, for most people the city where they will need to find one will be unfamiliar, and as a result, they might have trouble getting directions.

If you don't believe me, and you're bored on a trip some time, walk up to a gas station attendant and ask where the local Kinko's is, or the nearest library, or a cyber café. More often than not when I ask these questions, I get the blank "deer in headlights" stare. Not that there's anything wrong with the gas station attendants or the question; it's just that they're more accustomed to questions like "Where is Main Street?" (If you're really bored, ask them what the stupidest questions they have ever been asked are. You're likely to get some very interesting answers.)

Check-In Wait Time

Presuming you are able to find an Internet access point, you still have to get signed up to use a computer. In the office service locations, this is generally a painless process, because they want you to start using the computer as soon as you can. However, you never know how busy it's going to be when you walk into one of these places. I had to wait 10 minutes before getting signed onto a computer, and another 15 minutes to get signed out on one particularly nasty trip. Luckily, I wasn't in a hurry.

Libraries and other public Internet access points, although free, have been known to have some rather unorthodox and painful procedures for accessing the Internet. The process can sometimes take a while.

Cyber cafés are usually pretty laid-back about getting you checked in, and although there isn't much paperwork, it's sometimes hard to figure out what they will charge you. If you're too quick, you might end up being done on the computer before you've finished your espresso.

In general, plan on checking in and checking out taking approximately 15 minutes, no matter which type of Internet access point you choose.

Privacy

After you've signed in, you'll notice that most computers are arranged in the middle of the room. There might not be privacy walls to protect the information on your screen from the prying eyes of the people around you. Sometimes there are situations where you might have to reconsider opening an e-mail or document because you're not sure what it has in it and who might see its contents over your shoulder.

I consider myself to be pretty low-key about privacy issues. I don't routinely shred my bank statements, nor do I have any particular aversion to giving someone my Social Security number. However, I have to admit that using a computer in an office service location has set me on edge. There have been times when I felt the need to look around to see if someone was looking over my shoulder. What is it they say about paranoia? You're not paranoid if the world really *is* out to get you.

The other issue, although admittedly not as urgent as the first, is that someone could look back through your activities on the computer, review the sites that you visited, and if you're not careful, see copies of the material that you viewed. Take a look at the "Tips and Tricks for Internet Access Points" section later in the chapter to see ways that you can prevent other people from tracing your steps.

Infrastructure Costs

Infrastructure costs might not be an issue for you when you're using Internet access points. If all you are doing is checking a Web-based e-mail account hosted by a free service, such as MSN Hotmail, you have no infrastructure costs to worry about. Similarly, if your organization has Microsoft Exchange and has made Outlook Web Access available, your costs are minimal.

However, if your goal is to access more than e-mail, it's possible that the corporate systems will have to be rewritten to support a connection from the Web to use the application from an Internet access point. The cost for custom software development to convert systems to run over the Web is not trivial. Unless you're planning to use only services that are already available, such as Web-based e-mail, the costs of retooling systems might far exceed the benefits.

Tips and Tricks for Internet Access Points

The earlier tips and tricks for remaining productive while away from your desk primarily covered performance enhancements. The tips and tricks for Internet access points are mostly about maintaining your privacy.

Use Secure Socket Layer

Secure Socket Layer (SSL) encrypts traffic across the network so that no one can capture your data and read it. It can't protect your data from someone looking over your shoulder, but it can help protect it from people between the Internet access point and the location where you're getting the information.

SSL sites are accessed via *https://* instead of *http://*. They require installation of a certificate at the server level. Those certificates are available from trusted certifications authorities for less than $500 per year. They're a good investment for your servers if you're going to be sending confidential information via the Internet.

Don't Allow Internet Explorer to Cache Pages

By default, Microsoft Internet Explorer will cache the Web pages you see so that if you want to look at them again, you won't have to retype the URL. This is a good idea for performance, but a bad idea when you're using a computer at an Internet access point, where the pages will remain for someone else to snoop through. There are settings you can use to prevent Internet Explorer from caching pages and to force it to erase any pages that it does cache.

The following procedure shows you where to find the settings that you'll need to change:

1. Open Internet Explorer.

2. On the Tools menu, click Internet Options to display the Internet Options dialog box.

3. Click the Advanced tab to see the advanced options as shown in Figure 1-4.

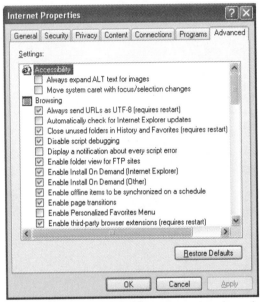

Figure 1-4 *Internet Explorer has a number of advanced features.*

4. Scroll down, and select the Do Not Save Encrypted Pages To Disk option. This will prevent Internet Explorer from saving pages accessed through SSL to the disk.

5. Select the Empty Internet Files Folder When Browser Is Closed option. This will cause Internet Explorer to delete any cached files that it saves when you exit the browser.

6. Click OK to return to Internet Explorer.

These two quick changes in the configuration will ensure that your information isn't lingering around on the disk for the next person to find.

Clear the History and Temporary Files Before Leaving

If you followed the previous advice about erasing cached pages, there won't be any temporary files left for someone to find. It is not a bad idea to manually clear the temporary files
and the history before you leave as well. The temporary files contain the information you
downloaded, if Internet Explorer cached them. The history file contains the sites that
you went to during your session. Follow these steps to clear the files:

1. Open Internet Explorer, if it's not already open.

2. On the Tools menu, click Internet Options to display the Internet Properties dialog
   box as shown in Figure 1-5.

Figure 1-5　*The Internet Properties dialog box enables you to clear the temporary files
and history manually.*

3. Click the Delete Files button.

4. In the Delete Files dialog box, click OK to delete all the temporary files. You don't
   need to worry about the Delete All Offline Content check box, because you
   wouldn't have created offline content.

5. Click the Clear History button.

6. In the Internet Options dialog box, click the Yes button.

7. Click OK to return to Internet Explorer.

Don't Ever Save Passwords or Allow Sites to Save Cookies

Some Web sites offer to send your computer a cookie that identifies the computer. The cookie can then be used to automatically log you in. Accepting a cookie on your own computer or password-protected notebook might be a good idea, but it's unsafe when you're on a public computer. If a Web site offers to create a cookie for automatic logons, be sure to decline so that future users of the computer can't use your identity on that Web site.

Internet Explorer has a similar feature that offers to save your password for you so that you don't have to type it in each time that you visit a page. This is not something that you should take advantage of on a public computer. Remember to decline these offers so that your password isn't stored on the computer.

Choose Wisely

Even if the Internet access point is empty when you walk in, don't just sit down at the first computer that you see. Try to find one that's tucked back into a corner and situated so that your face, not your back, is toward everyone else. If you stay in any Internet access point long enough, it will get busy—quickly. It's best to pick your spot wisely before you start so that you won't feel like you have to move.

Summary

Selecting the right devices is a difficult decision, and one that tends to evolve as your needs evolve. In this chapter, you learned about the basic types and categories of devices and the fundamental advantages and disadvantages of each one.

Notebooks are the most popular devices for ensuring productive mobility, but their weight and lack of an instant start-up feature make them suitable only when you have to do serious work.

PDAs are great for lightweight tasks such as calendar and contact management, but they might be difficult to use for large projects because of their limited screen size and their lack of keyboard and power.

Internet access points offer the ability to travel without carrying anything, but they require that you locate one before you have access to your information. They also raise some privacy concerns.

Here are some thought-provoking questions that you should consider before deciding what devices to purchase:

- How often do you travel, and what information do you need access to when you're on the road?

- How much of your time in the office is spent away from your desk (in meetings, for example)?

- Do you take short, regional trips or long, trans-continental trips?
- How concerned are you about privacy and the security of your information?
- Do you need to run Windows applications while traveling?

Choose Your Transmission: Connectivity

One of the advantages that today's PDAs have over their historical brethren is their ability to connect to your desktop computer, notebook, and corporate network, and to the Internet. They can connect through cables and through infrared and radio waves, using a variety of mechanisms. The ability to make these connections makes PDAs very valuable tools.

This chapter explores connectivity options—from the painfully slow to the blazingly fast and every stop in between. My goal in this chapter is to help you to understand your options for connecting your PDA.

You'll see how some of the same mechanisms you use to make connections from your PDA can be used to make connections from your notebook. You'll also discover how wireless technology can make you even more mobile and flexible.

The information in this chapter can also be considered background information for Chapter 5, "Park It in the Garage: Synchronization." In Chapter 5, I'll explain how to control what information gets onto your PDA and how frequently it gets updated.

Connections with Cables

The most basic forms of connectivity—those that have been around since shortly after PDAs came on the market—rely on cables. These cables are composed of at least two strands of copper that make a circuit, across which electrical information is communicated. Samuel Morse couldn't have realized the legacy that his invention of the telegraph would leave. Ever since those days when we communicated across long distances by applying a small amount of voltage to a wire to communicate a signal, we've made slow, methodical advances—and sometimes great leaps—in the way we communicate.

The communication mechanisms used today are far more technically sophisticated than running power down railroad tracks, but the process isn't all that different. Each wired communication method sends a signal by controlling the voltage on a pair of wires.

The next few sections look at the wired options available for PDAs today. All PDAs on the market will default to one or the other (or both) of these communication methods for their synchronization with a notebook or desktop computer.

Serial Connections

The oldest type of connection used with PDAs is the serial connection. Serial connections are so named because they send information one bit at a time, in a series. The serial connection dates back to before the original IBM Personal Computer. Figure 2-1 shows a serial cradle for a Compaq iPAQ, including the end of the serial connection.

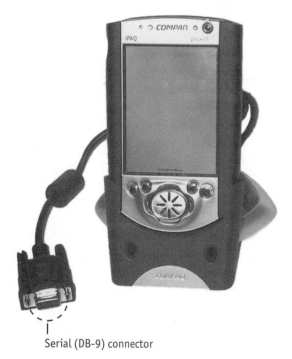

Serial (DB-9) connector

Figure 2-1 *Compaq's iPAQ can use both a universal serial bus (USB) connection and a serial connection.*

Serial connections generally run at speeds of 115 kilobits per second (Kbps) or less. Compared to today's high-speed connections, this is slow. However, it's much faster than some of the wireless connections we'll be looking at. Figure 2-8 at the end of this chapter shows the relative speeds of serial and all other kinds of connections.

Advantages of Serial Connections

Serial connections are perhaps the most stable type of connection. This should be no surprise, because the computer industry has had dozens of years to make this technology work. There was once a time when high-speed serial communications could be problematic, but that time has long since gone.

Disadvantages of Serial Connections

The two key disadvantages of serial connections are that they are slow and sometimes difficult to set up. Because many devices, including the mouse and modem, use serial connections, it's possible to run out of serial ports. Having multiple ports can make it difficult to determine to which serial port you're connected.

Microsoft Windows operating systems refer to serial ports as COM1 and COM2, but many hardware manufacturers label them Serial A and Serial B on the back of the unit. This inconsistent labeling can be confusing. Most people will translate A to 1 and B to 2, but serial ports are still not user friendly.

Where Serial Connections Fit

Serial connections are a good choice only when you don't have any other options. Their slow speed, need for a cable to connect the devices, and difficulty in correctly setting up the cables mean that serial connections are a last resort. Serial connections are, however, supported by almost every device, so it's not a bad fallback position.

Tips for Serial Use

- If you get an error message from the synchronization utility stating that the port cannot be opened, try setting the software to use the second serial port, COM2. Sometimes a modem, mouse, or other device might be using the first serial port, and you actually plugged the device into the second serial port.

- If you want to use your PDA some distance from your computer, you can buy a serial extension cable. You can run a serial connection as much as 1000 feet away from your computer.

Universal Serial Bus Connections

In the last five years, a newer, better, and faster connection method has become available. Universal Serial Bus (USB) connections offer faster connection speeds, automatic device detection (Plug and Play), and you can connect up to 127 devices per bus. The result is a faster connection that is easier to set up and is in most cases more stable. A USB connector is small, flat, and easy to use. Figure 2-2 shows a Compaq iPAQ in its USB cradle and a view of the USB connector.

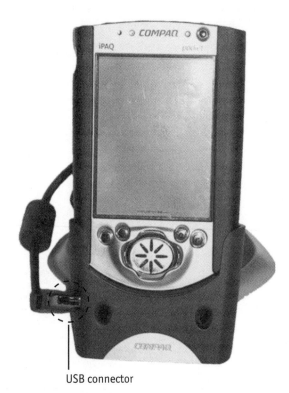

USB connector

Figure 2-2 *A Compaq iPAQ in its cradle, and its USB connector.*

Advantages of USB Connections

USB is capable of sustained transfers at 2 megabits per second (Mbps). That's roughly 20 times as fast as a serial connection. The additional speed that is available from a USB connection can't be overstated.

Automatic device detection eliminates the need for you to manually determine which port your device is plugged into. With USB, one port isn't different from another; they are all connected and all available. This makes connectivity a snap. USB is definitely the preferred method for connecting to your notebook or desktop computer.

Disadvantages of USB Connections

The one downside to USB connections is that your computer has to support them. You'll need Microsoft Windows 95 OSR2 or later, and your computer must have a USB connection port built in or you will have to buy and install a separate add-in card. Most reasonably new hardware will support USB connections, though.

Where USB Connections Fit

USB is the preferred primary connection method for newer PDAs and other devices. Its high speed and Plug and Play characteristics make it ideal for the mobile professional who doesn't have time to fiddle with options or wait a long time for data to synchronize.

Tips for USB Use

- Install the PDA software before plugging the PDA into the computer. This will prevent Windows from attempting to install the device without the correct drivers.

- Don't use a USB hub unless you have to. When you have problems, remove the USB hub before you start troubleshooting. Many problems can be traced to USB hubs. (A USB hub allows you to plug in more devices by providing multiple ports on the hub and using only one USB port on the computer.)

- If you encounter a problem with a USB device, unplug the USB cable, wait five seconds, and plug it back in. This will reset the connection and sometimes even fix mysteriously broken connections.

Local Connections Without Cables

Today's advertisements show teenagers communicating wirelessly at concerts, business people talking on unseen telephones in the middle of city squares, and a variety of scenarios that make it seem like someone beamed back some science-fiction technology for use today. A lot of what appears in the advertisements isn't available right now—but some of it is.

This section covers the local wireless connectivity options. By *local*, I mean within a few feet. These options are really just replacements for cables connecting two devices. In theory this is great—no wires, nothing to get tangled, less to carry, and so on. The reality leaves a little bit more to be desired.

Infrared

Infrared, sometimes called IR or IrDA, has been around for years. It's the technology that enables you to change the TV channel using a remote control. It's a low cost technology that is included in practically every PDA. Infrared is sometimes even supported on desktop computers and somewhat more frequently on notebooks.

Figure 2-3 shows the infrared port on a Compaq iPAQ, and Figure 2-4 shows the infrared port on a Palm V. On both of these units, the infrared ports are located on the top of the unit; however, there are many PDAs with infrared ports positioned elsewhere.

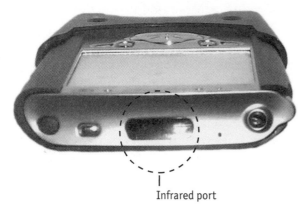

Infrared port

Figure 2-3   *A view of a Compaq iPAQ's infrared port, as seen from above.*

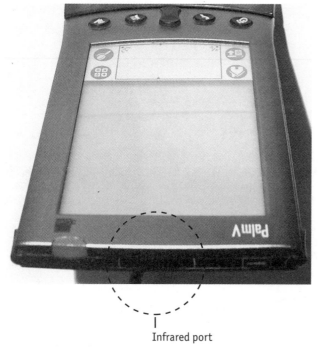

Infrared port

Figure 2-4   *A view of a Palm V's infrared port, as seen from above.*

Advantages of Infrared

The biggest benefit of infrared technology is its low cost. Because it's so inexpensive to implement, more and more devices support it. A fair number of notebooks and a few desktop computers use IR as well, so you can transfer information between your PDA and your desktop fairly easily.

Almost every type of PDA supports IR. With the right software, it's the perfect way to communicate small bits of information, such as contact information or notes. Microsoft Windows CE allows you to transfer information back and forth between Windows CE devices. With software like Peacemaker from Conduits Technologies (*http://www.conduits.com /products/peacemaker*), you can even transfer contact information to your friends and co-workers who don't have the Pocket PC platform yet.

Another key advantage of infrared is that it uses very little power. Transmitting data between devices won't prematurely drain your batteries, as is the case with some other technologies.

Disadvantages of Infrared

Because infrared is based on the serial technology I addressed in the previous section, it has the same 115 Kbps speed limitation. This limitation isn't a problem for small amounts of data, but can get tedious when you're working with larger blocks of information.

Infrared also requires "line of sight" communications—the infrared transceivers on the two devices must be able to "see" each other. In practical terms this means that the infrared transceivers must be facing each other and within a few feet of each other.

Note Alignment of infrared ports on two devices can have a great impact on the success of a transfer. The infrared port on your PDA should be easy to locate; it's the very dark red (almost black) lens, and it looks similar to the lens on a TV remote. The ports on the two devices should be at least 3 inches apart, and they should be directly facing one another.

Where Infrared Fits

Infrared is good for quick connections requiring minimal data transfer. It requires the attention of both parties transferring the data, so it's not very useful if you can't guarantee perfect alignment of the lenses.

Infrared is sometimes appropriate for synchronizing your PDA with a notebook, because it doesn't require a cable, and you can manage the synchronization process. Synchronizing your PDA with a notebook by using IR ports isn't difficult to set up and can help lighten your load, because you don't have to take the cradle with you.

Tips for Infrared Use

- Keep the devices about 1 foot apart. Less distance is better only up to a point. If the devices get too close (or too far away), your results will be unpredictable.

- Keep the infrared windows lined up as directly as possible.

- Don't attempt to use infrared in direct sunlight. The normal infrared waves in the sunlight will sometimes confuse the receiving unit.

Bluetooth

This isn't something your dentist will talk to you about after you eat a grape Popsicle. It's the name of a technology designed for short-range data transmittal when infrared isn't appropriate—for instance, when there's not a direct line of sight between the two devices that need to communicate.

Advantages of Bluetooth

Bluetooth supports connections between two devices that are roughly 10 meters, or 30 feet, apart. The devices do not need to have an unobstructed "view" of one another, nor do they have to be aligned in a particular way. In special conditions, the range of the signal can be extended to 100 meters, or 300 feet, but that requires higher-powered transmitters than most PDAs and notebooks have.

Bluetooth also allows devices to communicate at 1 Mbps, roughly ten times faster than infrared. That is certainly fast enough to synchronize your PDA with a notebook computer.

Disadvantages of Bluetooth

The downside to Bluetooth is that it's an emerging technology that isn't supported by many phones, PDAs, or notebook cards. Finding two devices that can use Bluetooth might be a problem. Although Bluetooth-enabled cellular phones and Bluetooth headsets have been regarded for many years as perfect examples of this new technology, at the time of this writing there are very few commercially released Bluetooth products.

Initially, Bluetooth was designed to be a low cost way of connecting two devices wirelessly. It was expected to be more expensive than infrared, but less expensive than some of the wireless LAN options that I'll explain in the next section. However, because there's not been market acceptance of Bluetooth products yet, the prices for the few devices that are available remain fairly high.

Note There are members of the industry who are beginning to question the application of Bluetooth. Although there's not a lot of opposition to Bluetooth yet, many people believe it's not quite finished. As a result, many are suggesting that other existing standards, such as 802.11b, be used instead of Bluetooth. 802.11b is a wireless LAN standard that I'll address in the next section.

Local Area Networks

So far I've explained relatively slow connections. Sure, USB is 2 Mbps, but when you compare that with the 100-Mbp rate possible over wired Ethernet connections, it seems slow. (Ethernet is a networking standard that's popular in most organizations.) Comparing the data transfer rate of a Fast Ethernet network to the communications rate of a serial connection is much like comparing the output of a fire hose to that of a squirt gun. (There is roughly a 1000 to 1 ratio between the two speeds.)

This section will address the options to connect your PDA to the local area network (LAN). Connecting a PDA directly to the wired Ethernet in your building might seem weird at first, but it does eliminate any speed problems that you might have felt you had connecting with any other method. I'll also cover wireless LANs, what they can do, and why you want one.

The following sections are intended for readers who use PDAs, but all of these options are available for notebooks as well. Almost every notebook uses a wired Ethernet connection, and wireless options are certainly suitable for notebook use. The options in the section "Connections for Travelers," however, might not be good solutions for your notebook, because their speeds are lower.

Shared Bandwidth

A LAN links together computers and equipment within one location, such as an office. Before looking at LANs and comparing their speeds to other types of connections, I must mention that LAN connection speeds are higher in part because LAN technologies are designed to be used by multiple computers at the same time.

Even though LANs have much faster speeds than the other technologies, you might have to compete for this bandwidth with other users. In small offices and properly set up corporate networks, this isn't usually an issue. However, having shared bandwidth is a bit different from having your own bandwidth, and might mean that there are times when you have noticeable slowdowns.

Wired Ethernet

Taking a device as portable as your PDA and subjecting it to a heavy LAN cable might seem a lot like chaining down a butterfly. However, there are situations where connecting your PDA to a network makes sense.

The way wired Ethernets for notebooks are connected to the corporate network makes them advantageous to mobile workers. However, the same cannot be said for PDAs. Generally, people do not directly attach a PDA to their corporate network; they synchronize their PDA with a computer.

However, there are some situations where network connectivity is a must, but a notebook just isn't socially acceptable. People sometimes frown on the use of notebooks in a meeting, whereas the use of a PDA is often considered acceptable. Although the corporate distinction between using PDAs and notebooks in a meeting is a fine line that doesn't always make sense, it is still something to consider.

Advantages of Wired Ethernet

The main advantage of wired Ethernet is speed. Ethernet runs at 10 Mbps. Most networks run Fast Ethernet, which has a speed of 100 Mbps. Other than the increase in speed, Fast Ethernet is the same as Ethernet. Ethernet is the clear winner in any speed race; it means that the network will run faster than a PDA. It also means that if an application can run on a PDA, it can run while the PDA is wired for Ethernet.

Disadvantages of Wired Ethernet

The biggest disadvantage is that plugging a PDA into a network is awkward. The heavy cable needed for Ethernet sometimes outweighs the entire PDA. That can make handling the PDA while it's wired to the network a little cumbersome.

You also have to contend with the lack of drivers for Windows CE network cards. Drivers exist for some PC cards and for the few CompactFlash network cards. You might have to buy a new network card to be able to use it with your PDA.

Note CardBus, a newer, faster standard designed to improve performance, is what most newer networking cards for notebooks are designed for. No Pocket PC or Handheld PC supports CardBus at this time. Either a CardBus card or PC Card can be inserted in a CardBus slot, because they both have the same physical dimensions, but most CardBus cards cannot be run in the PC Card slot. If your "PC Card" has a copper plate with raised dots in a row, it's really a CardBus card.

The last problem with using a PDA when wired to a network isn't a network problem; it is a problem with the size of the device. You can download information so quickly that you'll wish you had a bigger screen on which to view the data.

Wireless Local Area Network Connectivity

If wiring a PDA to a network is like chaining down a butterfly, the wireless network is like cutting that chain and letting the butterfly fly free again. Wireless LANs offer most of the benefits of wired Ethernet without the awkward cables.

A wireless LAN is, as you might expect, a wireless local area network. It combines the advantages of a local area network with the additional advantage of being wireless and therefore more mobile.

Most wireless LANs implemented today use the current IEEE 802.11b standard, which defines a networking speed of 11 Mbps and a range of roughly 100 meters. The 802.11b standard is based on technologies that have been around since World War II and were used primarily for concealing information from the enemy. However, the primary technique, called spread spectrum, proved to be a very reliable way of transmitting data.

Because wireless LANs use an industry standard, devices from many different vendors interoperate (play well) with each other. Although there is the occasional card that won't work with another vendor's products, mostly they work together. Because there are multiple vendors who make the equipment, the costs of these devices continues to come down.

Advantages of Wireless Local Area Networks

The obvious advantage of wireless LANs is that they are wireless. The biggest downside of a LAN is the heavy cable that binds the attached device. Wireless network cards generally weigh only a few ounces and do not add much more than an inch to the standard Compact-Flash or PC Card. With those exceptions, they are indistinguishable from a PC Card or CompactFlash card. Figure 2-5 on the next page shows a Symbol wireless LAN PC Card.

Note Symbol recently released a CompactFlash version of their 802.11b network card. This is a very impressive package and a great tool for Pocket PCs that cannot support a PC Card.

Figure 2-5 *Wireless LAN cards like this Symbol card need only an inch or so for their antennas.*

The speed of 802.11b wireless LANs is an impressive 11 Mbps—faster than even a direct USB connection, and fast enough for any task. I use a wireless LAN to back up my Compaq iPaq, because it's faster than backing up the unit in its cradle. It's certainly sufficient for synchronizing your PDA with a desktop computer and for routine browsing.

Wireless cards are more expensive than their wired cousins, and their access points—which are essentially the same as Ethernet hubs for wireless connectivity—are more expensive than their Ethernet counterparts as well. However, there are other costs that have to be considered, particularly for those who don't have LANs in existing buildings.

In offices that haven't been wired for Ethernet using Category 5 cables, the cost of running all of the wiring necessary to set up a wired network might far exceed the additional equipment cost. A new Ethernet cable run might cost $100. Add to this the need to install Ethernet cable runs in every location where you might want or need to use your notebook or PDA, and the cost of wireless technology starts to look more appealing.

Note With the correct settings and a wireless LAN in your home, you can even take your system from the office to home and start working immediately. You won't need to swap cards, hardware, or even settings. This can mean a simple transition from one location to another, and a level of convenience that hasn't previously been available.

Disadvantages of Wireless Local Area Networks

The biggest concern for wireless LANs is that someone might eavesdrop on your communications. Although there are security settings built into the 802.11b standard, they have been found to have vulnerabilities. It would take a sophisticated individual to capture the data going across the wireless LAN, but it's certainly not impossible.

The security solutions that I address in Chapter 3 minimize the likelihood of electronic eavesdroppers. However, any time information is sent over the airwaves, there is a risk.

Connections for Travelers

All of the connection types mentioned in this chapter so far are great for people working in offices or at desks; they aren't helpful to people traveling away from their offices to another city. There are different solutions for staying connected when mobility involves out-of-town travel.

Modems

Before the wireless LAN, before the LAN, and before infrared, modems were used to connect computers across the country. A modem, short for modulator demodulator, converts digital signals into analog signals so that they can be conveyed over non-digital media. The most common implementation of these is a modem that works over the public switched telephone network (PSTN). In other words, the most common type of modem uses an ordinary telephone line.

Modems of this type are not generally new to anyone who's been mobile, nor are they new to other computer users who have used them to share information or files with outside organizations. Most people are also familiar with the limitations of a modem.

Note This overview covers the traditional modem that uses analog phone lines. It doesn't apply to DSL modems, cable modems, or other devices that have *modem* in their name. Some would question why *modem* is in some of these devices' names if they don't modulate and demodulate signals, but that's a marketing decision.

Speeds

Most people describe communications that travel through a telephone modem as slow. Although Internet connection speeds have climbed dramatically, the telephone modem has stayed relatively slow at 53-Kbps. That's half the speed of a typical serial connection.

In reality, to get the 53-Kbps speeds that are possible today, the service providing the line must be digital, and the analog connection on the computer end must be a short, static-free line. If either of these isn't true, the real connection speed of a modem is much less than 53 Kbps. Typically, consumers can have 40-Kbps connection rates through most of the U.S. If the host of the line isn't digital, the limit is 33 Kbps.

Note The reason for the digital requirement on the host end is to get around a limitation of the analog-to-digital conversion process. Shannon's law limits the amount of data that can be sent across a phone line to 33 Kbps. If the host of the line is digital, this rate is increased to 56 Kbps. In the U.S., the Federal Communications Commission (FCC) limits the speed to 53 Kbps.

One other quirk of modems is that 56-Kbps modems transmitting at 53 Kbps only upload, or transmit, information at 33 Kbps. This is due to the limitations of the phone line. This means that uploading a long e-mail with an attached file, such as a PowerPoint file, can be excruciatingly slow.

Another problem with modems is their need to identify the appropriate speed at which to communicate. This happens during a training or identification phase of the call initiation. (Training is the process of establishing a usable set of frequencies to communicate on.) Between the time it takes to dial the number, the time for the telephone network to establish a connection, the time for the host to answer the line, and the time to train, connecting two modems can take 45 seconds or more. Modems are not conducive to getting a little bit of data quickly.

Digital Phone Systems

By my definition, digital should be good. A digital phone system should make it easier to relay digital information from one computer to another. Unfortunately, nothing could be further from the truth. Digital phone systems often use much higher power levels than standard analog phone lines. Occasionally, when a modem is plugged into a digital phone system, the additional current fries the components in the modem, making it completely unusable.

This can happen over and over again when mobile professionals try to access an analog phone line to connect to the corporate e-mail system to get their mail.

A variety of line testers are available at a reasonable cost that allow you to test a phone line before attempting to plug your modem into it. Additionally, most hotels have phones that provide a modem line from the base of the phone itself. The beauty of these phones is that you don't have to worry about whether the phone system is digital or not, because the phone always provides an analog phone line to your modem.

Advantages of Modems

Access is the clear advantage of using modems. It's usually easy for travelers to access analog phone lines to use with modems to connect to their offices. That doesn't mean that it might not be difficult from time to time.

It's also relatively cheap. Some of the other options I'll go over later in this chapter might require more expensive equipment and sometimes even service contracts. The cost for these other plans can be prohibitively expensive.

Disadvantages of Modems

The biggest complaint people have with modems is their slow throughput and the relatively long time it takes to connect. This is particularly frustrating when long distance dollars are adding up as you download your e-mail.

The other problem with modems is that they are very difficult to use. Every hotel has its own requirements for dialing out—requirements that have to be fed into your notebook or PDA before you can use the line. When traveling between different hotels, you might wish that modems could figure out how to get an outside line and dial your closest access point. Unfortunately, that's something modems can't do on their own.

Tips for Modem Use

- Start your connection as soon as you can, and start your software to synchronize with your remote server. Because modems are slow, it's often best to get the system to start synchronizing your e-mail or other data and then come back to work on it after you're connected.

- When you check into a hotel, ask the desk clerk how to connect your modem. You won't be the first one to ask this question, and they can sometimes give you helpful hints or even suggest settings.

- Look for alternatives. Just because you have your modem with you doesn't mean you have to use it. See if Ethernet or a wireless LAN is an option. It never hurts to ask.

- If you can't find an analog phone line, look for a fax machine. Almost all fax machines use analog phone lines, even when connected to a digital phone system. If you or the organization you're visiting can live without the fax machine for a few minutes, you might be able to use the fax line to get your information.

Cellular Modem

Although similar to regular modems, cellular modems are specifically designed for use with cellular or mobile telephones. In some cases, these cellular modems are included in the same package as regular modems; in other cases, they are available separately.

There is a whole series of wireless systems that cellular modems can use. The differences between the various mechanisms used by cellular phones are beyond the scope of this book, but the phone that you choose will determine which wireless system you can use. From the standpoint of a cellular modem there is no difference.

You'll also notice that I use the term *cellular*, although that isn't technically correct for every type of wireless system. Personal Communications Service (PCS) phones, for instance, are mobile phones, but are not cellular. However, for our purposes there is no difference.

Note I'm not personally a fan of using a cellular phone and cellular modem in this manner, but I can say that Socket Communications (*http://www.socketcom.com*) makes a very nice series of products that come bundled with a CompactFlash card and the cable you need to connect to your cellular phone.

Advantages of Cellular Modems

Cellular modems enable you to access your information whether or not a phone line is available. This is convenient when you're riding a train or you are a passenger in a car. By using a cellular modem and a proper cellular phone, you can connect wirelessly to the main office.

Another advantage that cellular modems have over other wireless connections is that they use your existing cellular service; you won't have to subscribe to another service and pay another monthly fee. Although carrying a cellular phone and a PDA or notebook might seem like you're carrying two things when you might be able to get by with one, it's unrealistic to expect that you'll be able to travel without a cellular phone in today's business environment.

Yet another advantage of cellular modems is their wide service areas. You can use a cellular modem any place where you can use a cellular phone. These coverage areas greatly exceed the coverage areas of dedicated data solutions, such as Cellular Digital Packet Data (CDPD). I'll address these solutions in the next few sections.

Disadvantages of Cellular Modems

There are four drawbacks to using cellular modems. The first is that the already slow speed of a regular modem is further reduced to either 14.4 or 19.2 Kbps, depending on the cellular network. This can be painfully slow if you're waiting for an e-mail to download.

The second drawback to cellular modems is that they don't work everywhere. Generally speaking, you can establish a cellular connection anywhere you can get a cellular signal; however, if you are too far outside a major city, particularly in the Midwest and through the mountains, you'll find yourself without service.

Even when you do have service, there might be brief periods when your cellular modem isn't able to send or receive data because the signal isn't good enough. Couple this with the slow speed, and connecting with a cellular modem can be very frustrating.

Finally, this can be an expensive option, particularly when you are roaming outside your home area or use up all the minutes in your cellular plan. This means you can be paying as much as $.70 per minute to get a slow, poor quality connection.

When Does a Cellular Modem Make Sense?

Cellular modems are best for infrequent access when no phone lines are available. For example, cellular modems might be beneficial if you're on a boat or commuter train—situations where you don't have the option to use a wired connection.

Cellular modems also tend to have a slightly wider range of places where they can be used when compared with other wireless alternatives. You might have to use a cellular modem if you're in a remote area.

Cellular Digital Packet Data

Cellular modems connect your cellular (or mobile) phone to your notebook or PDA. Not that great a feat. However, juggling the two devices that are now connected by a cable can be complicated. Having to hold your cellular phone and your PDA means an end to one-handed operations—one of the reasons why PDAs are so appealing in the first place.

Enter Cellular Data Packet Data (CDPD). CDPD integrates the transceiver in a cellular phone into a radio card that can be inserted into you PDA or notebook. This card eliminates the need for you to connect your cellular phone to your PDA. Figure 2-6 on the next page shows a Sierra Wireless AirCard 300. The card slides into a PC Card slot and has only a tiny, flexible antenna extending beyond the PC Card socket.

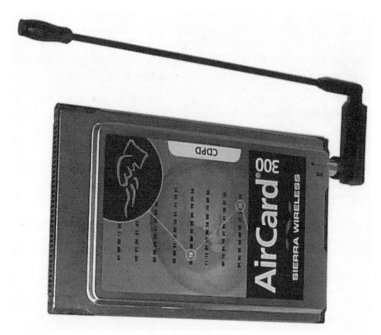

Figure 2-6   *Sierra Wireless' AirCard 300 enables CDPD access with the right service subscription.*

Advantages of Cellular Digital Packet Data

Regaining the one-handed operation of your PDA and obtaining the faster connection times of CDPD top the list of reasons why CDPD is better than a cellular modem. Because the card is self-contained and has only a small antenna, it can slide into the PDA's PC Card slot and doesn't require special effort to manage.

A CDPD modem takes a few seconds to track down a cellular signal that it can use to register with the network, but it's generally connected within 15 seconds—about one third to one quarter of the time it takes for a typical cellular modem to connect.

Disadvantages of Cellular Digital Packet Data

The biggest disadvantage to CDPD service is the cost. CDPD service requires that you purchase the CDPD card and pay for the service. Although the service fees for CDPD aren't outrageous, they do become a factor when you add them to all the other services that you're supporting, including your cellular phone plan. CDPD plans are generally in the range of $75 to $99 per month for unlimited access.

When does Cellular Digital Packet Data Make Sense?

CDPD service doesn't make sense for most people. The exception is the person who has applications that take advantage of wireless connectivity on his or her PDA. It will take a specific need that can't be filled any other way to justify the additional expense of CDPD services.

Alternative Wireless Services

CDPD isn't the only service available if you want to have a one-handed operation of your PDA and wireless connectivity, but it is the one with the widest coverage area. Other services exist or are being tested in major markets. These services offer much higher connection speeds and sometimes a few more "bells and whistles."

The premiere alternative to CDPD was Metricom's Ricochet service, which was only implemented in ten U.S. cities. This service was substantially superior to CDPD. It offered better connections at 128-Kbps speeds. The service was recently purchased by Aerie Networks, Inc. The most up-to-date information on Ricochet is available at *http://www.aerienetworks.com/ricochet.html*.

There is a great deal of talk about the new, third generation (3G) mobile telephone systems that cellular communications companies are planning on putting in place, but by and large these services are not real yet. Several providers have indicated that they will take an incremental step to improve wireless communication with a so-called 2.5G hybrid merging of new technologies. The designation 2.5G implies that it is neither the second generation, which is in use today, nor the third generation, which is expected to be available a few years from now.

Note A variety of mobile communications companies are beginning to roll out these 2.5G services. Their acronyms are starting to proliferate in the news. All you need to worry about is how fast the connection is and whether your current mobile provider offers the service. Don't get caught up in the acronym game.

The third generation (3G) wireless system and the hybrid (2.5G) systems might not be widely available for years to come. Mobile providers are just now scrambling to upgrade their systems. You can expect an adoption curve similar to what happened with digital cellular implementation, or the so-called second generation system. The service initially appeared in cities with a very large subscriber base and is slowly being rolled out to the rest of the country. In some rural areas, even the digital second generation system still isn't available.

Special Considerations for Traveling

While talking about the different wireless options for traveling, I knowingly skirted a few issues that deserve special attention because they are unique challenges, and you'll want to monitor the ever-changing information about what these options entail. Coverage areas are changing very rapidly and vary from provider to provider. The next two sections are dedicated to this topic.

Coverage Areas

I mentioned that in wide area networking products, the coverage areas vary. The coverage area issue will probably be the one that determines which wide area wireless solution you select, unless you live in a major metropolitan area.

Coverage in rural or even small metropolitan areas is not always available. When it is available, it's often through only one provider. This can make the service solution very simple: You pick the provider that has service in your area.

The best place to start your search for wireless products is the wireless providers' Web sites. Although coverage maps are usually buried three or four levels deep in most providers' Web sites, they can be a quick way to determine whether the provider will be able to service your needs.

Some wireless providers also allow you to search for coverage by ZIP code, which will give you a more definitive answer as to whether you can expect service in your area. The coverage maps available on the Web sites make looking at a small area difficult. For instance, take a look at Figure 2-7, which is a Verizon Wireless map.

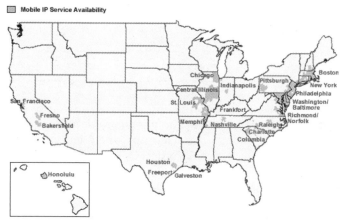

© 2001 Copyright Cellco Partnership d/b/a Verizon Wireless. All rights reserved. Actual coverage varies from the area depicted above. The mapped territory contains areas with no service. Wireless service is subject to network and transmission limitations, including cell site unavailability, particularly in remote areas. Customer equipment, weather, topography, and other environmental considerations associated with radio technology also affect service. The map represents coverage as of November 2001. For current coverage, visit *http://www.verizonwireless.com/mobile_ip/svc_availability/index.html.*

Figure 2-7   *Verizon Wireless CDPD coverage.*

Note During the writing of this book, I used CDPD service from GoAmerica (*http://www.goamerica.net*). It utilizes a Sierra Wireless card and both the Verizon and AT&T wireless networks. I was able to get signals well beyond the coverage area shown on the coverage map. You might be pleasantly surprised to find the service working beyond the coverage area, but you shouldn't expect it.

Worldwide Access

If you're traveling between continents—for instance, between the U.S. and the U.K.—your solutions are going to be much more complicated. Because the cellular systems and regulations differ dramatically between continents, it's unlikely that you'll find a single provider able to give you service on both continents.

Note The situation is changing, and there is hope for the future; however, there are currently only a limited number of phones that are "multi-lingual" enough to handle travel throughout the world.

This applies to wireless services as well as cellular phones. It does not, however, apply to your wireless LAN cards. The IEEE 802.11b standard is in use both in the U.S. and abroad. You can probably get wireless access to your systems at your company's local offices, but you won't likely be able to rove the streets enjoying your wireless freedom.

For wireless phone service, you're probably stuck with one of the few satellite-based phone systems that, because of their satellite basis, are available any place on Earth. The most popular satellite phone system is Iridium (*http://www.iridium.com*).

The death knell for these satellite-based systems might be that their coverage in densely populated areas is spotty at best. Electromagnetic interference from people, cellular phones, radios, and electricity usage makes their reliability in urban areas less than perfect. Unfortunately, these are exactly where most people who need the service tend to be.

All that being said, the old axiom "the only game in town is the best game in town" holds true. The technology might not be perfect, but it is what we have available to us today.

Summary

In this chapter you learned about the options that you have to connect your PDA to your desktop computer or notebook. Figure 2-8 shows you a quick overview of the speeds and distances supported by the various connectivity options that we've covered in this chapter. (Notice that the scale of the figure is logarithmic, indicating that speed and distance increase exponentially toward the upper right corner of the chart.)

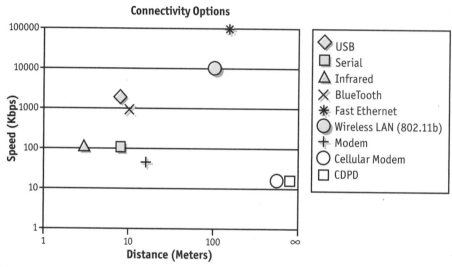

Figure 2-8   *The speeds and distances of most major connectivity options.*

When determining your connectivity options and needs, here are some questions that you might want to ask yourself:

- What option are you going to use for local connections? You will always need one connection method, so what's it going to be?

- Will you ever transfer information to other PDA users? How will you do it?

- What are some of the things you want to be able do with a wireless LAN? Send e-mail? Surf the Web? Access corporate systems?

- Where do you frequently travel? What service providers have coverage in those areas?

- What wireless solutions have your friends used? How did they like them?

- What other devices do you have that can be used instead of or in addition to your PDA, notebook, and other data options?

Choose Your Alarm: Security

In this chapter, we look at the necessity of protecting your mobile devices and the information they contain from theft.

We've all seen the news stories about computer hackers who steal hundreds of thousands of credit card numbers from Web sites. It seems like there's a new story every month about a site that has become a victim of malicious hackers and about the losses those attacks cause.

Your information might not be as valuable as hundreds of thousands of credit card numbers, but I'm sure you want to take reasonable precautions to prevent it from ending up in the wrong hands. This chapter will explore what security is, how to define what level of security you need, and what specific techniques you can use to protect your data.

Note Hackers would prefer that the term *cracker* be used to describe those people who use their technical skills for illegal activities. Hackers are proud of their technical prowess. They see hacking as a skillful way of solving a problem. However, because the distinction is not clearly understood by most people and my goal is to maintain readability here, I'll use *hacker* to describe the people who perform these activities.

Understanding Security

The first step toward understanding how to secure your information is to understand the key concepts of security. These concepts differ only slightly from the physical lock-and-key security we're all used to. As you'll see in a moment, installing a lock and key is no different from challenging a user to see if he or she knows a device password. In the digital world, it's easier to make security a little more complicated, and in some ways more secure.

Note Unfortunately, some people find security to be a very dull topic. It's an area of computer science that uses mathematical techniques to hide information in plain sight. My approach in this chapter is to explain the concepts you might need to know, or might run into. Although I recommend that you read each section, if you find yourself getting bored, you can skip some sections. You can always come back to them later when you need to learn more about security.

Logical, or digital, security is usually composed of three components:

- **Authentication**   The process of identifying a user uniquely.

- **Authorization**   The process of determining whether a user who has been authenticated has permission to use the resource he or she is requesting. For instance, a user might have to be authorized before being allowed to open a file.

- **Encryption**   The process of transforming or *ciphering* information to prevent unauthorized access to it. In other words, you need the computer equivalent of a "secret decoder ring" to access the information. Without it, the information is useless.

Note The use of both *authentication* and *authorization* is unfortunate because in English these words are so similar in appearance that they are sometimes confused. Please pay special attention to these two different words, because the distinction is important in this section.

Encryption mechanisms are not perfect; given enough time with your device, someone will be able to decipher it. For this reason, physical security is also covered in this section. I'll go over the options for physical security and some of the basic habits you should develop to prevent theft of the devices themselves.

Authentication

As I mentioned earlier, authentication is the process of identifying a user uniquely. It's similar to going to a teller at your bank. The teller first makes sure that you are who you say you are. Typically, the teller requests a piece of information that only you should know, such as your social security number, but he or she might also ask for a picture ID, such as a driver's license or passport. In either case, the bank teller authenticates your identity.

Authentication can take many forms—from a user name and password to fingerprint or retinal analysis. Most of the time, the authentication methods used for computer systems are knowledge based. You're asked for a user name and password (or sometimes just a password) to verify your identity.

Knowledge

The most common type of authentication mechanism is clearly knowledge based. Most of us have had to log in to a corporate network with a user name and password, or enter a personal identification number into an alarm system to disarm it. Knowledge-based authentication systems work on the assumption that the user is the person associated with a user name and password combination, or in some cases with just a password.

The user should be the only person who knows the information used to authenticate him or her. Because only the user knows the information, it is safe to assume that the person entering the information is the user to whom the information belongs.

One of the fundamental tenets of knowledge-based authentication is that the user does not share the authentication information with anyone else. This prevents one person from supplying another person's authentication information and being falsely authenticated.

Note Don't share your passwords with anyone. This includes help desk staff and systems administrators. For reasons of auditing, which we will cover in the next section, you should ensure that your authentication information isn't used by anyone else. Systems administrators shouldn't need your password anyway—they can access everything you have access to with a little work. If you must share your password, remember to change it as soon as you can after the other person has used it.

Password

Password-based authentication can be used to authenticate a user's identity or to authorize access to a resource. When used as an authentication method, passwords are a single string of letters and numbers that uniquely identify you. No one else should be able to guess this password; this guarantees that it's you and only you who can use the password.

If the password is an access method, it isn't used to identify you; it's used to indicate your authorization to use a resource. It allows you access to the resource, but doesn't provide any clue to your identity. When a password is used in this way, you can think of it as a key. A key doesn't identify you; it only indicates that you are presumably authorized to access what is behind the door. When passwords are used in this manner, the step of authenticating your identity is skipped and the next step of authorization is tested.

To understand this, think of an alarm system. In some cases, there's one code that is used by everyone. The code simply turns the system on or off. This is an example of an authorization code. Knowledge of the code indicates the user's authorization to turn on or off the alarm system. However, for most alarm systems, each user has his or her own unique code. This code both identifies, or authenticates, the user and authorizes access.

The biggest problem with a system that uses passwords is that it's too easy for the password to be found by or disclosed to someone who isn't supposed to have it. If you need to change a password used for authentication, it's relatively easy—you just change it. It's more difficult to change the password if it's being used for authorization, because you must distribute the new password to all the people who use it for authorization. This often leads to a repeat of the problem—the password being accidentally discovered and thus requiring another password change.

User Name and Password

Requiring a user name in addition to a password helps to improve knowledge-based authentication. The user name is used to identify the user. The password is then used to verify the user's identity.

On the surface, this seems like a minor change, but it solves the relatively important problem of two users who want to use the same password. With a password-only system, if a person learns that a password is already in use, he or she knows that password can be used to gain access to the system.

Requiring a user name and password eliminates this problem and makes it considerably more difficult for someone to use "brute force" to gain access to the system. Brute force is a semi-random guessing strategy for finding out the user names and passwords in the system. This method is sometimes used when a hacker is trying to gain access to a system but has little or no information about the system.

User name and password combinations ultimately have the same weakness all knowledge-based systems do. You must carefully guard the password so that no one else can masquerade as you. With knowledge-based authentication methods, there's little you can do to prevent the eventual exposure of the secret password.

Biometric

A totally different approach to authentication uses not what you know but who you are to prove your identity. It uniquely identifies you based on characteristics of your body that are unique to you. Biometric systems require additional hardware, which makes them substantially more expensive; however, they are much more effective at preventing false authorization. In this section I'll address the common biometric authentication mechanisms, as well as some of their limitations.

Fingerprint

The commanders on *Star Trek* acknowledge the receipt of information by placing their thumbs on a work pad, and then they go along their merry way. *Star Trek* is, of course, science fiction; however, it's a scientific fact that no two fingerprints on the planet are identical. That is why you can use a fingerprint to uniquely identify a person.

For decades, law enforcement has used the unique qualities of fingerprints to identify criminals. Fingers secrete oil that is deposited on the things a person touches. By dusting something a person has touched with powder, law enforcement officers can determine the fingerprint pattern of the person. Then the fingerprints can be compared to the fingerprints of known offenders. The process for getting an electronic fingerprint system to work isn't that complicated, but it can be negatively affected by the same thing that law enforcement officers use to catch criminals. The oils that are secreted from our skin tend to build up on the fingerprint scanners, confusing the system.

However, for the most part fingerprint recognition is simple, quick, and painless. You place your finger or thumb on a small scanner. The scanner takes an image of your finger or thumb and stores it in the database. When you want access to the system, you place your finger on the scanner again. The software then compares your fingerprint to the one on file. If it matches, you are authenticated and presumably authorized for the device or service that you're attempting to access.

However, there are a few problems with fingerprint analysis. The first problem is that oils from a person's skin are deposited on the scanner. This can cause the scanner to see part of the previous person's fingerprint in addition to your fingerprint, causing a match failure. The solution is to continually clean the fingerprint scanner or to use pressure-based scanners instead of optical scanners.

Another issue with fingerprint identification is that injuries such as burns can temporarily disfigure the fingerprint so that a match is no longer possible. This can also happen with other minor injuries, such as small cuts from chopping vegetables in the kitchen. When fingerprint identification is used, there is usually a backup identification mechanism—such as a secure password—that can be used when fingerprints are not available.

Fingerprint recognition systems cost less than $300 per unit. Some units support Microsoft Windows CE devices such as Pocket PC and HPC 2000 hardware, in addition to notebooks and desktop computers. Support for Windows CE devices is increasing so rapidly that fingerprints might soon be a popular authentication method for Windows CE devices.

Facial Recognition

We identify most people we know by their facial features. Most of us are quite good at differentiating between two people, because their faces are built differently, even if the differences are subtle. This is true even of identical twins, although distinguishing between twins' features is much more difficult.

A computer facial recognition program identifies the locations and sizes of your basic facial features and uses them to create a mathematical model. Such a program records the location and size of your nose, eyes, and mouth as a string of numbers in a database. When you are being verified by such a program, the image of your face is again converted into a string of numbers and compared with the images on file. The program confirms a match when a certain number of your features are within a certain level of variation from the mathematical representation of your face on file.

Facial recognition is quite likely to be a footnote in the journals of security research. It seems much more useful as a tool for identifying specific people than it does for authenticating that the person using the system is a specific person. For example, it's being used in casinos and at sporting events to spot people authorities want to keep out. In a casino, this might be a known cheater or card counter. At a sporting event, the system might be looking for known trouble-makers. These systems are quite expensive; they start in the tens of thousands of dollars.

Retinal Scanner

Another unique attribute of a person that most of us are not aware of is the pattern of blood vessels in the back of the eye—more specifically, the pattern of blood vessels in the retina, or seeing part of the eye. Because these patterns are unique and not normally visible to most people, it's difficult to get the information necessary to forge a retinal scan.

Retinal scans are perhaps one of the most secure biometric solutions available today, but because the scanner needs to "see" the back of a user's eye, they are generally large, expensive devices used to protect only the most secure locations. They are, unfortunately, completely impractical for mobile devices.

Alternate Authentication Methods

So far I've addressed knowledge-based systems and biometric systems. Neither of these systems is appropriate for every need: Knowledge-based systems are cheap to implement but vulnerable to security leaks; biometric systems are often prohibitively expensive and are sometimes vulnerable to user injuries. This section explores alternative forms of authentication that don't fit neatly into either of the two previous categories.

Smart Card

In many ways, the idea of smart cards might seem like a step backward in security, because they are similar to keys. It's true that smart cards are essentially keys, but they differ from keys in two important ways: They cannot be copied easily, and they are designed in such a way that if they are copied, they won't be valuable for long. Because the actual code on the card is frequently changed and stored for new authentication, having an older copy of the information isn't useful. Think of this as a password that resets itself for you.

Smart cards are a great addition to a knowledge-based system that requires a password, but they aren't a replacement for a password. Smart cards work best when used in conjunction with a password. That way, a criminal would need to obtain the smart card (or a copy of it) in addition to the user's password to gain access to the user's information. The required smart card readers cost less than $300 per computer, and the cards cost approximately $10 per user. Although the costs are not excessive, they can be enough to rule out this solution for most businesses.

Most smart card readers are not portable enough to be considered mobile. Smart card readers are lightweight and fairly small, but they are not set up to be transported all the time. They are probably not the best choice for mobile security. Their need to be attached to the system with cables makes their use while traveling awkward.

Tokens

RSA Security sells a system that uses a small token with a frequently changing number to authenticate a user. The system uses a mathematical formula to change the number on the token once a minute. To log in, users must supply their password as well as the information displayed on the token.

Token-based authentication requires something that you know—your password—as well as something you have—the token. This type of authentication is relatively inexpensive; it costs less than $100 per user. It's also a very effective method of authentication because the user must have both the password and the token.

RSA offers software for the Palm environment that emulates the token so that you can use your PDA as your authentication token. This software will presumably be available for the Pocket PC sometime in the near future. The software will recognize your Pocket PC as part of your authentication so that you can prove you are who you say you are.

Signature

Signatures, like fingerprints, have been used for a long time as a form of legal identification. For most legal documents, signatures are the primary mechanism used to authenticate a person's identity and indicate their agreement on contracts. Because of this, signatures are a natural choice for an authentication mechanism.

The problem with signatures is that they can be forged. Signature authentication programs look at more than just the appearance of a signature to determine whether it is authentic. Signature recognition for authentication also takes advantage of the varying amounts of time people take to create different parts of their signature. I might, for instance, take more time making the *R* in *Robert* than you would. Or you might have trouble replicating the *b* in *Robert,* causing your writing to have a different flow than mine.

By gauging how a signature is created as well as the final result, signature-based authentication systems can accurately identify users. This was tested on CEOs and high-level executives whose assistants regularly signed their employer's name on correspondence. In many cases, the assistant's copy of the executive's signature was visually indistinguishable from the executive's original signature. However, because signature recognition systems use timing in addition to the final result, and the assistant's rate of signing the name differed from the executive's, the system was able to distinguish between an assistant's attempt at the executive signature and the real thing.

You can get signature-based authentication systems for your Windows desktop computer from several vendors. The only signature-based authentication system available for the

Pocket PC at the time of this writing is Sign-On. You can find more information about this product at *http://www.a2000d.com.*

Authorization

Up to this point I've focused on technology that ensures that users are who they say they are. However, just because you know who someone is doesn't mean he or she should have access to a resource. For instance, I can readily identify my mother-in-law. I know her face, her voice, and her signature. However, that doesn't mean that if she showed up at my doorstep at 2 in the morning, I would let her in. That is to say, I can authenticate who she is, but I can decide not to authorize her for entry.

Returning to the bank analogy from earlier in the chapter, after the teller has confirmed that you are who you say you are, he or she has to make sure you have the authorization to complete the transaction you want to make. For instance, if you want to withdraw money from a trust account, the teller has to make sure you're allowed to remove the funds.

One of the things that makes computer authorization confusing is that for every resource, there are often several different operations that can be authorized. For instance, a file might be listed in a directory, read from, or written to. Each of these operations can be authorized individually. As another example, printers or print queues might allow a user to print a document, delete a document, or control the print queue. In most cases, the different operations that can be authorized for a resource are kept together for simplicity. I won't address authorizations for specific operations because *which* operations are authorized has no impact on *how* the operations are authorized.

Controlling Access

Operating systems such as Microsoft Windows 2000 and Microsoft Windows XP commonly use an access control list (ACL) to determine whether you can have access to something. An access control list, as its name implies, lists users or groups and the status of their access to a particular resource, such as a file.

Users belong to a set of groups that the system administrator can control. The access control list can contain only lists of groups and their accesses. The system can determine whether a particular user should or should not be allowed access.

Access control lists are implemented in advanced operating systems. Because they are complicated and require more memory space to implement than password-based systems, ACLs are not frequently used with PDAs. You'll also find that some operating systems, such as Linux, don't have native support for ACLs. They use a more basic form of security that identifies the user and group (singular) that the file belongs to, and their authorized access. There's also space to indicate the authorization that the world (everyone) should have.

Auditing

One of the benefits of accurately authenticating specific individuals is the ability to audit their activities for later review. Card access systems and alarm systems have auditing turned on by default. Every time you use your card or transponder to gain access, a record is made of who you are and which "door" you went through. Similarly, a record is made whenever you turn on or off an alarm system by using a code. When these codes are assigned to individual users, they can identify the user who armed or disarmed the system.

Auditing is a useful tool, because, although you trust a person enough to give him or her access, you might still want to monitor his or her activities to some extent. On computer systems, though, auditing is usually turned off; so many people access so many different files and programs that it would be unrealistic to expect that you would want to track every access to every resource. For this reason, you can control auditing from within Windows 2000 or Windows XP on both a user and resource level. You (or the system administrator) can monitor only the directory C:\SECUREFILES, or only the user jobrown, or only when jobrown is accessing files in C:\SECUREFILES.

Auditing is often very useful when an organization suspects that someone might be doing something wrong but can't prove it. Auditing is used to collect information on the person's activities until it can be determined whether or not the person is doing something improper. Auditing is also sometimes used to perform random checks of confidential or restricted information.

Authenticating for Authorization

On the Pocket PC platform, there's not a lot of memory space to implement the access control lists and auditing features that you'll find in Windows 2000 and Windows XP. The Pocket PC is a personal device rather than a shared device, and this makes security authorization a bit different.

Because only one person generally uses these devices, the authentication step should also indicate authorization, or access. Earlier in this chapter, I suggested using a password as an authentication mechanism and explained that often it also implied authorization. This is how the Pocket PC's security works. If you know the password to the device, it's assumed that you should be able to have access to everything on the device.

If multiple users share a Pocket PC, you'll have to add your own security to it to prevent one person from accessing another person's information. One form of security that you can add is file-level encryption.

Encryption

Encryption is the protecting of data by converting it into a form that's unreadable except through a further transformation with a decryption key. All forms of encryption can be broken by someone with enough time, but the encryption techniques used today are generally very difficult to break without the correct key.

Note Sometimes you'll see *encryption* referred to as *ciphering*. These terms are interchange-able. Ciphering is the process of encryption. Deciphering is the process of decryption.

There are two primary uses for encryption. The first is as an additional level of security. Even if a user is able to read a file, he or she might not be able to decrypt it and use the information. The second use is to protect data over communication lines so that it cannot be recorded by a party other than the one for whom the data was intended.

The first step in the discussion of encryption is understanding how encryption works.

Keys and Certificates

The primary concern for encryption is the management of the keys. Keys are used with encryption algorithms to encrypt the data, and keys decrypt the data on the other end. A cryptographic key is a series of binary digits (ones and zeros) of a specific length that can be used to encrypt or decrypt a message.

Secret Keys and Public Keys

When encryption was first used, it was *symmetric*. In other words, the key used to encrypt the data was used to decrypt the data. This technique is also called *secret key cryptography*—the key used to encrypt the data is a secret that, when exposed, allows anyone to encrypt or decrypt the information.

The biggest challenge with symmetric or secret key cryptographic systems was sharing the secret key. Sharing this secret key and ensuring that only the person supposed to receive it did in fact receive it represented a huge challenge. At some point, the information had to be communicated, or transmitted, and there was no real way to provide 100 percent assurance that someone else wouldn't receive the key. There was always the possibility that someone could get the secret key—by overhearing you, by making a copy of the key if it was written down, or in numerous other ways.

Mathematical algorithms were eventually employed that use two different, paired keys. One key is used for the encryption process, and the other key is used for the decryption process. This public/private key pair allows information to be transferred by exposure of only the public key. After the message is encrypted with the public key, only the proper recipient with the private key will be able to decrypt the message.

For example, you could provide someone with a public key with which to encrypt a message he or she sends you. When that message arrives, you could use your private key to decrypt the message. No one who sees the message can decrypt it without your private key.

The problem with public/private key systems, sometimes also called *asymmetric key systems*, is that they are computationally intensive. This makes them difficult to implement as a general-purpose encryption method with reasonable performance. However, these asymmetric key systems can be very useful as a method of exchanging secret keys for symmetric cryptographic systems. By transferring secret keys within an asymmetric encryption system, you can be reasonably assured that a third party will not discover the secret keys.

Typical encryption methods use both public/private key systems and secret key systems. The correspondence is initiated when the first party sends an encrypted request to use a symmetric encryption mechanism and the secret key to be used in that conversation. The recipient uses the first party's public key to decrypt the secret key and tells the sender to begin communication. From that point on, the agreed upon secret key and symmetric encryption mechanism are used.

Encryption Methods and Key Lengths

The function of encryption is to prevent others from learning what was encrypted. As mentioned above, this is done by the use of keys. Ultimately, the quality of the encryption that you get—and how difficult it is for someone else to decode—are based on two things. The first is the encryption formula or algorithm itself. The second is the length of the key. The longer the key, the harder it is to guess what the right key is.

As mentioned in the previous section, there are two types of encryption, each with its own advantages. For the most part, public/private key systems are used to exchange the secret key information needed by the symmetric key system that will encrypt the bulk of the traffic. Several public/private key encryption mechanisms are available, but the most popular is RSA.

On the symmetric encryption side, there are several different methods of encryption. The U.S. standard for encryption is aptly named Digital Encryption Standard (DES). This standard is well known and well understood, and as a result, it is considered relatively secure. The problem with DES, however, is that because it uses a rather short fixed-length, 56-bit key, it's no longer considered sufficiently secure. Because DES is implemented in the hardware of many devices, it's impractical to change the length of the key.

Note Generally speaking, only well-understood encryption methods are accepted by the industry as being secure. This is because the encryption community has thoroughly evaluated the algorithm to ensure that there aren't any mathematical shortcuts to determine the key and break the encryption.

Given the impracticality of changing how DES works, a mechanism was developed that runs the DES on the same information three times with three different keys. This mechanism effectively increases the DES key length without changing the hardware. However, because three DES encryption iterations are required, it takes three times as long to encrypt information with Triple DES (3DES) than with standard DES. Despite the additional processing necessary to encrypt data, 3DES is rapidly becoming the new standard for data encryption.

Other mechanisms for symmetric encryption include the RC2 and RC4 methods; they are used in environments such as products designed for export. However, by and large, the encryption methods used in the United States are RSA and DES or 3DES.

Note The U.S. State Department tightly controls which encryption tools can be exported. Encryption is, by law, considered a weapon system. The National Security Agency (NSA) is responsible for observing the communications of foreign nations and parties. It sees strong encryption tools as a hindrance to its primary mission and advises the State Department on which tools to allow for export. In general, this means strong encryption tools are not available outside the U.S.

The length of a key is one of the primary factors determining how difficult it will be to regenerate the key or to decrypt a message without it. The longer the key, the harder it is for someone to break the code. However, the longer the key, the more time it takes to encrypt the data, as well.

RSA encryption typically uses key lengths of 512 bits or longer. Key lengths of 1024 bits or more are recommended to help ensure that the encryption is not unnecessarily weak.

Conversely, because of the need for speed and the differences between public/private key and secret key systems, a typical key length for a secret key system is between 40 and 128 bits. This is, of course, only for those secret key encryption systems that allow variable key lengths, such as the RC2 and RC4 previously mentioned. The U.S. standard states that 40-bit key encryption can be exported almost anywhere, 56-bit key encryption can be exported to the foreign offices of U.S. companies, and 128-bit key encryption cannot be exported from the U.S. at all.

Digital Signatures

One of the benefits of public/private key encryption is that it is possible to ensure that a specific person created a message. The ability to validate a specific sender creates, in essence, a digital signature that ensures that the message was not tampered with in transit.

To create a digital signature, you must first create a message digest for the message. A message digest is the result of a function that reduces the entire length of a message into a string of fixed length that is difficult to reproduce. The algorithm for converting the message into the fixed-length string must generate strings that are not similar to strings in other messages, and that are distributed over the entire range of possible values that the fixed length string might hold. This makes the message digest similar to a fingerprint. It is reasonable to assume that the correct fingerprint with a message indicates no one has tampered with it.

Message Digest 5 (MD5) is the most popular message-digesting algorithm used. (It doesn't eat the message; it creates a message digest.) It is popular because it does a good job of creating a message digest in almost any circumstances, and it is only marginally slower than the less secure MD4 algorithm.

This message digest is added to the message and encrypted with the sender's private key. After the message is received, the recipient can decrypt the message digest using the sender's public key. If the decryption is successful, the sender originated the message. If the message digest received from performing a message digest algorithm on the message matches the one deciphered from the signature, the message was not altered in transit.

Certificates

Certificates fill an important role in encryption and digital signatures. In the section about digital signatures, I mentioned that the recipient uses the author's public key to verify the identity of the author. The problem comes in verifying the author's public key. More often than not, the author and the recipient never meet face-to-face. They need a mechanism that assures them of a person's public key, and thus his or her identity.

Certificates create this assurance by encapsulating the identity of the person or entity to whom the certificate belongs, along with his or her public key, within a document encrypted by the private key of a certification authority. The certification authority states that it has verified the sender's identity and public key contained in the message. Most people trust the certification authority and accept its assurance that the person and public key are matched.

Certificates often include the public/private key pair so that you don't have to generate a key and then have the key authenticated by the certification authority. Because of this, getting your own digital certificate might be a good idea if you routinely send confidential information.

File Encryption

Now that I've covered the basics of what encryption is, what it can do, and how it works, it's time to put it to work. Windows 2000 and Windows XP support file-level encryption, which is integrated into the Windows security system. File-level encryption enables users of Windows 2000 and Windows XP to encrypt files individually. This way, sensitive information can be protected without affecting the speed of operations for non-sensitive files.

For instance, you might decide to encrypt the customer database on your notebook, but you wouldn't generally want to encrypt your program files. You would incur decryption overhead when you access the customer database, but not when you open or run a program.

If you encrypt your sensitive files and your Windows 2000 computer is stolen, the thief will be unable to access your files unless he can crack your password or the administrative password. The typical tactic of reinstalling Windows 2000 in a new directory and using the new administrator account to open the files will not be successful.

Tip Turn on file-level encryption on your Windows 2000-based notebook so that even if it is stolen, the thief will be unable to access your information.

In addition to the Windows 2000 integrated file-level encryption, there is a host of utilities that offer file encryption. These utilities are available for both Windows 95/98/ Me/2000 and Windows CE. They generally must be run separately from your application to encrypt or decrypt data.

If you keep particularly sensitive data on your PDA, you should consider using a file-level encryption utility to add another layer of security to your system.

Digital Wallets

For most people, some of the most sensitive information they carry is the information in their wallets. The information kept there—such as passwords, Social Security number, and credit card numbers—could cause some serious damage if the wrong person got them.

A digital wallet is an application that securely holds this information. It has its own passwords that a would-be thief would have to crack before gaining access to this sensitive information.

Several digital wallet applications for your PDA provide you with easy access to this information so that you can use it with Web sites or phone calls. This saves you the trouble of pulling your actual wallet out to search for information. Most of these applications offer built-in encryption to prevent your data from being stolen.

Communications Encryption

For communications encryption, the techniques of encryption don't change, but the way it is implemented does. Although Windows 2000 can protect your data with transparent file-level encryption, it doesn't offer a transparent communications-level encryption. There are, however, several different mechanisms you can use to encrypt your data over a communications channel. A communications channel is any kind of real-time communications system that carries data. This includes any connection to the Internet or between any two modems. The two most popular ways to encrypt data are virtual private networks and Secure Socket Layer.

Virtual Private Network

Using a public network to transfer data has always been cheaper than using a private network; however, the challenge has always been preventing your data from being copied in transit. A virtual private network (VPN) uses encryption to protect the data being transferred from being viewed by a third party during transmission. The encrypted data stream is private because no one else can read the data.

There are two types of virtual private networks with which you should be familiar. The first is the Point-to-Point Tunneling Protocol (PPTP) used by Windows NT, Windows 2000, Windows XP, and some other VPN products. This VPN method is easy to set up and maintain. A PPTP VPN client is built into Pocket PC 2002 devices, so you can use this type whenever you need to protect your communications to a Windows-based network. Because PPTP doesn't require certificates or special software to get started, you or your IT staff can set it up quickly and easily.

The other form of VPN in common use utilizes both the Internet Protocol Security (IPSec) and Layer 2 Transport Protocol (L2TP) protocols. Most of the time people refer to this type of VPN only as IPSec because L2TP can be used with multiple protocols, and it's the IPSec piece that actually provides encryption. IPSec-based VPNs are supported natively by Windows 2000, but there is not a native client in Windows CE. You can, however, purchase an IPSec VPN client from Certicom. For more information on Certicom, go to *http://www.moviansecurity.com*.

In addition to the absence of a native Windows CE client, there's the requirement that IPSec-based VPNs have certificates installed on the VPN server. This authenticates the server so that your data can't be hijacked, but it also makes the system more costly and difficult to set up. For now you'll probably find that most of your VPN access to the corporate network is with PPTP, not IPSec.

Secure Socket Layer

Secure Socket Layer (SSL) encryption is a mechanism put forth as an Internet standard by Netscape. SSL encrypts a hypertext transfer protocol (HTTP) channel so that its contents cannot be seen in transit. This means that the Web pages you view are secure.

SSL works only for Web pages, but if you're using a Web application, SSL is a very effective way to secure your data. Because SSL is transparent, it's as easy to use as a regular Web site. The only change in the URL is typing in *https://* instead of *http://*. The setup on the server is relatively simple as well. You install a certificate on the Web server and then enable the Web site to use the certificate.

SSL can be used with either 40-bit or 128-bit key lengths and when 128-bit encryption is used, it is considered secure for commercial applications, including those that transmit medical records.

Note By default, Pocket PC 2002 doesn't have 128-bit security installed. You can add it with the Microsoft High Encryption Security Pack, which is available at *http://www.microsoft.com /mobile/pocketpc/downloads/ssl128.asp*.

Theft and Loss

Although not technically a security issue, theft of the device itself is an issue that you will have to take into consideration when choosing your mobile equipment, and one that will be intertwined with your overall security policy. When you're considering the possibility of the theft of your devices, there are two key points: prevention and recovery. I'll start with prevention, because that's where your primary focus should be.

Prevention

There is no real way to prevent someone from stealing your mobile equipment. If someone has you targeted and they want your equipment, they will eventually get it. However, in general, thieves aren't out to steal from just anyone. Typically, thieves look for easy targets. They want something they can take with low risk of confrontation and low risk of getting caught.

All you really have to do is to deter thieves from stealing your equipment. You want to make it more difficult for them to steal your equipment than it would be to steal someone else's. This is a cold reality, but it *is* reality.

Consider your home: One of the most basic and highly recommended security precautions is a lot of light around it. Does this prevent burglars from targeting your home? No, but it does discourage them. Thieves in general don't want a lot of light around a home they are attempting to burglarize.

Techniques

Deterrence is something that generally is very simple to do. Here are a few suggestions:

- Be observant. Good thieves blend into the crowd—otherwise they wouldn't be good thieves. You should be on the lookout for people who seem to be too interested in the details of what you or others are carrying.

- When traveling, keep your bags near you at all times. The more distance there is between you and your bags, the higher the chances are that you won't notice if someone takes them.

- When setting bags at your feet, put the shoulder straps of your bags around your foot. That will make it difficult for thieves to steal the bags without your knowledge.

- At the airport, don't place your bags on the X-ray scanner until just before you walk through the metal detector. Keep an eye on your bags while you are walking through the metal detector. Make sure your bags don't leave before you do.

- Put your PDA in your front pocket if it will fit. It's very difficult to pick someone's front pocket. By sliding your PDA into your front pocket, you'll make it hard to forget and harder to steal.

These techniques won't prevent every theft, but keeping a keen eye and managing the location of your luggage will definitely help to deter a thief.

Products

A few reasonably priced products can make it easier to protect your equipment from theft. Here are a few suggestions:

- Buy and use luggage locks. These won't prevent thieves from getting into your bags if they are stolen, but they will prevent thieves from opening the bag and taking something from it while you're looking away. I use combination locks so that I don't have to look for keys if I need to open my luggage while traveling.

- Buy a cable lock system that will keep your luggage or notebook in place when you are not looking. Systems come in either keyed or combination varieties, and some, such as the Targus DEFCON 1 system, are available with motion sensors and alarms that are activated if the unit is moved.

- Buy a non-traditional computer bag. The less your luggage looks as though it contains expensive electronics, the less likely would-be thieves will target it.

As with any loss prevention techniques, buying products such as these and using them can't prevent all theft, but it will make it more difficult.

Recovery

Whether your mobile devices have been stolen or just misplaced, recovering the device might seem hopeless. However, there are solutions.

Communicating

The first thing to do when you discover that you've lost a mobile device is to communicate. Call the places where you might have left the device, or the lost and found departments of locations where you last remember having it.

If you lost the device in an airport and you're still on the plane, talk to the flight attendants and see if they can help you by contacting the ground crew and security at the airport you left. If none of these people are able to help, you'll probably want to pick up the air phone and call the airline's customer service number for the airport's security personnel. Air phone rates are outrageous, but your mobile device wasn't cheap either, and the information on it might be very hard to replace.

You might be tempted to continue with your journey, go to your meeting, and come back to look later. However, your odds of recovering your device get lower as time passes. Consider calling ahead to your appointment and letting them know you'll be a few minutes late.

Taking Precautions

Look into using a return service. Returnme.com and StuffBak.com both offer services that help you get your mobile devices back. The system works by putting unique identifier tags on your equipment and registering your contact information on the service's Web site. The identifier tags include the return service name, the unique identifier, a Web site address, and a toll free phone number to contact the return service.

When you lose a device, the person who finds it can call a number to report that they've found the device. The service then makes all the arrangements to get the device picked up and returned to you. Both services allow you to offer a reward for the return of the devices.

Although the pricing for the services varies somewhat, both are very inexpensive. The largest costs are the startup fees to install labels on all your devices and the shipping costs when the device is found. However, this is generally a quick, easy, and inexpensive way to get your devices back when you misplace them.

Both of these systems rely on people being fundamentally honest—either that or they rely on the expectation that people would choose feeling good about themselves for returning something and getting a reward over keeping it and feeling bad.

The results from these systems have been surprisingly positive. They can't guarantee that you'll get your device back, but they do offer a better chance of recovery than if you weren't using the service. If someone finds your device and contacts the service, you might have your device back in as little as a day. For most people, that's a pretty good deal.

Using LoJack for Mobile Devices

You might have heard of a system called LoJack that helps the police locate stolen cars. LoJack uses transmitters hidden inside the car to lead the police to the car and, presumably, the thieves.

This idea has been applied to computers. CompuTrace (*http://www.computrace.com*) works with a piece of software that periodically sends a report of its location to Compu-Trace, either from the Internet or a phone line. The software is virtually undetectable. The company claims that there is no way to remove the agent from the hard disk without the appropriate password, but in reality, nothing is impervious to attack. However, removing the agent is well above the technical expertise of the average thief.

CompuTrace is a bit expensive—$49.95 for one year of monitoring—but it's cheap compared to the loss of your notebook. The software also works only for computers running Windows 95/98/Me/NT/2000. It won't work with your Windows CE powered PDA.

Implementing Security

So far this book has addressed options and products to improve your understanding of the mobile market. In this section, however, I will walk you through some important steps to ensure the security of your information and your devices.

Setting a Device Password

The information on your device is sensitive. The first thing to do is to set a device password so that if your device is lost or stolen, the person who gets it won't be able to access your information. Without the device password, no one can access your data. Also, with a password set, when the device is rebooted, the password will be required for access; there is no way to get past this password.

One of the other advantages of the device password is that it is difficult to crack. This is largely because each time someone types an incorrect password, the device waits for a short time before allowing the user to attempt it again. Each time you type an incorrect password, the device doubles the amount of wait time before the next attempt can be made. After five or ten incorrect password attempts, the delay between attempts becomes exceedingly long.

The process of setting a password for your device is painless. Follow these steps:

1. Open the Start menu, and select Settings. Tap the password applet.

2. If you've previously set a password, you'll be prompted to enter it now. The Pocket PC prohibits anyone else from changing your password.

3. The Password Settings screen, shown in Figure 3-1 on the next page, enables you to set your own password. Choose whether you'll use a simple, numeric password or an alphanumeric password by selecting the appropriate option button in the upper left corner of the screen.

Figure 3-1   *Password settings: plain and simple.*

Tip Unless you have particularly sensitive data on your device, you might want to use a numeric password, since they are easier to enter. Entering an alphanumeric password can take significantly more time. This is important if you want to be able to quickly use your device when you turn it on.

---

4. If you chose a simple password, enter the password you want to use for your device by pressing the keypad. If you chose an alphanumeric password, enter the password in both the password and the confirm text boxes.

5. Set the amount of inactive time that should elapse before you are required to reenter the password. This helps to reduce the number of times you must enter the password while using the device. If you select a time that is too short, you'll have to reenter the password over and over again.

6. Click the OK button.

The trick with setting up your password is finding settings you can live with. Entering a complex password every time you want to use your device will soon get annoying. Conversely, you don't want the settings so loose that anyone will be able to pick up your device and use it.

Establishing File Encryption in Windows 2000

Establishing file encryption in Windows 2000 or Windows XP is a trivially simple process. Turning file encryption on is as simple as a few mouse clicks. Here's what you need to do:

1. Locate the file you want to encrypt.

2. Right-click the file, and then on the shortcut menu, click Properties.

3. In the file's Properties dialog box (Figure 3-2), click the Advanced button.

Figure 3-2 *The file's Properties dialog box displays only the basic file attributes, not the encryption settings.*

4. In the Advanced Attributes dialog box (Figure 3-3, on the next page), select the Encrypt Contents To Secure Data check box.

Figure 3-3   *You can establish encryption for the file from the Advanced Attributes dialog box.*

5. Click OK to close the Advanced Attributes dialog box.

6. Click OK to close the file's Properties dialog box.

Summary

This chapter explained all the details of security and what authentication, authorization, and encryption mean. Authentication identifies the user and is a necessary component for effective auditing. Authorization indicates what a user can access. Finally, encryption protects data from people who snoop.

The possibility of someone else gaining access to your information is very real. The proper understanding and respect for security issues can help to ensure that you don't become a victim.

Here are some questions to help you evaluate which security options are appropriate for you and where you might need to improve your security:

• Does anyone know any of your passwords? Ideally, you should be the only person who knows your passwords.

• How valuable would the information on your laptop or PDA be to someone else? Could they get your address? Your credit card numbers? Passwords?

• How valuable would the information on your laptop or PDA be to your competitors? Do you have your entire customer list on the laptop?

• How difficult would it be to reproduce the information you have put on your laptop or PDA since the last time you backed the device up? (You do back it up, don't you?)

• Do you need access to the corporate network while you're away, or can you work with only Web access?

• What are you willing to do to prevent your information from getting into the wrong hands?

Customizations You Can't Live Without: Accessories

OK, I admit it: I'm a gadget freak. I love all kinds of things, whether they have a purpose or not. I'm so bad about it that I've often considered starting a Gadget Users Anonymous (GUA) 12-step program. If gadgets have a decidedly cool look to them, I'm hooked. It's true that I bought my Compaq iPAQ because of the business it helps me get done, but its sexy look didn't hurt the sale. One of the challenges I face—and I think we all face—is which gadgets to get. Which ones will provide real help when you're on the road?

This chapter will explain gadgets of both the software and hardware variety. I'll tell you what's good about them, what's bad about them, and when you might want them. The list—by no means exhaustive—is designed to help you find mobile accessories that will make staying productive while you are traveling easier.

Near the end of this chapter, I provide you with a few recommendations of Web sites and magazines so that you can do your own research into the latest and greatest gadgets.

Software

Software can't be called a gadget in its own right; however, it can certainly make your mobile devices more useful and more fun. I think of software as a gadget because most software serves a specific purpose. It enables your Pocket PC or notebook computer to do what it couldn't do before.

Pocket PC Software

Software on a Pocket PC is different than on your notebook. Notebook hard disks often have in excess of 8 gigabytes (GB) of storage capacity; a typical Pocket PC has a total of 64 megabytes (MB) of RAM for storage and running applications. (Each gigabyte is 1,024 megabytes.) This difference will lead you to be choosier about what you load on to your Pocket PC.

Tip You can always install all the software you want on your Pocket PC and then use the Remove Application applet to remove the program from Pocket PC memory. The beauty of this is that you can go into Active Sync on the PC, and on the Tools menu, tap Add/Remove Programs to reinstall the application on your device without having to go through a complete reinstall process. In essence, your PC can help you manage your Pocket PC's memory.

Monitoring Software

A Pocket PC has two critical resources that you must manage: power and memory. You can check your power by going to the Start menu, pointing to Settings, and then tapping System and then tapping the Power icon; you can check your memory by going to the Start menu, pointing to Settings, and tapping System and then tapping the Memory icon. Unfortunately, both of these settings are in rather out-of-the-way locations. PowerLevel by Scary-Bear Software (*http://www.scarybearsoftware.com*) displays your memory and power status on your Today screen. Figure 4-1 shows what the power level looks like on a Compaq iPAQ 3670 with an attached PC Card expansion sleeve. PowerLevel shows the status of both the main battery and the expansion pack battery, as well as the status of both program and storage memory.

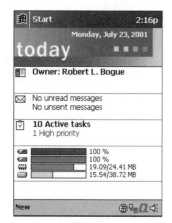

Figure 4-1   *Power and memory status displayed on a Pocket PC with PowerLevel installed.*

Infrared Communications

As you read in Chapter 2, most PDAs, notebooks, and even some desktop computers have infrared ports for communication. Microsoft Windows CE comes with an array of utilities to facilitate the transfer of information to other Windows CE devices and personal computers, but it doesn't come with utilities to communicate using infrared.

The Conduits Technologies Peacemaker Web site (*http://www.conduits.com/products/peacemaker*) is one of several utilities that enable your Windows CE device to communicate with Palm Pilots. This utility is particularly handy if most of your colleagues use Palm devices.

A few utilities claim to enable your Pocket PC to become a remote control for your audio/video components as well. Most of them have severe limitations and don't work on the latest Pocket PC devices, though, so you won't really be able to turn your Pocket PC into a remote control—yet.

Games

Whether or not you regularly play computer video games, adding a few games to your Pocket PC can be a lot of fun. Games will help you to while away the hours when you're sitting in a distant airport waiting for your next flight.

If you're new to computer games, a good way to start is by augmenting the solitaire game that is installed on the Pocket PC by default with Microsoft's Entertainment Pocket-Pak. The Entertainment PocketPak includes classic card and board games including Blackjack, Chess, FreeCell, Hearts, Reversi, and Taipei. In addition, it includes the familiar Windows Minesweeper game, a word game called Cinco, a Battleship-like game called Sink the Ships, and a Missile Command-like game that has you defending your outpost from incoming lasers.

If you're really interested in solitaire card games, you should take a look at King Sol from Rapture Technologies (*http://www.rapturetech.com*). It features 60 different solitaire games. Rules are included for each one, and if you need a little help, the Auto Play will play some cards for you. Rapture Technologies also produced the Games PocketPak for Microsoft, so they know what they are doing when it comes to creating games for the Pocket PC.

If you're looking for something classic but a little more exciting than a board game, the Microsoft Arcade PocketPak (*http://www.microsoft.com/mobile/pocketpc/downloads/arcadepak.asp*) includes Pocket PC versions of Pac-Man, Ms. Pac-Man, and Dig-Dug. Maybe you remember playing these classic arcade games when you were younger. At least now you don't have to drop quarters in the machine. Personally, I never caught Pac-Man fever, but I'm absolutely addicted to Dig-Dug.

If, on the other hand, you're looking to take out your office frustrations, maybe Microsoft Games PocketPak is for you (*http://www.microsoft.com/mobile/pocketpc/downloads/gamespak.asp*). It contains five office-themed games, which are slightly reminiscent of the adventure games of yesteryear. There are games similar to Breakout, Frogger,

Lemmings, and Burger Time, if you remember any of those titles. If you're looking for a new twist on office and action adventures, you might want to try this wild PocketPak.

No matter what your game of choice is, from Asteroids to Yahtzee, you'll probably find a Pocket PC version of the game. If you can't get excited about the idea of playing games on your Pocket PC, you can still use your Pocket PC for diversions while you're waiting for a flight. In Chapter 12, "Reading Time: eBooks, News Clippings, and Agents," I'll cover eBooks and eBook readers that you can use to read the latest novel from your favorite author or an old classic.

Notebook Software

Most personal computer software does decidedly boring—but necessary—things. You can use Microsoft Word to write letters, articles, and books. With Microsoft Excel you can plot your debts over time. Microsoft Project creates schedules so you can see how far behind you are on things. However, there is some software on the market that is of particular interest to the mobile professional.

Windows Media Player

Windows Media Player is the Microsoft operating system's native music and video files player. Media Player is integrated into desktop Windows operating systems, but the latest versions have a lot to offer to the Pocket PC as well. Of particular interest to the Pocket PC owner is the ability of Media Player to shrink or *transcode* music files on your personal computer so that they will take up less memory on your Pocket PC.

The process is simple: Just set up the playlist you want, and then select the portable device. This brings up a window like the one shown in Figure 4-2. If you want to copy the whole list to your Pocket PC, click the Copy Music button. After Media Player has transcoded the file (if necessary), it will copy it to your device.

I'll go into more detail about how to use Windows Media Player and how to listen to music on your Pocket PC in Chapter 11, "Music and Dictation."

Figure 4-2   *Windows Media Player is a great way of moving music to your Pocket PC.*

Back Up Software

If your information technology (IT) department isn't responsible for backing up your notebook regularly, you'll probably want to take on this responsibility yourself. Notebooks need backups even more than desktop computers for two reasons: First they are subjected to more stresses—hot-to-cold cycles, jarring, and the like—that increase the likelihood of a hardware or hard disk failure. The second reason is that notebooks are much more likely to get stolen or lost than desktop computers.

You can back up your notebook to another hard disk (preferably one you don't take with you), to a tape backup device, or to rewritable CD-ROMs. Backing up to another hard disk will be the quickest and often the least expensive, then you're likely to have only one or a few different backups of your data. If you should happen to have a hardware failure during the backup and have only one hard disk to which you do backups, you'll probably have destroyed your previous backup—making things just as bad as if you had never backed up your data at all.

Tape backup devices can be expensive, particularly those with capacities that match or exceed the size of current hard disks. In addition, they are much slower than a typical hard disk. You'll want to do a tape backup over the course of an evening so that you can leave your notebook to run the backup on its own.

Rewritable CDs seem to be a good option, because you can create multiple backups through the use of additional rewritable CDs. However, CD writers are often slower than equivalent hard disks, and each rewritable CD will hold less than 700 MB. This isn't a problem for small hard disks, but backing up 20 GB of data onto CDs could take more than 20 discs—not something you're likely to want to supervise.

No matter how you decide you want to back up your notebook, you'll need backup software. Veritas Software makes its BackupExec products for every desktop version of Windows. It will back up onto another hard disk, a tape, or a rewritable CD. You can find out more about BackupExec at *http://www.veritas.com*.

Hardware and Accessories

A true gadget has to be something you can hold in your hand. Maybe it's not an exploding pen from the James Bond movies, but it is something that is useful nonetheless. Just as the right accessories can make an outfit work, the right mobile accessories can make your trips less frustrating.

Input

If you've tried using your Pocket PC to enter a lot of data, you've probably found that the lack of a keyboard makes the process difficult. The built-in "soft" keyboard, handwriting recognition, and transcriber are ways you can enter information, but they're not exactly efficient.

Keyboards

One thing a Pocket PC clearly lacks is a keyboard. Its absence was intentional and has helped to make the device lightweight and functional; however, it can be frustrating when you're trying to enter data.

Fortunately, there are two keyboards you can purchase for your Pocket PC that will enable you to enter data as if you were using a notebook. One of those options is the Key-Sync keyboard from iBIZ (*http://www.ibizcorp.com*). This keyboard is smaller than even a standard notebook keyboard, but it's still workable. Its primary advantages are that it's one piece—you can use it on surfaces that aren't entirely flat, such as your lap—and because of its design, it can be used with a wide variety of devices, including several Pocket PC hardware platforms and other PDA-type devices as well. Figure 4-3 shows a KeySync keyboard connected to a Compaq iPAQ Serial Cradle.

The one downside to the KeySync keyboard is that you must have a serial connection to your device. Because a lot of devices use USB connections instead of serial connections, you'll probably have to buy a serial cable or cradle to use the KeySync keyboard.

Figure 4-3   *The KeySync keyboard can be used in tight spaces.*

Targus (*http://www.targus.com*) offers a Stowaway keyboard that unfolds into a full size keyboard. This might sound odd, but typing on it is comfortable—the keyboard is the same size as a full-size desktop keyboard. When folded up, it is only 3.6 inches by 5.1 inches and 0.8 inches thick. It easily tucks away into your baggage, so you can carry it with you.

The advantage of the Stowaway keyboard is that it has its own built-in PDA holder and doesn't require a separate serial cable. The disadvantage, however, is that the keyboard is only available for certain PDA models. The keyboard has a reputation of being hard to work with because it tends to fold back up when it is used on a surface that's not completely flat. Still, it's a great solution if you want to sit down and type something into your PDA.

Screen Protectors

One of the disadvantages of a touch-sensitive device is that because the surface of the screen is constantly being touched, it's more likely you will scratch the glass. Scratches can make it difficult to see what is on the screen. The solution to this is a screen protector—a thin sheet of clear plastic that keeps your stylus from touching the surface of the screen.

Fellowes (*http://www.fellowes.com*) makes a product called WriteRIGHT—a small plastic sheet that adheres to your PDA screen using static electricity. You can take it off without fear that it will leave a sticky adhesive on the surface of the unit. The process of installing this plastic protector sheet is simple, and instructions are included. When you've marred the surface of the plastic protector sheet, you simply remove it and replace it with another.

WriteRIGHT is a must-have accessory. I occasionally hear complaints about how it makes the appearance of the screen a little weird, but the first time you put a scratch on your PDA screen or accidentally write on it with a pen rather than a stylus, you'll appreciate the protection.

Stylus Replacements

Every PDA comes with its own stylus. Sometimes the vendor will even include an extra stylus, so you can afford to lose one. Ultimately, however, you'll probably find that you want a single pen you can use on your PDA as well as on a sheet of paper.

Today there are several companies offering multi-point pens. These multi-point pens have a stylus point, one or more pens of varying colors, and in some cases a highlighter. I use the multi-point pen (shown in Figure 4-4) that I received as a gift when I joined Club Pocket PC (*http://www.microsoft.com/mobile/pocketpc/club*). It has four points: stylus, black pen, red pen, and pencil.

Figure 4-4   *Multi-point stylus pens aren't much bigger than traditional pens and are much more versatile.*

Selecting a multi-point stylus is largely a matter of personal choice, so you'll have to go shopping for yourself. At least one site on the Internet, Stylus Central (*http://www.styluscentral.com*), offers a wide selection of stylus replacements and multi-point stylus pens for a variety of PDAs.

Bar Code Readers

Even after you've chosen a keyboard and a stylus, entering data manually is never fun. It's much easier to let devices do the data entry for you. Bar codes and bar code readers were developed to enable faster and more accurate collection of information. If you're planning on doing a lot of data collection with your PDA, you should look into simplifying the task by using bar codes.

Both Symbol (*http://www.symbol.com*) and Socket Communications (*http://www.socketcom.com*) offer bar code readers for PDAs. Symbol is the longtime leader in bar code scanning equipment. You've probably seen their bar code scanners at grocery or department stores. Socket Communications is a big developer of PC Cards and CompactFlash cards.

Bar code readers come in three varieties: wand, laser, and integrated units. The wand systems use a small wand that you swipe across the bar code. These will work in a pinch, but take longer to recognize a bar code than either of the other methods. The laser systems shoot a laser across a few inches or a few feet to read the barcode. This is probably the kind of bar code scanner that you are used to. The integrated systems are essentially laser units that are physically attached to the PDA or are integrated into the PDA itself. Integrated systems offer the most convenient access, because you don't have to juggle your PDA and the scanning device.

Symbol offers completely integrated units that include your PDA and the bar code scanner. These are a great choice if you need to do a lot of bar code scanning. Because the scanning unit is integrated into the PDA, you don't have to worry about it accidentally breaking off or getting disconnected. In addition, Symbol units are more rugged than the consumer devices from other manufacturers like Compaq and HP.

Digital Cameras

When most people think about input devices, they wouldn't automatically include digital cameras. However, digital cameras are the input mechanism for images (that is, unless you can draw really well and really fast with your stylus). Digital photography has radically changed how many businesses work. For example, in the insurance industry, photos of damage can now accompany an electronic claim form. Companies that sell products through retailers can take pictures of how the products are displayed so that they can see how things look in stores in different parts of the country.

The proliferation of digital cameras and printers capable of producing good quality printouts of digital images has led to an explosion in the way digital photography is used. Even if you can't currently think of a way your business can use digital photos, it might not be too long before they become an integral part of your day-to-day business.

There are two ways you can incorporate digital imaging into your other mobile devices. One way is to buy an add-in CompactFlash card that plugs into your Pocket PC and then record images directly into the memory of your Pocket PC. This is an agreeable method, because it reduces the number of devices you must carry. However, the picture quality is lower than you can get from a dedicated device—typically only 0.3 megapixels (640 by 480). Right now, only the Casio Cassiopeia, HP Jornada, Compaq iPAQ, and U R There @MIGO support plug-in digital cameras.

The other approach is to select a digital camera that can easily upload pictures to your Pocket PC or notebook. Digital cameras come in all shapes and sizes and with image resolutions in the several-million-pixel range. This means a picture taken with a digital camera can produce a lifelike picture that can be printed out as large as 12 inches by 18 inches. This should certainly meet most people's photographic needs.

In addition to supporting different resolutions, digital cameras also differ in the type of memory they use for storing photos until they are downloaded. The Sony Mavica series of cameras were popular because they stored images on a standard 3.5-inch floppy disk. Other cameras available today use rewritable CDs to store the photos. However, most cameras store images on memory cards rather than on floppy disks or CDs. This memory is commonly packaged for cameras in one of two ways: The first way is on a CompactFlash card, and the second is on Smart Media. The differences between these two memory packages are relatively small—but critical.

CompactFlash-packaged memory can be directly inserted into any PDA that has a CompactFlash slot. When used with an inexpensive PC Card adapter, a CompactFlash memory card can be put into any notebook computer. The CompactFlash card looks like a removable hard disk. From the CompactFlash "hard disk," you can copy the photos onto the hard disk on the notebook. You can access and view your photos on your Pocket PC through a special Storage Card folder, or send them through the Inbox application.

Smart Media, on the other hand, requires a special piece of equipment and its own software to be read from a notebook computer. You can still use the connectivity software bundled with the camera to download the pictures, but you won't be able to simply insert the card into your Pocket PC or notebook without an adapter.

Mobile professionals who want to move all kinds of information will find that cameras designed to use CompactFlash memory cards are useful. These cameras also use memory cards quite efficiently. Later in the chapter, I'll explain the other uses for CompactFlash cards.

Storage

Providing a safe home for your mobile devices while you are traveling is essential to their long-term survival. The ability of devices to withstand the rigors of mobility is often touted—and sometimes tested—by magazines. These accessories store and protect your equipment.

Notebook Cases

A notebook case is a common accessory for almost everyone who uses a notebook. Most notebooks today come with at least a basic case to help protect them from the hazards they are subjected to on the road.

In Chapter 3, I advocated getting a less conspicuous notebook bag to help reduce your risk of having your notebook stolen. This is certainly one good reason to consider replacing the original notebook bag, but there are two other important considerations.

Notebooks seem to be the most common devices that mobile professionals leave at home. Notebooks don't weigh that much by themselves, but the weight of the bag adds considerably to the burden. It feels like it weighs more than 20 pounds. When you shop for a notebook bag, look for one that fits inside your larger luggage. It won't lighten the load, but at least it will make it more manageable.

The second consideration when selecting a new notebook case is convenience. Most mobile professionals eventually find themselves trying to work while they are en route to their destination. They find themselves digging through their bags for information while walking between concourses at the airport or reaching into the back seat to grab a copy of the map that they received from the rental car company. (Hopefully they do this while stopped safely at a red light.) The accessibility of the pockets is an important consideration.

My favorite notebook bag is one that Targus sold approximately seven years ago. The reason I like it so much is that it is set up so the notebook is loaded from the top—it's essentially dropped into place. This makes retrieving and storing the notebook quick and easy. The bag isn't the lightest one I've ever used, and in some ways it's not the most convenient. However, it doesn't look like a notebook bag, and it is reasonably convenient.

Pocket PC Cases

When you start getting accessories for your Pocket PC, it will become harder and harder to keep all of them together. Cases can help keep everything in one place and protected. Cases for Pocket PCs come in two basic varieties.

The first variety of Pocket PC cases has a fold-over lid or cover. Often, these have a tuck-in flap or use small magnets to seal the case. These cases provide some storage for business cards or a CompactFlash card or two. They won't, however, hold much else.

Note If you're interested in this type of case, check out Vaja cases at *http://www.vaja.com*. They make some simply excellent cases.

The second type of case is more like the Franklin Day Planners of years gone by. They have a small pad of paper and some storage room. Frequently, these cases zip shut rather than employing the simpler closing mechanism used by the smaller units. One of the biggest advantages to the larger cases is that they include a pad of paper and have a spot for a multi-point stylus.

Note To quote *Monty Python's Flying Circus*, "And now for something completely different." An organization called e-Holster (*http://www.eholster.com*) is offering a holster system for your PDA and cellular phone that looks like a weapon shoulder holster system.

Of course, the type of Pocket PC case you get will be dictated by your own personal preferences. However, I suggest you try the minimalist approach first—choose a small, compact case that fits most of your needs. The larger the case is, the less likely most people will be to carry it. If you're interested in doing some research, there's a list of PDA accessories including cases at *http://www.wincecity.com/accessories.html*.

Note A holster system was recently released for the Compaq iPAQ. It uses a similar holster mechanism to the mechanism used by cellular phones and pagers. You can find out more about it at *http://www.iproductsonline.net*.

Car-Mounted Hardware

If you're using your PDA in the car, you might have noticed that setting it on the seat next to you isn't convenient because PDAs have a tendency to slide around while you're driving. I've had mine slip off both the front and the side of the passenger seat, requiring a sort of fishing expedition while sitting at the next red light.

Using a PDA holder keeps your PDA from wandering around the car on its own and helps you to access the PDA when you come to a stop, rather than spending that time trying to locate it. Some holders are set up with quick-release mechanisms that provide easy access to the device: You can pull the unit out of the holder, use it, and return it to the holder before the light changes.

Car-mounted hardware for your PDA comes in four basic varieties: those that attach to the windshield; those that attach to the air vent; those that fit in a cup holder; and those that are permanently affixed.

The type of holder you select will be based largely on your preferences regarding how high you want to mount the unit in your car and whether you want to take your holder with you while you are traveling. If you want to take your holder with you while traveling, you'll probably find that air vent holders are the most portable, because they are generally the smallest and lightest.

If you're interested in car-mounted hardware, you might want to check out Arkon Resources at *http://www.arkon.com*. They have a wide variety of options to choose from.

Memory

When you travel, you must choose what to bring with you. Whether you're traveling down the hall or across the country, you've got to decide how much you are willing to carry and what you can live without. In electronic terms, this means deciding which files you can take with you on your notebook or PDA. The following devices help you take more information with you.

CompactFlash Memory Cards

CompactFlash memory cards provide extra storage space after you've filled the built-in memory on your Pocket PC. CompactFlash cards come in varying sizes from 4 MB up to 640 MB.

You might think that your PDA has plenty of memory—most Pocket PC–based PDAs have 64 MB of RAM. That seems like tons of RAM—until you start installing applications and adding data to the PDA. You'll find that when you start trying to listen to MP3 or Windows Media Audio (WMA) music files, add a few eBooks, download a map or two for Microsoft Pocket Streets, and begin to fully use the functionality of your PDA, you never have enough room.

Note Even on my 64 MB–equipped Compaq iPAQ 3670 I've had to move things off the device and onto a storage card. Music and eBooks were the first files that I removed. Even after removing almost all the data on my iPAQ, I've still got less than 25 MB of free memory—just from all of the installed applications. It adds up quickly.

CompactFlash cards can easily store your maps, music, and eBooks, so you don't have to use the precious memory on the PDA itself. With enough memory cards, you can have a virtually limitless supply of music, books, and other files to keep you entertained. CompactFlash memory cards are available from a wide variety of vendors.

Micro Drives

A few years ago, IBM announced they were developing a hard disk that would fit within the space of a CompactFlash slot. These disks, dubbed *micro drives*, offer higher capacities than any CompactFlash memory card. Initially, IBM offered these in capacities of 170 and 340 MB. More recently, IBM has offered micro drives with capacities up to 1 GB.

The biggest problem with micro drives is that they consume a lot of power. They can substantially reduce battery life in a Pocket PC—so much so, in fact, that some users recommend copying files from the card onto the Pocket PC's main memory and then unplugging the drive until it's needed.

If you have serious storage needs for your Pocket PC and you can't use your notebook to manage the information on the Pocket PC, look into micro drives. You can find more information on the IBM Web site at *http://www.storage.ibm.com/hdd/micro*.

CD Burners

If you're running out of room on your notebook, a CD-ROM burner is the answer. You can store files that you don't need to modify frequently on a CD and free up valuable hard disk space for something else. You probably don't need to travel with a CD burner, but it's helpful to have access to one when you're in the office.

There is still a limit to what can be stored on notebook hard disks. If you store enough data, eventually you'll fill up any hard disk. That's why the CD burner is a great solution. In today's "20 GB hard disk in a notebook" world, a 650 or 700 MB CD might not seem like much of a savings, but it starts to add up as you burn more and more CDs.

CD burners for desktop computers have dropped to only a couple of hundred dollars; external units that will work with a notebook will set you back a few hundred dollars. Often, software is included with the unit to make the process of creating CDs relatively painless.

Power and Protection

No matter how cool or useful a digital tool is, it won't work without power. People are accustomed to having notebooks start when they press the power button and hearing the friendly chirp of a PDA to remind them that it's time for a meeting. What people sometimes forget, however, is that it takes power to make this happen, and when you're traveling, it's not always possible to find power when you need it.

The products in this section either help you power your digital device or help protect it from too much power.

Air and Auto Adapters

Your notebook computer will come with a power adapter to convert the AC power found in your home into something usable by the notebook. Pocket PCs require the same power conversion. However, the kind of power available to you on a transcontinental flight is neither the AC power in your home nor the kind of power your notebook is able to use.

If you spend a lot of time on long flights, you might consider purchasing an air adapter for your notebook. These adapters work with the power systems in specially equipped planes and enable you to work and charge your notebook batteries while on the flight. Not every plane is equipped to support air adapters, but more planes are becoming so equipped, particularly those frequently used for long flights.

An extra benefit of air adapters is that most of them double as car adapters, so you can plug your notebook into the cigarette lighter while you're on the road. Please don't try to use your notebook while actually driving, though.

DC to AC Inverters

If you have many devices or change your devices every few years, the cost of all of the extra adapters that you have to buy is enough to make you wonder if there's a better way. One solution to the problem of having to buy a new auto adapter is to use a DC to AC inverter. These devices convert the power found in your car into something very close to what you would expect from a wall outlet at your home.

An inverter can be used with the power adapter that came with the device to charge it, or to enable its use while traveling. However, DC to AC inverters tend to weigh more than simple auto or air adapters, so you'll be carrying a little more weight when you're traveling, unless you travel in your car and can leave it there.

Electric Fuel

Electric Fuel has a pretty high cool factor. Electric Fuel is a disposable zinc air-powered battery that can recharge one of your mobile devices. Whether it's your phone or your PDA that needs a charge, you can plug an adapter into your device, remove the fuel cell from its vacuum wrapper, and plug the fuel cell into the other end of the adapter.

These zinc-air batteries power the attached device and charge its onboard battery. Although results vary by device, the Electric Fuel Web site *(http://www.electric-fuel.com)* says that an individual fuel cell can recharge a typical device three times. Between uses, it should be stored in its resealable vacuum bag. This will prevent the battery from discharging. When you've used it up, simply throw it away.

This device is a lightweight, small, and simple insurance policy against running out of power. By taking different adapter cords and only one cell while traveling, you can protect your PDA and cell phone from running out of power. If you happen to leave your Electric Fuel at home, you can stop by a computer store and pick one up. Although most computer stores don't stock adapters and batteries for every type of phone, many of them have started to stock Electric Fuel. Enough stores carry Electric Fuel that you might be able to get yourself out of a jam.

Extra Batteries

Electric Fuel is a great alternative to being without power, but a disposable battery isn't really designed for situations in which you'll frequently need to have additional power. It's designed specifically to be the exception, not the rule. When you routinely need to have more power than a single battery can provide, you need to look for additional batteries.

Batteries for notebooks can add a fairly substantial amount of weight. Adding another few pounds to a notebook that weighs only 7 pounds can make a big difference. The unfortunate reality is that the battery represents a significant amount of the total weight of a notebook. Having another battery for your notebook is often a necessary evil. If you do get another battery for your notebook and you're sure you won't need it for a particular trip, consider leaving it at home and give your back a rest.

Extra batteries for PDAs are another thing altogether. Some PDAs, such as the Cassiopeia and Jornada, have replaceable rechargeable batteries, but other PDAs, such as the Compaq iPAQ, don't have user-changeable batteries. This makes carrying a spare difficult. However, the Compaq iPAQ can use external expansion packs with batteries in them (such as the PC Card and Dual PC Card), which can provide some additional power to the base unit in a pinch. Officially, this isn't sufficient to run your iPAQ.

Note I dare you to try to get a straight answer about how the power in the main unit of an iPAQ and the power available in the expansion pack are related, or for that matter, how much power is really in the expansion pack. Compaq has conflicting information posted on their site about how the expansion pack battery will and won't share power with the main unit battery. It's probably best to assume that sliding an expansion pack onto your iPAQ will help it enough that it won't lose its memory, but probably not enough for it to run.

You might have to get creative with ways to power your Pocket PC if the main battery is drained. One solution is a battery pack designed for digital cameras. These power packs are not as convenient as expansion packs, but they can provide extended power when you need it. If you can find a battery pack that works with your digital camera too, that's even better.

Note You can now find battery packs that run on standard AA batteries. You can find out more about one for the Compaq iPAQ at *http://www.data-nation.com*.

Notebook Surge Suppressors

Surge suppressors are designed to protect your electronic equipment from electrical surges that travel down the power line, and in some cases, the phone line. A surge suppressor protects by shunting, or diverting, the energy before it reaches your electronic device.

Inexpensive notebook surge suppressors are available to protect your power supply from surges. Some of these units plug inline with the power supply where the power comes in from the wall; others plug into the wall, and the power supply is plugged into them. The ones that plug inline with the power supply are simple, because you disconnect the cord from the power supply to the wall, plug the cord into the surge suppressor, and plug the surge suppressor into the power supply. In either case, replacing a surge suppressor that has died because of an electrical surge is much quicker, cheaper, and easier than replacing a power supply that has died because of too many surges.

You should carry some sort of surge suppressor with you while traveling. Surge suppressors designed for notebook use are both lightweight and inexpensive.

Phone Line Testers

In Chapter 2, I mentioned that some phone systems at hotels and businesses are digital, and the additional power they use to drive the phone lines can damage your modem. If you're uncomfortable with asking whether a line is digital or not, or you're not willing to risk using a line, you can use one of several available line testers. They'll tell you whether the phone system is digital or not and whether it's safe to use your modem. Targus (*http://www.targus.com/prod_faq.asp?sku=* CMD5395) sells one for $29.99 that is slightly larger than a pen.

Digital Phone Line Enablers

If you want to be able to use almost any phone line, whether it's digital or not, you might want to look into a digital phone line enabler. These devices enable you to use even a digital phone line with your modem, with the expense of a little extra complexity.

These units cost around $150, but might be ideal for people who absolutely must make calls from businesses with digital phone systems or connect while on the road. Information can be found at *http://wwiv.targus.com/prod_faq.asp?sku=PA040U*.

Phone Cords

One of the most unfortunate things to forget while traveling (I know from experience) is the phone cord needed to connect a modem to a phone line. Phone cords are not particularly heavy or bulky, but because they always seem to get tangled up in the power cords, they can be a hassle.

To make phone cords less of a hassle, use one that is retractable. Retractable phone cords cost less than $20 and can spool a phone cord up into a small box about the size of a cassette tape. Targus also sells this helpful accessory. To find out more, go to *http://www.targus.com/prod_faq.asp?sku=PA200U*.

Miscellaneous

Some accessories refuse to fit neatly into a category. They're an important part of being mobile, but they're difficult to classify.

Global Positioning System Receivers

One of the biggest challenges that I face when traveling is figuring out quickly how to get from the airport to my meeting location. In some cases, my first challenge is to figure out how to get out of the airport. A Global Positioning System (GPS) receiver and its bundled software can help guide you to where you're going when you don't have a clue how to get there.

A GPS receiver sends a message to your notebook or Pocket PC that indicates exactly where you are at any given moment. Originally designed by the military for precision navigation, GPS receivers have started to become commercially available tools. Newer products support voice prompts, which tell you what direction you'll need to turn and how long before you need to make that turn. Although these directions occasionally turn out to be wrong, by and large they are a way to reduce your stress if you're running late for a meeting and don't know how to get where you're going. A GPS receiver can quickly become your favorite accessory, particularly if you frequently travel to unfamiliar cities.

I've devoted all of Chapter 10 to GPS, maps, and getting directions.

Headphones

A set of headphones is essential if you're planning to use your notebook or PDA to play music. With your Pocket PC's ability to play MP3 and WMA music files, there's virtually no reason not to listen to music while you travel. An inexpensive set of headphones that is small enough to be packed in your bags is something I consider essential.

FlyLight

Typing on a notebook keyboard in the dark isn't all it's cracked up to be. Most of the time when I have to do this, I'm forced to turn the notebook screen's lighting to its highest setting, burning through battery life, just to get enough light on the keyboard to see well enough to type. That's where the ingenious FlyLight comes in. The Kensington FlyLight (*http://www.kensington.com*) plugs into your USB port and provides a flexible light you can shine on the notebook keyboard or your work papers.

Of course, the FlyLight will consume some of your precious battery power too, but according to Kensington, the power drain will be negligible for most notebooks. It will certainly be less than turning the notebook screen's lighting to its highest brightness setting. At $20, the FlyLight is a steal.

Additional Resources

A funny thing about the computer industry is that there isn't a single most-respected Web resource for information. The resources listed here are broken into some broad categories to help make the list manageable.

Distribution Sites

A few PDA-specific sites on the Internet are large distribution points for software developers selling their wares:

- Handango.com (*http://www.handango.com*)   This large site offers hardware and software for a broad range of devices including Palm and Pocket PC. Handango is one of the larger software distribution sites, and it also offers some accessories. It's definitely worth a look.

- PocketGear.com (*http://www.pocketgear.com*)   This Pocket PC–focused software distribution site is rapidly gaining software titles and becoming the place to shop for Pocket PC software.

- MobilePlanet.com (*http://www.mobileplanet.com*)   This mail order and online shopping site offers a variety of PDA and notebook hardware and accessories.

Other companies that distribute software have some titles for Pocket PCs and might be your best bet for notebook software, but the three sites just listed can help you meet your Pocket PC needs.

Pocket PC Enthusiast Sites

One thing the Pocket PC has going for it is the strong support of a community that believes in the Windows CE and Pocket PC technology. The following sites are just a few of the many sites dedicated to the support of the Pocket PC platform:

- **PocketPCGallery.com** (*http://www.pocketpcgallery.com*)   This is a jumping-off point to many other Web sites and Internet resources. Although PocketPCGallery doesn't offer any content of its own, it's a good place to find Pocket PC resources.

- **Pocket PC Thoughts.com** (*http://www.pocketpcthoughts.com*)   This is the news and review site run by Jason Dunn, a long-time Windows CE supporter and the technical editor for this book. Pocket PC Thoughts is a community site with a running discussion on a variety of topics and issues. Jason archives all the discussions, so you can come back later to see what people were saying about an upcoming technology before it came out.

- **Pocket PC Passion.com** (*http://www.pocketpcpassion.com*)   This Web site, run by Dale Coffing, reflects his enthusiasm for the Windows CE platform. It also has links to other Pocket PC and Windows CE sites.

- **PDAStreet.com** (*http://www.pdastreet.com*)   This Web site deals with all things PDA, including Palm, RIM Blackberry, Psion, and others. A special part of this site, Windows CE City (*http://www.windowscecity.com*), is dedicated to Windows CE.

- **PocketMatrix.com** (*http://www.pocketmatrix.com*)   This Web site includes news, forums, and software downloads (both freeware and shareware). Its coverage of development issues for Pocket PCs and various unique FAQs make it a good stop.

- **PocketNow.com** (*http://www.pocketnow.com*)   This site includes the standard news and articles that you might expect, plus a careers section, a free classified ad section, and a variety of other areas that you might not expect from a news site.

- **CEWindows.net** (*http://www.cewindows.net*)   This is a comprehensive collection of Windows CE information, including frequently asked questions all the way back to Windows CE version 1.0. (Today's Pocket PCs run version 3.0.)

The nice thing about all these sites is that there aren't huge corporate ad banners cluttering up the design; it's just the site administrator, you, and the rest of the community. Also, because these are community-supported Web sites, you'll often find that they all link to each other, so after you've visited a few of these sites, you'll find the rest, including new ones that pop up.

Magazines and Magazine Sites

There are a limited number of magazines whose market is mobility devices and PDAs. The magazines listed below have at least part of their content dedicated each month to mobility issues:

- **Pocket PC Magazine** (*http://www.pocketpcmag.com*)   This magazine has articles and reviews on Pocket PCs and related devices. They are now publishing their issues in electronic as well as printed format. I'll revisit them in Chapter 12, when I review eBooks.

- **On-Magazine** (*http://www.onmagazine.com*)   This online-only magazine (*ezine*) is a guide to technology. Many of the technologies covered are mobile technologies, including PDAs, notebooks, and cellular phones.

- **Laptop Magazine** (*http://www.bedfordmags.com/lbg*)   This magazine is ostensibly focused on laptops; however, they frequently include coverage of mobile technologies and devices.

- **Mobile Computing Magazine** (*http://www.mobilecomputing.com*)   This magazine, a longtime player in the mobile computing arena, has been there and done that. You can look through the magazine archives dating back to April 2000.

- **Mobile Info** (*http://www.mobileinfo.com*)   This is another ezine whose focus is on mobile technology. It particularly focuses on how to build mobile infrastructure and develop mobile applications.

- **Brighthand** (*http://www.brighthand.com*)   This is an ezine with a good selection of in-depth product evaluation and comparison articles. Its authors seem obsessive about finding the "perfect" solutions.

Certainly, there are more magazines that offer some coverage of mobile computing, but this list should give you a good start on places to go when you want to know whether the newest gadget that you want to buy is any good or not.

Summary

This chapter took you on a whirlwind tour through some of the best accessories and software available for the mobile professional. This chapter is only a start for finding the right accessories for your mobile needs. You could spend countless hours finding new gadgets that will help you be more productive on the road with fewer frustrations.

Here are a few questions you might want to answer about the products you might want to add to your personal mobile magic bag:

- What is the most frustrating thing for you while you are traveling? Is there a product (or service) that can alleviate this frustration?

- Have you ever been prevented from being productive while traveling? What caused this? Was this a one-time situation, or could it potentially happen again?

- How many of these "cool gadgets" are you willing to carry? How much software will fit on your PDA or notebook?

- Will the accessory that you're thinking of buying solve a real problem, or is it just cool? Are you willing to buy it, use it twice, and never use it again?

Park It in the Garage: Synchronization

To be productive while traveling—and therefore be truly mobile—you need both the information that will enable you to make decisions and the information you will update during the course of your travels.

Most people can't remove information from their corporate network, because others might need the information too. As a result, there's always the quandary of how to effectively manage information on your mobile device and keep it in sync with the information on the corporate network.

It's possible to do this manually, but because of the complexity of the task, it's easy to make a mistake or forget some information and lose valuable work. For instance, if you updated a financial analysis spreadsheet while you were away but forgot to copy the spreadsheet to the network when you returned, your colleagues would be working with outdated information. Conversely, if you made changes to the financial plan and copied everything from your notebook to the network but, unbeknownst to you, one of your colleagues had updated the financial plan while you were away, you would have copied outdated information to the network and overwritten your colleague's work.

The tools mentioned in this chapter are designed to automatically find the files that need to be updated on your notebook or Pocket PC and copy the up-to-date information over them. Conversely, files that you updated while you were away are updated on the corporate network. These are intuitive tools that "know" when a conflict occurs because a file has been changed in both places. In these cases, you're informed of the conflict, and you can manually consolidate the changes.

Synchronization for your Notebook

Many people use their notebooks as their mobile office. Notebooks enable them to work on all their information while traveling. Keeping the information on a notebook synchronized with the network is an important goal for every mobile professional.

There are two basic types of information you can synchronize while you travel. The first type is your files: your Microsoft Word documents, Microsoft Excel spreadsheets, Microsoft Access databases, and so on. The second kind of information you can synchronize is your e-mail.

Synchronizing Files

Starting with the release of Microsoft Windows 95, there has been a feature in Windows called Briefcase. Briefcase is designed to support the synchronization of files between your local Windows system and a remote server. A Briefcase appears on your notebook system just like any other file folder.

After you set up Briefcase, you can work freely, ignoring that the Briefcase isn't just a normal file folder. When you get back to your office, a few quick steps synchronize your Briefcase with the network. The first step to using Briefcase is creating a Briefcase folder. Here is the process to do this:

1. Double-click the My Computer icon. In the My Computer window, select the location where you want to create the Briefcase. Alternatively, you can skip this step and create a Briefcase on your desktop.

2. Right-click a free area of the folder or desktop, point to New on the shortcut menu, and then click Briefcase.

3. Right-click the New Briefcase icon, and click Rename on the shortcut menu. Give the new Briefcase a name that makes sense to you, such as *Work Files*.

That's all there is to creating a new Briefcase. You can open the Briefcase by double-clicking it. The first time you open the Briefcase, you'll see a message like the one in Figure 5-1, telling you a little bit about the features of Briefcase.

Drag the files you want to keep synchronized into the Briefcase. The following procedure shows you how to put files into your Briefcase, in case you're unfamiliar with copying and moving files in Windows:

1. Open the Briefcase by double-clicking it. If this is your first time opening the Briefcase, click Finish to close the dialog box containing the introduction message.

2. Move the Briefcase window aside if necessary, and on your desktop, double-click the My Computer icon to open Windows Explorer.

3. Navigate to the folder that contains the files or folders you want to keep synchronized by double-clicking each drive and folder until you reach your intended folder.

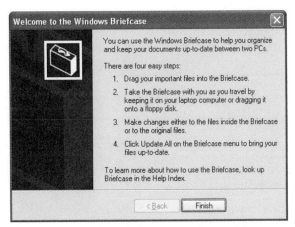

Figure 5-1   *Briefcase helps you understand how to use it the first time you open it.*

4. Right-click the taskbar, and on the shortcut menu, click Tile Vertically. The screen should look something like the one shown in Figure 5-2 when you are done.

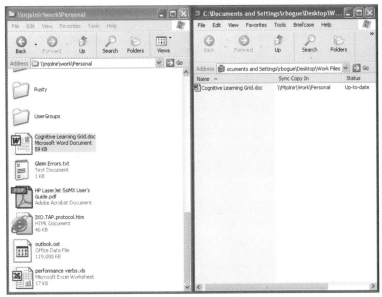

Figure 5-2   *Briefcases look almost exactly the same as an ordinary file folder, except for the extra menu.*

5. Position the mouse pointer over the first file or folder you want to move. Hold down the mouse button, drag the file icon to the Briefcase window, and then release the mouse button. The file or folder should appear in the Briefcase window.

Note The method described here is just one of many ways to move and copy files in Windows. If you're interested in becoming more effective at file management in Windows XP, read *Microsoft Windows XP Inside Out* (Microsoft Press, 2001).

---

6. Move the files and folders you want into the Briefcase. You can put files from many different servers and directories into one Briefcase.

7. When you are done, simply close the Briefcase and Windows Explorer.

Now you're ready to travel with the files you've gathered from the network. You can disconnect from the network and open files directly from your Briefcase. The modifications you make will be held in your Briefcase until the files are updated.

Synchronizing the files in the Briefcase with the files on the network is a simple process. Simply open the Briefcase, and click the Update All button. The Update All command is also on the Briefcase shortcut menu (available when you right-click the Briefcase icon).

When you click the Update All command, Briefcase compares the files on the network, the files currently in the Briefcase, and the files that were last copied into the Briefcase. From there, it creates four different lists of files:

- **Nothing Changed**   This is a list of files for which no action is necessary because the file didn't change on either the notebook or the network.

- **Only The Notebook Changed**   This is a list of files that must be copied to the network because changes were made on the notebook.

- **Only The Network Changed**   This is a list of files that must be copied to the notebook because changes were made on the network.

- **Both The Network And Notebook Changed**   This is a list of files that you have to manually synchronize because changes were made on both the network and the notebook. As a result, a simple file copy cannot be done in either direction.

These lists (with the exception of Nothing Changed) are then assembled in a confirmation dialog box that tells you what Briefcase is going to do with your files. If you're satisfied, click the Update Now button.

The confirmation list contains three icons. The first two icons are green arrows that point to the right or left, indicating which way the file will be copied. An example of a file that needs to be copied to the network is shown in Figure 5-3.

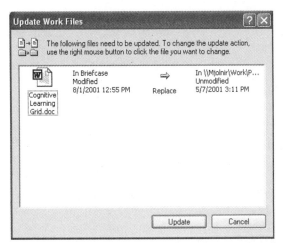

Figure 5-3   *An arrow that points to the right indicates a file that should be copied to the network.*

The other type of icon is a "skip" icon, which is a clockwise curved arrow. An example is shown in Figure 5-4. This indicates that a file was changed on both the network and the notebook, and therefore Briefcase can't automatically resolve the conflict. When this occurs, you'll eventually need to manually correct one of the files. To preserve the changes from both versions of the file, click the document icon to the left of the confirmation line, and select the option to skip the file. Then open both files in the appropriate application, and copy both sets of changes into a single file. Then rerun the process, and copy the file you changed to the other location.

Figure 5-4   *A clockwise curved arrow means you have to decide what to do.*

Briefcase is a good tool for synchronizing a reasonable number of files, but you should not attempt to use it to synchronize an entire network's information, even if you have the space on your notebook's hard disk. Briefcase tends to malfunction when you request the synchronization of too many files. Generally, this occurs when you want to synchronize thousands of files.

Synchronizing E-mail with Outlook 2002

One of the most important sources of communication and information today is e-mail. The average number of e-mail messages a person receives every day has increased over the last few years, and it's clear that e-mail is a very important tool for business workers. The research and consulting firm Gartner (*http://www.gartner.com*) recently released a report that said business workers spend 49 minutes a day on average managing e-mail. BBC News has reported that the average business worker in the U.S. receives 200 e-mail messages a day (*http://news.bbc.co.uk/hi/english/sci/tech/newsid_357000/357993.stm*). Clearly, mobile workers cannot afford to be without e-mail.

Since the creation of Microsoft Outlook—and its partnership with Microsoft Exchange server—it has supported mobile users by using offline files to store copies of information kept on the server, and it has offered remote mail capabilities to keep mobile workers connected. However, Outlook 2002 has significantly raised the bar in terms of flexibility for the mobile worker.

Before I explain how to turn on synchronization so that your e-mail is available while you travel, I will review a few things about Outlook and remote connections in general.

Outlook and the Microsoft Exchange server account to which it is connected contain more than just e-mail. They contain your tasks, calendar, and notes as well. Additionally, the public folders on an Exchange server can store many human resources and other business forms. Large amounts of information can be stored on an Exchange server and accessed through Outlook.

Unfortunately, when traveling you are frequently limited to slow connection speeds. As a result, you have to limit the amount of information you send across the wire so that you can get things done. This means you have to decide what information you want to synchronize.

Note In Chapter 7, I'll address corporate e-mail in more depth and explain Outlook's remote mail component for Exchange servers.

Outlook enables you to control what information you synchronize and when you synchronize it. This means you can use an older copy of an expense report form that's stored in a public folder on an Exchange server without needing to download the most recent version. In most cases, it's probably not vital that you use the newest form immediately. Accounting departments expect to get a few outdated expense forms.

Setting Up Public Folders for Synchronization

By default, some of your personal mailbox, including your e-mail, is available for synchronization, but only public folders that have been added to your favorites are available for synchronization. The process of adding a public folder to your favorite public folders is easy:

1. Open Outlook, if you haven't already.

2. On the View menu, click Folder List to display the Folder List, if it isn't already displayed.

3. Click the plus sign to the left of the Public Folders icon to expand the list.

4. Click the plus sign to the left of All Public Folders to display a list of all public folders.

5. Continue navigating through the public folders and expanding subfolders until you have located the folder you want to make available offline.

6. Right-click the folder, and then on the shortcut menu, click Add To Favorites.

7. In the Add To Favorites dialog box, click the Options button to reveal the subfolder options. The Add To Favorites dialog box is shown in Figure 5-5.

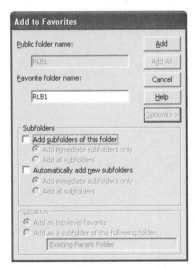

Figure 5-5 *You can control how subfolders are handled using commands in the Add To Favorites dialog box.*

8. If you want to automatically add subfolders, select the Add Subfolders Of This Folder check box. Then select the option that indicates whether to include only one level of folders or all the subfolders in the folder you selected.

9. Similarly, if you want to automatically add new subfolders, select the Automatically Add New Subfolders check box, and select the appropriate option.

10. Click the Add button to add the folder to your favorites.

After you've added the desired public folders to your favorites, you're ready to set up synchronization settings that will enable you to maintain local copies of the folders for traveling.

Setting Synchronization Settings

There are two basic steps to setting up synchronization of your mailbox and your favorite public folders. The first step is to ensure that you have an offline folders file created. The second step is to specify which folders you want available offline.

To set up an offline folders file, follow these steps:

1. Start Outlook, if you haven't already.

2. On the Tools menu, point to Send/Receive Settings, and then click Define Send/ Receive Groups.

3. In the Send/Receive Groups dialog box, click the Edit button. The Send/Receive Settings dialog box shown in Figure 5-6 appears.

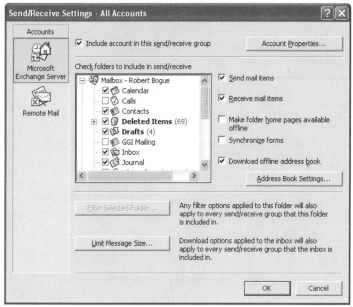

Figure 5-6   *The Send/Receive Settings dialog box can be daunting at first.*

4. Click the Account Properties button.

5. In the Microsoft Exchange Server dialog box, click the Advanced tab. The Advanced tab of the Microsoft Exchange Server dialog box is shown in Figure 5-7.

6. Click the Offline Folder File Settings button.

7. In the File Text box, accept the default file name, or enter your own path and file name.

8. Set the Encryption settings. You should use either Compressible Encryption or no encryption and use Windows 2000/XP's file-level encryption for the file that Outlook creates.

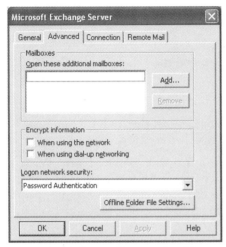

Figure 5-7   *The settings on the Advanced tab of the Microsoft Exchange Server dialog box are fairly easy to use.*

9. Click the OK button to close the Offline Folder File Settings dialog box.

10. Click the OK button to close the Microsoft Exchange Server dialog box.

Note If you want to determine which folders to keep in your offline folders, you can stop here and skip ahead to step 4 in the next set of steps.

---

11. Click the OK button to close the Send/Receive Settings dialog box.

12. Click the Close button to close the Send/Receive Groups dialog box.

Not all folders will be synchronized simply because you have an offline storage file. By default, only your Inbox, Outbox, Deleted Items, Sent Items, Calendar, and Contacts are synchronized. This can be particularly frustrating if you use the Notes folder in your Exchange mailbox to hold important tidbits of information, such as a rental car confirmation number or an account number.

In addition to specifying exactly which folders to synchronize, you'll also need to configure Outlook to synchronize these folders when you want them to be synchronized. I'll explain this procedure next.

> **Note** Although it's possible to set up several different groups in which you can synchronize some of your offline folders at one time and others at another time, an explanation of how to do that is beyond the scope of this book. For more information, search the Help file of Outlook 2002 or purchase an Outlook 2002-specific book, such as *Microsoft Outlook Step by Step* or *Microsoft Outlook Inside Out* (Microsoft Press, 2001).

1. Start Outlook 2002, if you haven't already.

2. On the Tools menu, point to Send/Receive Settings, and then click Define Send/Receive Groups.

3. In the Send/Receive Groups dialog box, click the Edit button.

4. In the Check Folders To Include In Send/Receive box, select the folders from your mailbox and public folder favorites to include in synchronization.

5. Unless you have a specific reason not to, select both the Make Folder Home Pages Available Offline and the Synchronize Forms So That You Always Have The Latest Information For The Folder check boxes. You might not want to synchronize forms if there are frequent changes to large forms in one or more of the folders that you synchronize.

6. Click OK to return to the Send/Receive Groups dialog box. Figure 5-8 shows the Send/Receive Groups dialog box.

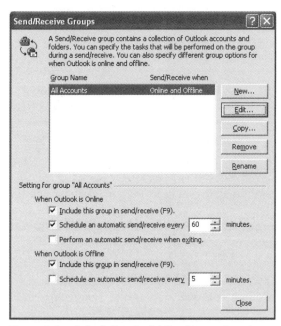

Figure 5-8 *Scheduling is the final step of setting up synchronization.*

7. Select the Include This Group In Send/Receive (F9) option in both the When Outlook Is Online and When Outlook Is Offline areas of the dialog box. This ensures that when Outlook sends and receives all messages, it will resynchronize all folders as well.

8. If you anticipate occasionally being in so much of a hurry that you won't have time to synchronize before closing Outlook, select the Schedule An Automatic Send/Receive Every check box, and set the number of minutes between synchronizations.

9. If you don't mind waiting a few minutes when closing Outlook, you can also select the Perform An Automatic Send/Receive When Exiting check box. This ensures that your offline folder file is completely updated when you disconnect.

10. Click Close to return to Outlook.

The process to set up folder synchronization isn't particularly complicated. Synchronization will greatly enhance your mobile experience, especially if you set up your offline folder so that you can take the information from your mailbox and public folders with you when you're traveling without needing access to a connection. (This can be handy when you're sitting in an airplane at 35,000 feet.)

Synchronization for your Pocket PC

Unlike working on a notebook, where you can manually move files back and forth, it's virtually impossible to work on a Pocket PC without synchronization. Because the Pocket PC doesn't have a built-in keyboard, it's challenging to manually enter data into the device. Its mobile nature leaves you open to the possibility of losing it or running out of battery power, resulting in the loss of all the data.

Luckily, the synchronization tool that Microsoft provides for Windows CE–based devices, including the Pocket PC, is a very solid application. It has all the features that you need to keep your data in sync and make the process relatively painless.

If you have experience with Palm, you'll be interested to note that Microsoft's Active-Sync synchronization tool is different from the HotSync tool provided by Palm Computing in two very important ways.

First, ActiveSync helps your computer and your Pocket PC maintain constant contact with one another by sending each other periodic updates when events happen. For instance, if you have Inbox Synchronization turned on, when you receive a new message in your computer's Inbox, it is transferred almost instantly to the Inbox on your Pocket PC. If you delete a message from your computer's Inbox, the message is removed almost instantly from the Inbox on your Pocket PC. This is an important feature, because you can leave with your device without worrying about manually synchronizing the unit first.

Second, with ActiveSync you can transfer files to and from your Pocket PC using the familiar File Explorer interface. This means that you can drag and drop files from a folder on your computer or the corporate network directly to your Pocket PC without going through a series of extra steps.

Selecting Connectivity for ActiveSync

For the most part, you have a primary form of connection to your computer, the one that you will most frequently use to connect your Pocket PC and your computer. This is the connection you use most, and the one for which you have a device cradle. The Compaq iPAQ, for instance, comes with a cradle that enables you to use USB to connect to your computer. If for some reason your computer doesn't have a USB port, you can also buy a serial cradle and connect the iPAQ to your computer with a serial connection. Your first connection from your device to your computer should always be made from the cradle, because that's the easiest connection to make, and most cradles provide power to the device. When your device detects that it is in its cradle, it will automatically attempt to connect with the computer and start ActiveSync. The first time your device attempts to synchronize your Pocket PC with your computer, it will ask you about establishing a partnership. I'll explore that in the next section.

After you've made the initial connection from the device's cradle, you can connect to your computer using infrared, a network connection, or the serial or USB connection you already made. Initially this might not seem a great a benefit; however, these options can be invaluable if you travel or spend a lot of time out of your office.

If you travel, you know that your number one enemy is luggage. The less weight you carry and the less space things take up, the better off you are. If you can synchronize your Pocket PC with your notebook using infrared (IR), you won't have to carry the cradle for your Pocket PC. You still have to carry a battery charger if you're concerned that you'll run down your battery, but one less thing to carry is one less thing to carry.

Conversely, if you get synchronization to work with a network and your office (or home) has a wireless network installed, you can carry your device with you and receive constant updates. Of course, you have to ensure that your Pocket PC doesn't turn off because of inactivity. To prevent your Pocket PC from turning off, follow these steps:

1. On the Start menu, tap Settings.

2. Tap the System tab in settings. The system options will be displayed, as shown in Figure 5-9.

3. Tap the Power icon. The Power applet will be displayed, as shown in Figure 5-10.

4. Under On Battery Power, clear the Turn Off Device If Not Used For check box.

5. Tap OK to close the Power applet.

You also have to change ActiveSync so that it doesn't disconnect when you manually synchronize. To do this, follow these steps:

1. On the Start menu, tap ActiveSync.

2. If your device is connected and synchronizing, tap Stop.

3. On the Tools menu, tap Options.

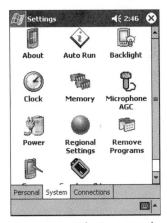

Figure 5-9 *The System tab includes many options.*

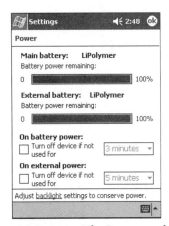

Figure 5-10 *The Power applet lets you keep the device on.*

4. In the ActiveSync dialog box, tap the Schedule tab. This tab is shown in Figure 5-11.

Figure 5-11 *Scheduling enables you to set up automatic synchronization.*

5. Clear the When Manually Synchronizing, Disconnect When Complete check box.

6. Tap OK to return to ActiveSync.

7. If your Pocket PC was synchronizing when you started, tap Sync.

Now you can connect to your computer with a wireless network card and keep it synchronized just as if it was in a cradle. This is useful when you're sitting in meetings and want to keep up to date with your e-mail.

Caution Keeping the unit on and constantly polling for updates will consume battery power. You might run out of power if you attempt to keep your Pocket PC connected all day.

Creating a Partnership

Creating a partnership between your Pocket PC and your computer is a simple task. In fact, your Pocket PC will attempt to create a partnership with your computer the first time you connect them. All you need to do is answer a few questions to ensure that the options you want are set on the device and on the computer. To establish a partnership between your Pocket PC and your computer, follow these steps:

1. Make sure ActiveSync is installed and running on your computer. If ActiveSync is not installed, on the Start menu, point to All Programs, and then click Microsoft ActiveSync.

2. Insert your Pocket PC into the cradle attached to your computer. ActiveSync will display a message like the one shown in Figure 5-12.

Figure 5-12   *ActiveSync detects the new device and asks whether you want to establish a partnership.*

3. Select the Yes option, if it is not already selected.

4. Click the Next button to move to the next page.

5. You are asked whether you want to create a partnership with just this computer. Click the Next button to move on to selecting the conduits to synchronize, shown in Figure 5-13.

6. Select the conduits that you want ActiveSync to synchronize, or just leave the defaults. You can always change the conduit settings later.

7. Click the Next button to continue.

8. Review the settings on the Setup Complete Wizard page, and click the Finish button when you're ready.

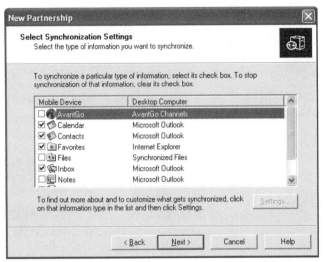

Figure 5-13   *Configuring conduits can be done when you set up the partnership or later.*

As you can see, setting up a partnership between your computer and your Pocket PC is very simple. Even if you make a mistake setting up the partnership, you can change your settings later (explained in the next section).

Establishing and Configuring Conduits

Conduits are the pieces of software that move information between the applications on the Pocket PC. These pieces of software are included with your Pocket PC (in the case of the built-in applications) and normally come with third-party applications.

Conduits are installed to ActiveSync, which activates them one at a time to exchange information with the Pocket PC. They also perform data conversion if the data on the Pocket PC is different from the data on the computer.

Two of the best examples of conduits are the one that synchronizes data between calendar applications and the one that synchronizes data between contact applications.

The Calendar conduit is responsible for converting the calendar data from Outlook into the calendar application built into the Pocket PC. These applications have very similar interfaces, but they don't have exactly the same internal data structure. As a result, the Calendar conduit converts the data from Outlook to the format required by the Pocket PC calendar application, and the other way around.

Similarly, the Contacts conduit converts the contact format used in Outlook to a format that the contact manager on the Pocket PC can understand. For contacts, this is particularly important, because you might have defined custom Outlook Contact forms that aren't supported on the Pocket PC.

Determining which Conduits to Activate

The following is a list of conduits that come with ActiveSync:

- **Calendar**   This conduit synchronizes the calendar on the Pocket PC with the Calendar folder in Outlook.

- **Contacts**   This conduit synchronizes contacts on the Pocket PC with the Contacts folder in Outlook.

- **Tasks**   This conduit synchronizes tasks on the Pocket PC with the Tasks folder in Outlook.

- **Favorites**   This conduit creates and synchronizes a Mobile Favorites folder in Internet Explorer with the favorites in the Pocket PC version of Internet Explorer.

- **Pocket Access**   This conduit synchronizes Access databases between the Pocket PC and the computer. This allows applications that use Access-format databases on the Pocket PC to have their information synchronized with the computer using third-party tools. Microsoft is encouraging developers to use Microsoft SQL CE edition; however, many have not made the transition yet.

- **Inbox**   This conduit synchronizes e-mail between the Inbox application on the Pocket PC and Outlook. E-mail folders can now be replicated between Outlook and the Inbox on the Pocket PC.

- **Notes**   This conduit synchronizes written, recorded, or sketched notes with the Notes folder in Outlook.

- **Files**   This conduit synchronizes files between a special directory on the computer, usually under My Documents, and the Pocket PC. I'll explain this conduit in more detail later in this chapter.

- **Mobile Link**   This conduit synchronizes AvantGo offline content with the Pocket PC. I'll address AvantGo and this conduit in Chapter 12.

In general, you need to activate conduits for any information you want to keep synchronized or backed up. There is a special mechanism for providing complete backups, but the easiest way to maintain continuous backups is to synchronize all the data that you use on your Pocket PC.

Because synchronization keeps a copy of the information on the computer in case information in the device or the device itself is lost, you already have an existing copy of the information. This copy of the information on your Pocket PC can even be used with a dissimilar device. Backups, as I explain later in this chapter, must be restored to the same type of device from which they were made.

Changing Conduit Settings

Most of the defaults for the conduits are just how you want them. They synchronize only the information you need to have on your Pocket PC. However, every once in a while you might need to change these settings because of a particular preference.

For example, I like to keep a complete record of my calendar for the past year with me. Although some might consider this silly, I often note in my calendar important deadlines or other information that might help me recall exact dates and times. On several occasions this has proven helpful. By default, ActiveSync and the Calendar conduit only synchronize recent events; thus, I wouldn't be able to get my historical information from my Pocket PC unless I changed the default settings.

To prevent my Pocket PC's memory from being totally consumed, I need to ensure that I've set the AutoArchive feature in Outlook 2002 to automatically archive appointments older than one year. Archiving this data deletes it from Outlook and puts it into a special file. This will not only remove it from Outlook's calendar, but—through synchronization—that data will be deleted from the Pocket PC as well. Setting up the AutoArchive feature in Outlook 2002 is beyond the scope of this book; however, if you search for *archive* in Outlook 2002, you will be guided through the process of establishing archive settings for your folders.

The next step in setting up synchronization for your Pocket PC is to reset the synchronization settings for the Calendar conduit. Here is the process for doing this:

1. Open ActiveSync. You can do this by double-clicking the ActiveSync icon in the system tray at the right end of the taskbar.

2. Ensure that there are no active synchronizations. You can remain connected to your device, but no operations can be pending while you proceed, because ActiveSync will disable any running operations.

3. Click the Options button in the ActiveSync window on the computer to open the Options dialog box. The Options dialog box is shown in Figure 5-14.

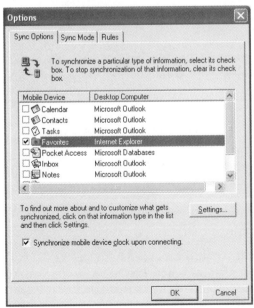

Figure 5-14 *You can control conduits from the Options dialog box.*

4. Select the Calendar conduit in the list.

5. Click the Settings button to display the Calendar Synchronization Settings dialog box. Note that the screen displayed is conduit specific. For instance, the Inbox conduit shows a different settings dialog box than the Calendar conduit. Figure 5-15 shows the Calendar conduit synchronization settings.

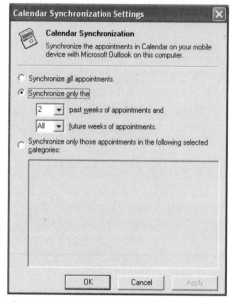

Figure 5-15   *You can control which appointments are synchronized through the Calendar conduit.*

6. Select the Synchronize All Appointments option. ActiveSync will synchronize the appointments on your Pocket PC with those on your computer.

Note As you can see here, you can synchronize appointments for a number of weeks, including 52 weeks, or one full year. However, I might decide at some point that I want to be able to review appointments for a different number of weeks. By synchronizing all events here, I won't have to change my settings in the future.

---

7. Click OK to close the Calendar Synchronization Settings dialog box.

8. Click OK to close the Options dialog box.

Each conduit has settings that control how it synchronizes data between the Pocket PC and the computer; however, each of the conduit settings is accessed in the same way. You might want to look at the settings for each conduit one by one so that you know how the conduits are set up. This will help you to make sure that the defaults for each conduit are what you expect.

Transferring Files

ActiveSync conduits are great for most situations. Data from the Pocket PC is synchronized with the appropriate application in the computer. However, synchronization doesn't apply to applications that use a basic file method of data storage. For instance, both Word and Excel can store data in many different files, so there is no central data repository for ActiveSync to synchronize with.

That is, in part, why you didn't see a Word conduit or an Excel conduit—because the files themselves are the self-contained data storage, it is assumed that you move them around as files.

Unfortunately, trying to move files to your Pocket PC will make you painfully aware of how precious memory space is on your device. People rarely worry about the size of the files they create—until they try to copy them to a Pocket PC.

In this section, I'll address several topics: how the Files conduit can be used to synchronize files; how Mobile Explorer can be used to move files back and forth manually; what file conversions are and how they work; and finally, ways to open files that aren't even stored on your Pocket PC, for those times when you just don't have enough memory.

Files Conduit

One of the easiest ways to move files to your Pocket PC is to simply drag and drop a copy of the file into a synchronized folder. The Files conduit automatically converts the file to a file type that the Pocket PC can handle (according to the file conversion settings I'll explain in upcoming sections) and copies the result onto the Pocket PC.

The first step to using the Files conduit is to select the check box for the conduit from the list of conduits in ActiveSync. The first time you turn on the Files conduit, you'll receive a message asking you to confirm that you want to create the synchronization directory. After that, the Files conduit will synchronize files.

A folder will be created in the My Documents folder, and it will be named with the profile name of your Pocket PC, followed by *My Documents*. If, for instance, your profile name is Merlin, a synchronized folder will be named *Merlin My Documents* will exist in the My Documents folder.

One caution about using the Files conduit: Because this folder is automatically synchronized with the Pocket PC, and because the file conversions that you set up might cause some formatting data to be lost, you should not use this folder as your primary storage folder for your documents—you should use it to hold copies of your documents. I'll explain about file conversions after the section on Mobile Explorer.

Mobile Explorer

Installing ActiveSync on a computer adds a new option to Windows Explorer. A new Mobile Device icon leads you to the files that are on the mobile device connected with ActiveSync. Figure 5-16 on the next page shows a My Computer folder containing a

Mobile Device icon that you can use to open windows for files on your Pocket PC. This enables you to perform the same file management tasks for your Pocket PC files that you can for any file on your computer, with a few minor exceptions.

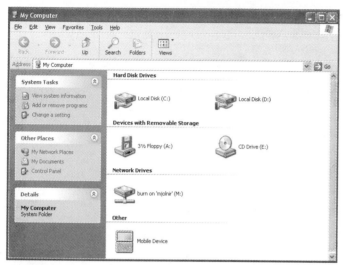

Figure 5-16   *Your Pocket PC looks like any other drive, thanks to ActiveSync.*

Tip If you attempt to open the Mobile Device icon without your device connected with ActiveSync, you see a blank folder. You must have your device connected to your PC to be able to perform this procedure.

Because these files aren't located on your computer, you can't open them directly from their windows. However, you can copy them to your computer and then open them. Likewise, you can't attach these files to an e-mail until you copy them to your computer.

Mobile Explorer will likely become the primary way you move files to and from your Pocket PC. Because it's convenient and familiar, it's a great way to get the information that you need for your next meeting onto the device.

Tip If you have a wireless network and are late for a meeting, your administrative assistant might be able to move the files you need to your Pocket PC while you're in transit. Just start ActiveSync on your PocketPC and leave it on while you're on your way to the meeting. As long as there is an ActiveSync connection between the computer and your Pocket PC, Mobile Explorer will work.

File Conversions

Conduits provide file translation between Pocket PC applications and their laptop and desktop computer counterparts. However, conduits are designed for applications that have one database. For file-based applications like Pocket Excel and Pocket Word, you need another mechanism to convert the data.

Although Pocket Excel and Pocket Word can read files created by their laptop and desktop cousins and do a passable job of enabling you to work with Excel and Word documents, they work better if the files are translated into a native Pocket Excel or Pocket Word format. The converted files contain only the information that Pocket Word and Pocket Excel can use. This conserves precious storage on your Pocket PC.

Caution Be very careful about copying files back and forth from your computer to your Pocket PC. "Round tripping" files like this might result in data loss. You should use file conversion in one direction only.

Table 5-1 shows you the conversion options for each type of file. Most of these are focused on translating Word and Excel files into Pocket PC versions.

Table 5-1   Pocket PC File Conversion Options

PC Format	Pocket PC Formats
Bitmap (*.bmp*)	2-bit, 16 shades of grey bitmap (*.2bp*)
Microsoft Word document (*.doc*)	ASCII (*.txt*) InkWriter/Note Taker/Notes (*.pwi*) Pocket Word (*.psw*) Pocket Word 1.0 (*.pwd*) Pocket Word 2.0/3.0 (*.pwd*) Rich Text format (*.rtf*)
Microsoft Word template (*.dot*)	InkWriter template (*.plt*) InkWriter/Note Taker/Notes (*.pwi*) Pocket Word (*.psw*) Pocket Word template (*.pwt*)
Font file (*.fon*)	Mobile Device Raster font (*.fnt*)
Microsoft Access application (*.mdb*)	Pocket Access database (*.cdb*)
TrueType Font file (*.ttf*)	Mobile Device Raster Font (*.ttf*)
Text document (*.txt*)	InkWriter/Note Taker/Notes (*.pwi*) Pocket Word (*.psw*) Pocket Word 1.0 (*.pwd*) Pocket Word 2.0/3.0 (*.pwd*) Rich Text format (*.rtf*)
Microsoft Excel workbook (*.xls*)	Pocket Excel 1.0 (*.pxl*) Pocket Excel 2.0/3.0 (*.pxl*)
Microsoft Excel template (*.xlt*)	Pocket Excel 2.0/3.0 (*.pxl*)

You can also elect not to do any file translation at all. For the most part, the default file conversions are good, but you might want to turn off file conversion under some circumstances. For instance, during the writing of this book I sometimes edited a chapter on my Pocket PC. (I don't recommend this, but it's what I did.) To preserve some of the styles in the document, I had to turn off file conversion or set it to Rich Text Format (*.rtf*). If ActiveSync had converted the files to Pocket Word, when I converted them back, all the style information would have disappeared. When I allowed this type of conversion, I couldn't see any information contained in styles, and as a result, headings looked just like normal text.

Of course, the process for converting files works both ways. ActiveSync can convert any format in the left column to any format in the right column, as well as the other way around.

The process for changing or reviewing file conversion is simple. To access the file conversions:

1. Start ActiveSync on the computer, if you haven't already.

2. Make sure that ActiveSync is not currently synchronizing data.

3. Click the Options button.

4. In the Options dialog box, click the Rules tab.

5. Click the Conversion Settings button. The file's Conversion Properties dialog box appears, as shown in Figure 5-17.

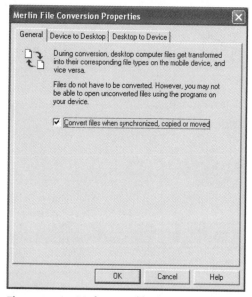

Figure 5-17   *Make sure file conversion is turned on.*

6. Make sure the Convert Files When Synchronized, Copied, Or Moved check box is selected.

7. Click the Desktop To Device tab. The dialog box should look similar to the one shown in Figure 5-18.

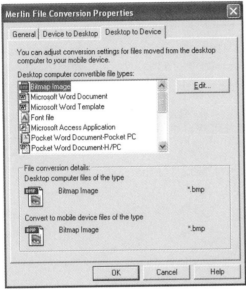

Figure 5-18   *Select the settings on the Desktop To Device tab.*

8. Select the file conversion settings you want to change in the Desktop Computer Convertible File Types list box.

9. Click the Edit button.

10. Select the type of conversion you want from the Type combo box, and click OK.

11. When finished, click OK to close the File Conversion Properties dialog box.

12. Click OK to close the Options dialog box.

You might want to experiment with the file conversion settings for Word documents in particular. Each file format has its own advantages and disadvantages when used with Pocket Word. Use either Rich Text format (*.rtf*) or an unconverted Word document (*.doc*) if you intend to "round trip" the document back to the computer. These two formats lose the least formatting data when they are round tripped.

File Explorer

So far, I've explained operations initiated on the computer; however, there might be a time when you want to transfer files from your Pocket PC. The most recent version of the Pocket PC can connect to network shares. In addition to transferring files with ActiveSync, you can connect to computers on the local network and transfer data manually from your Pocket PC.

The File Explorer on the Pocket PC is nearly identical to Windows Explorer on your computer, except that File Explorer can have only one window. All file transfer operations have to take place as cut-and-paste operations; you can't drag files from one window to another.

1. Find the file you want. To navigate up, select the location in the upper left corner, and then select a higher-level folder.

2. To open a network share, click the Open menu option at the lower end of the screen. Figure 5-19 shows the network share's Open dialog box.

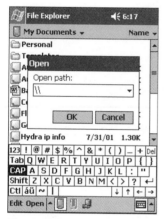

Figure 5-19   *Opening a network share requires that you know its name.*

3. In the Open Path box, enter the name of the system and share to which you want to connect. (You might need to enter your network authentication information the first time so that you can be connected to the server.) This will switch your view in File Explorer to the Remote view, as indicated in the lower part of the screen.

4. Right-click the file you want to move to your Pocket PC, and on the shortcut menu, click Copy.

5. Click the Pocket PC icon in the lower part of the screen.

6. Navigate to the folder you want to put the file in, and then on the Edit menu, click Paste. This will create a copy of the file on your Pocket PC.

Tip Storage space on your Pocket PC is precious. You might want to get in the habit of copying all files from the network to a storage card instead of to the device's main memory.

Shortcuts

File Explorer cannot open documents that are not local to the Pocket PC. This is a serious limitation of File Explorer. However, there is a solution to this problem that doesn't require you to copy the file to your Pocket PC.

Complete the previous steps, but instead of clicking Paste on the Edit menu, click Paste Shortcut. The shortcut won't take up much memory on your Pocket PC (slightly more than 50 bytes), and you'll be able to open the document by clicking the shortcut.

This tactic will really help when your Pocket PC is low on memory and you need to view a document on the network to verify some information.

Backing Up and Restoring

Conduits ensure that some of your data is backed up, and you can keep copies of the files on your Pocket PC and your computer as well, but you might still want to periodically back up your Pocket PC to save your configuration and settings, which aren't saved any other way.

Caution The ActiveSync backup and restore utility is simple and always available, but it's also got its own set of problems, not the least of which is that the restoration process is exceedingly slow. If your device didn't come with its own backup utility, you can buy one from Sprite Software at *http://www.spritesoftware.com*.

The process of creating a backup is simple:

1. In ActiveSync on the computer, on the Tools menu, click Backup/Restore.

2. In the Backup/Restore dialog box, select the Full Backup option, and click the Back Up Now button to perform a full backup. Figure 5-20 on the next page shows the Backup tab of the Backup/Restore dialog box.

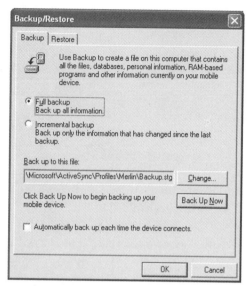

Figure 5-20 *Performing a full backup is an important precaution.*

After you have completed one full backup, you can return to the Backup/Restore dialog box and select the Automatically Backup Each Time The Device Connects check box and the Incremental Backup option. This will ensure that you always have a current copy of your Pocket PC files and settings backed up on your computer. However, the copy will take up a lot of space on your hard disk. If you're tight on space, you might want to skip doing incremental backups.

If you need to restore your device, take a look at the Help file in ActiveSync to learn the correct steps. For the most part, this process is simple, but you have to start an ActiveSync session before you can restore your data.

Resolving Conflicts

Every once in a while, ActiveSync indicates that there is an unresolved item or two. These unresolved items occur when you change an appointment on both the computer and the Pocket PC, and the two items don't match. As a result, ActiveSync doesn't know which change is the correct one.

The process of conflict resolution is simple. In the ActiveSync window on the computer, click the Resolve Conflicts link, and select the data that is correct. If there is more than one conflict, you will be prompted to resolve each item. However, the conflict resolution screens are conduit-dependent, so each screen will differ depending on the type of conflicting data.

Occasionally, a conflict will appear that can't be resolved by clicking the Resolve Conflict link. The Microsoft Money conduit has a tendency to generate this kind of problem, as do some third-party conduits. You should read the Microsoft Support Knowledge Base articles on these problems. Search for *Resolve Conflict* and *ActiveSync* in the Knowledge Base. One quick and easy fix, however, is to disconnect ActiveSync, reset your Pocket PC, and restart your computer. If that doesn't work, you can also try deactivating and then reactivating the conduit performing synchronization.

These steps don't solve every problem, but they sometimes solve problems caused when the computer and the Pocket PC get out of sync. By resetting everything, you'll often find that ActiveSync is able to resolve conflicts.

Troubleshooting Connectivity

Sometimes when you drop your Pocket PC into its cradle and ActiveSync tries to start, you get an error message indicating that ActiveSync can't recognize the device. This message prompts you to retry communications or disable the COM port. *COM port* is a bit of a misnomer when you're connecting via USB, but disabling the COM port will stop ActiveSync from using your USB port.

I usually encounter this error message when I already have an ActiveSync connection to the computer through a different port—for instance, when I'm connected to ActiveSync though the network. The solution is simple: Take the Pocket PC out of its cradle, wait five seconds, and drop the unit back into the cradle. Most of the time this solves the problem.

Occasionally, ActiveSync will not even try to connect, or will continue to display the connection error message even after you've removed and replaced the device. The best thing to do is to reset your device and try again. If that doesn't work, restart your computer and try again.

If all else fails, try connecting to your computer another way. If you usually connect through USB, try using a serial port or network. If you still can't connect, there might be something seriously wrong, and you'll have to call technical support.

Summary

Keeping your data with you and up-to-date is not as easy as it might sound. Problems arise when you need to keep your data synchronized with the data at your office. Fortunately, Briefcase and the offline folder settings for Outlook make keeping your notebook up-to-date while traveling a workable, if not perfect, proposition.

Keeping your Pocket PC synchronized with your computer is also easy. ActiveSync keeps all your working data, such as your calendar, e-mail, and contacts, up-to-date. In addition, the file transfer utilities help keep your files up-to-date.

As usual, I end this chapter with some questions to think about when you're using synchronization:

- What information do you need to take with you?
- How will you ensure that the information you have while traveling is kept up-to-date?
- What happens if you and a colleague at the office both alter the same document?
- How bad would it be if you lost the information on your Pocket PC? How should you protect that data?
- Does anyone else in your office need access to your information?

E-mail

Part II addresses the number one application that you'll need access to while mobile-messaging. The popularity of e-mail, which started in the early 1990s, drove the adoption of LANs for many organizations. Now e-mail is driving a wireless and portable market. Messaging, often called instant messaging, is now becoming popular as organizations struggle to find new ways of keeping their employees in touch.

Chapter 6 introduces you to the basic concepts that you'll have to consider when accessing e-mail from mobile locations. This chapter is really a foundation for understanding what you will and won't be able to do from remote locations. This chapter focuses on using Inbox with an ActiveSync connection.

Chapter 7 dives into the details of accessing other kinds of mail, the e-mail that you can get from your ISP or one of the free e-mail services on the Internet such as Hotmail. This chapter shows you how to apply the techniques in chapter 6 to other environments.

Chapter 8 explains instant messaging software. First it dispels the myth that instant messaging has no use other than wasting teenagers' time. Then it reviews a few different instant messaging clients, and how they might be appropriate for your needs.

Pocket PC E-mail Basics

Many years ago, I decided that I needed something better than a Day-Timer in which to keep my appointments. Microsoft Outlook was becoming popular, and I started getting meeting requests, which I would have to transcribe into my planner. Eventually this became so tedious that I gave up and bought a Palm.

The Palm solved my need to keep my calendar synchronized and made managing contacts much easier, but my attempts to send e-mail with it were a dismal failure. I finally had to turn it off after about three days of trying to make it work.

It couldn't keep up with the e-mail coming into my mailbox. It also attempted to resend the same message over and over again. I finally resigned myself to the fact that I just wasn't going to get e-mail working on my Palm.

To be fair, a good friend of mine was able to make e-mail synchronization work with his Palm. But the limited memory on the Palm meant he could have only the messages in his Inbox, not his entire mailbox, and he had to regularly clean out his Inbox or the large volume of e-mail would wreak havoc.

When I bought my Pocket PC, I expected the same kind of problems with e-mail—problems keeping my Inbox synchronized and messages getting sent out over and over again. Fortunately, I've had none of these problems, and despite the abuse I've given the Inbox application on the Pocket PC, it continues to work beautifully.

This chapter will help you synchronize your e-mail between your Pocket PC and your computer, and familiarize you with the user interface of the Inbox on the Pocket PC. In the next chapter, I'll address alternative ways of getting your e-mail.

Synchronizing E-mail

Making e-mail work on your Pocket PC depends on synchronizing it with your computer. If you accepted the default settings when you set up your Pocket PC Inbox, synchronization has already been set up for you. The quickest and easiest way to find out whether the defaults have been accepted is to check the Inbox application on your Pocket PC. If there is e-mail in your Inbox, synchronization is running. Figure 6-1 shows the Pocket PC Inbox screen.

Figure 6-1   *The Inbox will contain e-mail only if the Inbox conduit is working.*

There are two possible reasons why e-mail in your computer Inbox doesn't show up in the Inbox application on your Pocket PC. The first reason is that the e-mail in your computer Inbox might be too old. By default, the computer's Inbox synchronizes e-mail from only the last five days. The second reason is that your Inbox conduit might have been disabled. In any case, let's review the settings of the Inbox conduit. You can open the Inbox conduit settings by performing the following steps:

1. Open ActiveSync by double-clicking the ActiveSync icon in the system tray.

2. Tap the Options button to display the Options dialog box shown in Figure 6-2.

3. In the list box, tap Inbox. If the check box to the left of the Inbox conduit is not selected, the conduit is not active. Click the check box to turn the conduit on.

4. Tap the Settings button to display the Mail Synchronization Settings dialog box shown in Figure 6-3.

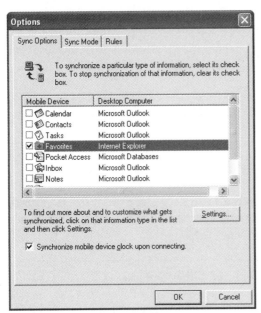

Figure 6-2   *The Options dialog box displays all the installed conduits.*

Figure 6-3   *The Mail Synchronization Settings dialog box displays a complete folder list.*

The Inbox conduit's settings aren't complex—with only four check boxes and a folder list, they are positively simple. The Mail Folders list box contains all the e-mail folders available in your mailbox. If there is a check box to the left of the folder, you can select it if you want the Inbox conduit to synchronize the e-mail in that folder.

Tip You won't be able to select your Sent Items folder. If you need to keep a copy of an important message on your Pocket PC, you'll have to send yourself a copy.

When I am done with a business e-mail message, I move it to the Business subfolder (under the Saved Mail folder), rather than leaving it in my Inbox or deleting it. This way, not only do I know I've finished with that message, but I can keep a copy of it in case I need it later. Because I move so much of my e-mail to the Business subfolder, I usually synchronize it along with my standard e-mail folders.

Note You can control the amount of e-mail synchronized with your Pocket PC by using the Inbox conduit settings. However, eventually you'll need to consider what to do with the e-mail that builds up in the e-mail folders in your mailbox. As I briefly mentioned in Chapter 5, you can use an Outlook 2002 feature called AutoArchive to manage the amount of e-mail stored in your mailbox.

The four remaining check boxes control how the memory used by the synchronized e-mail is managed. Selecting the first check box limits the total number of lines that can be retrieved per message. By default, this limit is 100 lines. If you routinely get long messages or digests from important mailing lists, you might want to clear this check box so that you can receive the entire message. Of course, this will allow a single message to consume more memory on your Pocket PC.

Selecting the second check box controls how long messages sit before they are removed from your Pocket PC. This setting also controls which messages are copied to your Pocket PC the first time you synchronize, and prevents old messages in your Inbox and other folders from being synchronized. The default for this setting is five days. A higher setting requires the synchronization of more e-mail, so the Pocket PC must have more memory available for e-mail storage.

Selecting the third check box enables file attachments to be synchronized with the Pocket PC. Because file attachments come in all sizes and can even be much larger than the amount of memory installed in your Pocket PC, select the fourth option if you want to limit the size of synchronized attachments.

These last two options are critically important if you receive documents from your office. If you receive Microsoft Word documents, Microsoft Excel spreadsheets, or other files you can review on your Pocket PC, you probably want to synchronize attachments.

However, you probably want to limit the synchronization to documents you can review on your Pocket PC. A limit between 50 KB and 500 KB is appropriate for most attachments.

Attachments do not run through the file conversion options I explained in Chapter 5. As a result, if someone sends you a Word document as an attachment, it will not be converted to Pocket Word, RTF, or any other format you might have selected in the file conversion settings. Pocket Word and Pocket Excel can display Word and Excel files, but they can't do it as effectively as they can Pocket Word and Pocket Excel files. You might notice some general weirdness, such as missing font characteristics or other display abnormalities, when you open these unconverted attachments on your Pocket PC.

After you have all the settings adjusted to your liking, you can close the Inbox Settings and ActiveSync Options dialog boxes by tapping OK twice.

Caution The settings for mail synchronization are global—meaning all folders must have the same settings. Thus, if you want to synchronize your Inbox for the last 30 days—because you keep only active items in it—and you want to save the mail in a special newsgroup folder for only the last three days to limit the amount of space in use, you will be unable to do so on the Pocket PC.

Reading Messages

As you might imagine, because there is no keyboard, composing new messages on a Pocket PC isn't easy. Even if you purchase an external keyboard, you might not have it with you all the time. However, the Inbox application excels at displaying e-mail messages.

Opening a message is simple. In the main Inbox screen, use your stylus to tap the message you want to read. The message appears on the screen, as shown in Figure 6-4.

Figure 6-4 *A message displayed in the Pocket PC Inbox application.*

Often, the message will be too large to read in one screen, so you'll have to scroll down to see the rest of the message. You can do this by using either the scroll bar on the right or the Down button on your Pocket PC device. The Down button will move the screen down, one page of information at a time.

If you chose to limit the number of lines retrieved in each message, you might see a *[Message Truncated]* message at the end of the text. This means that the message exceeded the number of lines you specified in the Inbox conduit settings. You can always go to your computer to read the rest of the message. Currently, there is no way to set your Pocket PC to download the rest of the message you're reviewing.

You have five options when you've finished reading your message:

- Close it.
- Reply to it.
- Forward it.
- Move it to a folder.
- Delete it.

Replying and Forwarding

Most of us have experienced the nagging feeling that an e-mail exchange has gone on too long. Perhaps the main reason that people over-respond to e-mail messages is that it is so easy to reply to them. On a Pocket PC, tapping the green arrow icon in the lower corner of the screen displays a shortcut menu from which you can reply to the message or forward it to someone else.

There are two ways to reply to a message. You can reply to the message sender alone by tapping the Reply button, or you can reply to everyone who received a copy of the original message by tapping the Reply All button.

The appearance of the message depends on the Inbox settings on the Pocket PC. By default, your reply message will include a copy of the original message. However, you can change that setting. To reset it, on the Tools menu, tap Options, and in the Inbox Options dialog box, tap the Message tab. Figure 6-5 shows what the Inbox Options dialog box then looks like.

Figure 6-5   *The settings in the Inbox Options dialog box control the workings of the Inbox.*

Selecting the first check box formats your reply message to include the original message in the body of the response. Selecting the check box indents the body of the original message when it is included in your reply, and selecting the third check box formats the message to have a prefix character before each line of the original message when it is included in your reply. Including the original message in your reply helps the recipient see how your reply is related to the original message. Indenting the text or preceding it with a prefix character helps the recipient determine which text is from the original message and which is new. You should consider both indenting and adding a prefix character throughout the text of the original message when you are commenting or responding to the message.

Reply messages formatted with all three of the options checked will look something like Figure 6-6 on the next page. The original header is shown, as well as the text of the message. If you could scroll down, you would see that the initial message has been included. It is indented, and each line is preceded with the greater than symbol (>), as specified in the options.

Notice that the sender of the original message is already in the To line, just as you would expect with a reply in Outlook. However, if you didn't tap Reply All, you might not see the Cc or Bcc lines, and thus can't immediately add recipients to these fields. To display these lines, tap the down-pointing chevron (double V) in the lower right corner of the header. This expands the message header to display the missing fields. Figure 6-7 on the next page shows the same message with the header expanded.

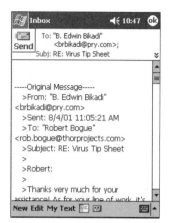

Figure 6-6   *Not all of the original message fits on the screen, but all of it is included in the reply message.*

Figure 6-7   *An expanded header takes up more room.*

To add recipients, tap the line you want them included in (To, Cc, or Bcc), and then type their e-mail addresses. You can also tap the To, Cc, or Bcc line, and then tap the Contacts button at the bottom of the screen. (The Contacts button is to the left of the Tape button.) A list of contacts and their e-mail addresses will appear on the screen. Tap the names of the people to whom you want to send the message. Another option is to tap the Search box in the Contacts dialog box and then enter part of a name. The resulting list of contacts will contain only those contacts whose names contain those letters. Figure 6-8 shows an example of this. When you're done, tap the Contacts button again to close the Contacts list.

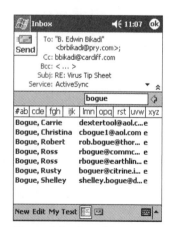

Figure 6-8   *Searching is an easy way to find the name you want.*

You can hide the header by tapping the upward-pointing chevron. This creates a little more space in which you can write your response to the message. When you're done writing your reply, tap the Send button in the upper left corner to send the message. If you need to discard the reply, tap the OK button in the upper right corner.

Forwarding a message is identical to the process just described, with one exception. When you reply to the original message, the Inbox application places the original sender's name and e-mail address in the To field. However, you can forward a message to anyone, not just those included in the original mailing. So when you tap the forward button, the To line is left blank. (This is true when forwarding in Outlook as well.)

Moving to a Folder

After you're done with a message, you probably want to get it out of your way. At least, that's the way I am when I'm done working on a message. I try to keep my Inbox clear of all messages except those I haven't finished working on.

Moving an open message to a folder is simple. On the Edit menu, tap Move to display the Move To dialog box shown in Figure 6-9. Then select the message's destination folder. A plus sign to the left of a folder name means the folder contains subfolders, as in Outlook. When you've selected the destination folder, tap the OK button.

Even if you're not reviewing a message, you can tap and hold a message you want to move from the Inbox. When you tap and hold a message, the shortcut menu that appears has the same Move To command that appears on the Edit menu when the message is open. Figure 6-10 shows the shortcut menu for an Inbox message.

Figure 6-9 *Select the destination folder for the message in the Move To dialog box.*

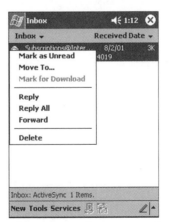

Figure 6-10 *The message's shortcut menu also contains the Move To command.*

Deleting

If the message you are reading is spam—sometimes the filters in Outlook 2002 don't catch them all—you'll want to delete the message. Deleting a message from either the Inbox or the message window itself is simple.

In the Inbox, tap and hold the message as I explained in the previous section. (Figure 6-10 shows the shortcut menu.) Tap Delete on the shortcut menu to immediately delete the message.

When you have a message open, you can tap the Delete Message button on the toolbar to delete that message. The Delete Message button is a small envelope with a red X in the lower right corner.

The settings in the Inbox Options dialog box (shown earlier in Figure 6-5) control what happens when you delete a message. To display these settings, on the Tools menu, tap Options, and in the Inbox Options dialog box, tap the Message tab. The settings control whether the next or previous message is displayed after you delete a message, or whether you return to the Inbox's message list. Often it's more convenient to redisplay the message list so that you can see the other messages in the folder.

You can also choose whether items in your Deleted Messages folder are deleted automatically, deleted the next time ActiveSync connects, or deleted manually by you. Because it's easy to accidentally tap the Delete Message button, I recommend that you do not allow messages to be deleted automatically. But manually emptying your Deleted Items folder seems like overkill in the other direction. E-mail that you don't want will eventually fill up the memory on your Pocket PC, so I recommend that you select the Empty Deleted Items On Connect/Disconnect option. That way, deleted items will be deleted periodically but not automatically.

Sending Messages

In this section, I'll cover sending messages that aren't related to a previous message. Along the way, I'll cover some of the Inbox options that help you get the most out of your Pocket PC.

Starting the Message

To start a message, tap the New button in the Inbox. A blank message screen, shown in Figure 6-11, appears. From here you can type the e-mail address of the person to whom you'd like to send an e-mail, or you can open the Contacts list by tapping the Contacts button, as I explained in the section on replying to a message.

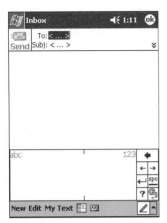

Figure 6-11   *A blank message screen.*

Adding a Standard Message

Because inputting text on a Pocket PC is so difficult, a feature called My Text enables you to create strings of frequently used text that can be inserted quickly into your e-mail message. To modify these text strings, on the Edit menu, tap Edit My Text.

You can have only ten text messages in the My Text Messages dialog box, shown in Figure 6-12. To edit a message, tap it, and then edit the message in the text box. When you're finished editing the message, tap OK to continue.

Figure 6-12   *You can create simple messages quickly in the My Text Messages dialog box.*

To send a message with My Text, on the My Text menu, tap the message you want. For instance, if I wanted to send a message to my wife telling her that I'm running late, I would tap the subject line in the message header, tap the My Text menu, and finally tap the *I'm running late* message. Then I would put my wife's address in the To line of the message header and send her the message.

Note In an always-connected environment where you're expected to respond quickly, the My Text option is quite helpful, but the difficulty of managing these options makes the feature less valuable if you're not expected to respond immediately.

Attaching Voice Recordings

Having predefined text messages is a good first step, but the My Text menu holds only so many messages—it's not possible to have predefined text for every eventuality. In the interest of making it easy to communicate with others without a full-sized keyboard, you can also include a voice recording in an e-mail message.

To access this feature, tap the Cassette Tape button at the bottom of the screen, and then tap the Record button. To stop recording, tap the Stop button. Figure 6-13 shows the Voice Recorder interface for recording messages.

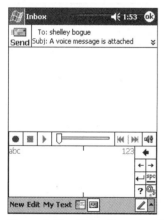

Figure 6-13 *Voice Recorder doesn't take up much space on the screen.*

After you record your message, you will see an attachment button in the message. (I'll address attachments in the next section.) This attachment contains the recording of your voice. The recipient can double-click the attachment in Outlook, and—if they have an audio card—they will hear your voice recording.

Voice recordings are particularly useful if you are in a time crunch and need to ask an administrative assistant to take care of several things for you. By using the voice recording feature, you can convey a lot of information in a short period of time.

To close the Voice Recorder interface, tap the Cassette Tape button on the toolbar again.

Attaching Files

Voice recordings are sent as message attachments, but they aren't the only kind of attachment that the Inbox supports. The Inbox enables you to send any file on your Pocket PC through e-mail. This means you can send the Pocket Word document you've been working on to your assistant to be formatted and printed, or to a colleague for review. However, as I mentioned previously, attachments are not converted by the ActiveSync file conversions, so you'll have to save the file in a format the recipient will be able to use. For Pocket Word, this is most often Microsoft Word format, but it might be Rich Text Format as well.

One file type you might send from your Pocket PC frequently is a JPG image file from a digital camera. In Chapter 4, I mentioned that you should select a digital camera that uses CompactFlash memory, because you can plug the CompactFlash card directly into your Pocket PC. From there you can review the images or forward them as attachments. Here's how to e-mail digital camera pictures from your Pocket PC:

1. Take the pictures with your digital camera.

2. Wait for the digital camera to finish copying the pictures to your CompactFlash card, and then turn the camera off.

3. Remove the CompactFlash card, and insert it in your Pocket PC.

4. Display your Inbox.

5. Open a new message form.

6. Enter the recipient's e-mail address and the subject of the message.

7. On the Edit menu, tap Add Attachment. The Add Attachment dialog box shown in Figure 6-14 on the next page appears.

8. Locate and tap the file you want to send from the list. My digital camera, a Kodak DC-260, stores the pictures it takes in the DC260_01 folder. Figure 6-15 on the next page shows the DC260_01 folder, which has a much shorter file list than the list in Figure 6-14. Figure 6-16 on the next page shows the message format.

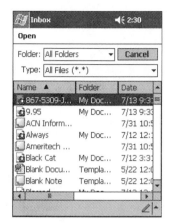

Figure 6-14 *The Add Attachments dialog box without a folder selected.*

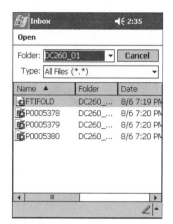

Figure 6-15 *The Add Attachments dialog box with a folder selected.*

Figure 6-16 *The attachment appears as an icon at the bottom of the message.*

9. Repeat Steps 7 and 8 for each file you want to attach.

10. Type a message to describe the pictures, and then tap Send.

Sending pictures as message attachments is simple, but there can be a few complications caused by newer digital cameras. Sometimes, trying to send multiple images in a single message also causes complications.

One complication is that Inbox makes a copy of the files to include in the message, using main memory. This isn't a problem unless you're attaching particularly large files that exceed the total amount of main memory available. Digital camera pictures are getting larger every year. The images are more detailed, and with that detail comes the need for more storage for each image. Newer cameras use in excess of 1 MB of memory per photo. It doesn't take long to fill your remaining memory if you are moving around several 1 MB images.

Another complication is that most e-mail systems have a maximum size they will accept for any given message. If you attempt to send too many photos in a single message, the message will be rejected, and you'll have to resend the files in smaller chunks.

Finally, if you use a slow connection, such as a dial-up phone line or wireless cellular network, it will take a long time to send the e-mail. When you send files, particularly photos from a digital camera, pay attention to how large they are. If you try to upload too much information, your Inbox might be prevented from synchronizing by accidental disconnections.

Tip You might want to check out tools that automatically resize images for you. One application is PQView, which you can learn about at *http://www.bitbanksoftware.com/ce /pocketview.htm*.

Spelling Checker

I can't spell. OK, I can spell, just not well. If it weren't for the Spelling Checker feature in Word and some wonderful editors, you might have trouble understanding what I'm trying to say. I can misspell the word 'I.' That's why I've become quite dependent on the Spelling Checker feature in e-mail and Word.

I hide my spelling deficiency behind some very good tools. In the most recent release of the Pocket PC operating system, the Inbox gained a Spelling Checker feature that had been noticeably absent from previous versions. Using Spelling Checker is quick and painless—just type the message you want to send. Figure 6-17 shows a message with many spelling errors in it.

When you've finished typing your message, on the Edit menu, tap Spell Check. If you have any spelling errors, Spelling Checker selects the word and displays a list of possible correct spellings. The list also enables you to ignore the misspelled word the first time it appears, or every time it appears, or to add it to the dictionary. Figure 6-18 shows an example of how Spelling Checker handles the misspelled word *the*.

Figure 6-17   *Friends don't let friends send messages like this.*

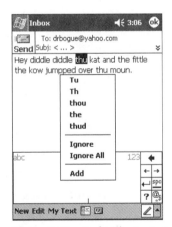

Figure 6-18   *Duh!* The *isn't spelled* thu.

After you've selected your action, Spelling Checker continues, highlighting other misspelled words. Occasionally, you might run into a situation where your spelling is so bad that the Spelling Checker feature can't figure out what you were trying to spell. When that happens, you won't see the correct word in the suggestion list, as shown in Figure 6-19 on the next page. You have two options: You can tap outside the suggested list window and cancel the spelling check, or you can ignore the word and fix it manually. If you choose to cancel the spelling check, the Inbox displays a message stating that the spelling check is not complete. If you continue the spelling check, the Inbox displays a message stating that the spelling check is complete. You can then fix any words that Spelling Checker couldn't recognize. Figure 6-20 on the next page shows the much improved e-mail message.

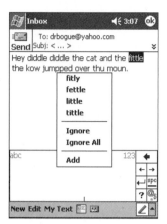

Figure 6-19 Fiddle *can't be spelled*
fittle *if you want Spelling Checker's help.*

Figure 6-20 *You can now see that*
this message is a nursery rhyme.

The Spelling Checker feature on the Pocket PC is a great help for people who can't spell and a good safety check for any important e-mail you're sending from your Pocket PC.

Summary

Sending e-mail with the Inbox application on the Pocket PC isn't quite as snazzy as Outlook 2002 on a computer, but it does the job. You can send, respond to, and forward messages; send attachments; and perform all the other critical functions you expect from an e-mail program.

I'll close this chapter with a few questions to help you think about how you can use the Inbox on your Pocket PC to be more productive:

- How much time do you waste waiting for meetings to start? How much time do you waste in meetings listening to things that don't pertain to you?

- How many e-mail messages do you get each day that don't require a response? How many require just a simple Yes or No answer?

- How many evenings have you been late getting home because you were catching up on e-mail you didn't get to because you were in meetings all day?

- How many times have you waited for people who had forgotten about the meeting and were working at their desks?

- How much more could you get done if you could dictate what you wanted your assistant to do and include a draft you've already created?

- How difficult is it to download and send pictures from your digital camera to your notebook?

Other E-mail Access

In the last chapter, I walked you through how to use the Inbox application on your Pocket PC with an ActiveSync connection. In this chapter, I'll cover other ways you can get e-mail and other information from your Microsoft Exchange mailbox while you're on the road.

I'll start with how to get e-mail from your Internet service provider or other services that provide Post Office Protocol version 3 (POP3) or Internet Message Access Protocol version 4 (IMAP4). (POP3 is the most common type of e-mail if you don't work with a Microsoft Exchange server.)

Next we will look at Web-based e-mail and how it differs from e-mail programs that are not Web-based. You might remember the section in Chapter 1 that explained Internet access points; they enable you to get e-mail while you are traveling so that you don't have to carry any devices. I'll explain Outlook Web Access, which is included with Microsoft Exchange Server. Outlook Web Access is a completely Web-based way to get your corporate e-mail.

I'll conclude this chapter with coverage of Microsoft Mobile Information Server. In the introduction, I mentioned that I was not going to cover mobile telephone products, except for the Microsoft Smart Phone. I'll break this rule because with Mobile Information Server, you can use your Web-enabled phone as an e-mail message reader and browser. Admittedly, viewing e-mail messages on a four-line screen can be a little tedious, but it's a good way to keep on top of urgent e-mail messages.

E-mail from Your Internet Service Provider

The trend with free e-mail services is to provide a Web interface to your e-mail. However, many Internet service providers (ISPs)—even those that also provide access to your e-mail messages through a Web interface—offer connectivity via POP3 and IMAP4 so that you can use the e-mail client on your computer or, in this case, your Pocket PC.

POP3, the older of the two standards, has been around longer than the Internet. It is a popular way to communicate and share messages. It is a relatively simple protocol that enables you to download all the messages in your mailbox at one time. It doesn't attempt to filter the content of the messages in any way.

IMAP4, on the other hand, is a newer protocol in which the header of the message—including the subject information and size—can be transmitted and reviewed before you download the entire message. You can control which messages are downloaded, because you can learn a little about a message before it is downloaded.

The distinction between IMAP4 and POP3 is that with IMAP4, you can control which messages you download. One of the big problems with POP3 is that if someone sends you a 2-MB spreadsheet, you have to download that spreadsheet before any other messages can come through. You must download it whether or not you intend to review it.

Large files aren't a problem when you have a fast connection at the office, but when you're in a rural area and you're barely holding onto a slow, dial-up Internet connection, even medium-sized file attachments can take an excruciatingly long time to download. If you should happen to get disconnected while downloading e-mail, you have to start all over. In some cases, this makes it impossible to download your e-mail.

Because most ISPs and e-mail services provide instructions for setting up and using ISP-based e-mail in your computer-based e-mail program, I won't show you how to do that. However, I will show you how to set it up and use it on your Pocket PC.

Setting Up Your E-mail Account

Setting up your POP or IMAP account involves five wizard pages, with another three pages if you want to change some of the advanced settings. After you complete the following steps, your Pocket PC will automatically send and receive e-mail whenever you are connected to the Internet. Here is the process to set up the account:

1. On your Pocket PC, open the Inbox. To do this, on the Start menu, tap Inbox, or press any hardware button you've mapped to launch the application. The Inbox application is shown in Figure 7-1.

2. On the Services menu, tap New Service. The E-mail Setup Wizard appears, as shown in Figure 7-2.

Note The E-mail Setup Wizard works a little differently for e-mail domain names for which Microsoft has configuration information. If you have Internet acess through a large, well-known ISP, these steps might be slightly different for you.

Figure 7-1 *The Inbox opens with ActiveSync.*

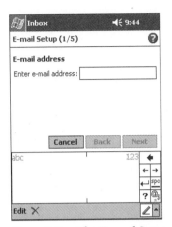

Figure 7-2 *The E-mail Setup Wizard contains five pages.*

3. Enter the e-mail address associated with this e-mail account.

4. Tap the Next button. The second page of the wizard is displayed, as shown in Figure 7-3.

5. If you want to cancel the configuration process, tap the Skip button. (With fast Internet connections, the process might finish before you get a chance to tap the Skip button.) During the configuration process, the Inbox determines the correct settings based on the e-mail address you provided.

6. Tap the Next button to continue. Figure 7-4 shows the User Information page of the wizard.

Figure 7-3 *Automatic configuration shouldn't take long.*

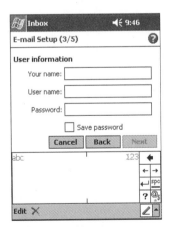

Figure 7-4 *You can use any name, including a nickname.*

7. Enter your name in the Your Name box. You can include your middle name if you like. The name you enter is the name people who receive messages from you will see.

8. Enter your user name and password for the e-mail system. This should be the information provided to you by your ISP. Generally, this user name is different from the user name you use to sign on to the service.

9. If you want to store your password on your Pocket PC so that you won't have to keep re-entering it, select the Save Password check box. For most people, the effort to re-enter their password each time isn't worth it.

10. Tap the Next button to display the fourth page of the wizard, shown in Figure 7-5.

11. In the Service Type box, choose the type of server you are contacting. If you are unsure what kind of service your ISP provides, it's generally safe to assume the service is POP3.

12. Enter the Internet name of the POP server. Generally, this will be *pop* followed by the Internet name of the provider.

13. Tap the Next button to display the final page of the wizard, shown in Figure 7-6.

Figure 7-5   *The service type is still POP for most providers.*

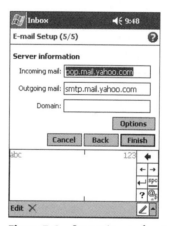

Figure 7-6   *Incoming and outgoing servers are normally named similarly.*

14. In the Outgoing Mail box, enter the outgoing e-mail server name.

15. If your e-mail server belongs to a Windows 2000 or Windows NT domain, enter the domain name in the Domain box.

16. Instead of tapping Finish, tap the Options button to display the Advanced Options Wizard. Although you can complete the setup from here, you will almost always want to change a few settings. Figure 7-7 shows the first step in setting the advanced options.

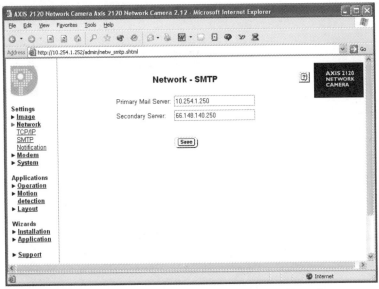

Figure 7-7 *The first page of the Advanced Options Wizard.*

17. On the wizard's first page, select the Check For New Messages Every check box, and then set the frequency to check for e-mail. If you don't want this server connected until you manually connect, make sure the Check For New Messages Every check box is cleared.

18. If your outgoing server (SMTP server) requires that you log in before you send e-mail, select the Outgoing E-mail Server Requires Authentication check box. Some e-mail servers require that you log in before sending e-mail to prevent them from being used to generate spam e-mail.

Note Most ISPs do not require authentication. They use other verification mechanisms to ensure they are not used to send spam e-mail. Spam e-mail is unwanted marketing information distributed to many e-mail users.

---

19. Tap the Next button to display the second page of the Advanced Options Wizard, shown in Figure 7-8 on the next page.

20. If you are using an IMAP server, tap the down arrow to the right of the Options box, and select either Get The Whole Message or Get Message Headers Only in the drop-down list. If you select the Include check box, make sure to type a number in the Include box to specify how much of the first part of the message will be downloaded with the header. These options have no effect if you are using a POP3-based e-mail server.

21. Tap the Next button to display the final page of the Advanced Options Wizard, shown in Figure 7-9.

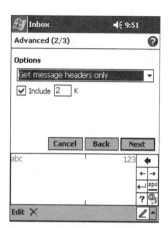

Figure 7-8 *These options work only with IMAP.*

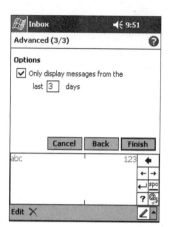

Figure 7-9 *Generally, you want to increase the number in the Days box.*

22. Clear the Only Display Messages From The Last check box. This will ensure that all your messages are retrieved. You can also increase the number of days for which messages are retrieved by changing the number in the Days box.

23. Tap Finish to return to the Inbox.

Now that you have set up your e-mail account, it's time to test it to make sure it is working. That's the topic of the next section.

Downloading Your E-mail

Downloading your e-mail is a quick and easy process after you've got your Pocket PC connected to the Internet. (I don't cover connecting to the Internet here, because it varies widely by device and provider.) Downloading your e-mail is done in three steps:

1. Connect your Pocket PC to the Internet. You can do this directly or through an ActiveSync connection to your Internet-connected computer.

2. Tap the Connect button at the bottom of the Inbox screen, to the right of the Services menu option.

3. Tap the Send/Receive button.

Reading and responding to your e-mail is identical to using the ActiveSync connection, except that you have to repeat the process just described whenever you want to send the messages you've written.

Outlook Web Access

In Chapter 1, I mentioned that by using Internet access points and Web-enabled or Web-based applications, you can travel and remain productive without needing to bring any devices with you. Outlook Web Access (OWA) provides complete access to your Microsoft Exchange Server mailbox, including e-mail, calendar, and contacts.

In addition to being able to access your Exchange mailbox while traveling, with OWA you can quickly check your e-mail while sitting at a co-worker's desk—or in another location. The speed and ease of OWA make it a great option when you don't want to configure a computer.

Note If you happen to be designing solutions for manufacturing shop floor needs, you might find that allowing staff to log into OWA to get their personal e-mail rather than setting up specific network profiles for them might be quicker and easier.

Most professionals are familiar with Outlook. Even if your organization doesn't use Exchange Server, because Outlook is included in Microsoft Office, you're probably familiar with it. OWA doesn't provide the same level of functionality as Outlook, but the interface will be familiar to users of Outlook.

Note The OWA software that shipped with Exchange Server 5.5 was a huge step forward, because it provided, for the first time, Web access to your Exchange mailbox. However, many interface quirks and limitations made it difficult for most users to get accustomed to it initially. Exchange Server 2000 dramatically improved the Outlook Web Access component. If your organization hasn't upgraded to Exchange Server 2000, you might want to do so, if for no other reason than to get the updated OWA client.

Outlook Web Access is bundled with Exchange Server, and can be installed on any server running Microsoft Internet Information Services. In other words, any server running Windows 2000 with the Web Services component installed can be an OWA server.

Note It is strongly recommended by the computer industry that you use a Secure Socket Layer (SSL) connection to your Web server. This is particularly important when your e-mail server isn't the same as your Web server. Because your password must be transmitted in plain text when Exchange Server and the Web server are not installed on the same server computer, use SSL to encrypt this information. SSL connections are prefixed with *https://* rather than *http://*. If you need a refresher on encryption and security practices, refer to Chapter 3.

In the following sections, I will show you how to log on to OWA and create messages using OWA.

Logging On to Outlook Web Access

Logging on to OWA is nearly as simple as pointing your browser to the correct Web server and location. When you point your Web browser to OWA, you might be prompted for your password, depending on how the administrator set up the system. A prompt for a password looks something like Figure 7-10.

Figure 7-10   *OWA uses standard http authentication.*

If you are not prompted for a password, your system administrator has configured OWA to accept your Windows logon as your authentication for OWA as well. This can be problematic if you're trying to log on to your e-mail account from someone else's desk. If this happens, the only way to get OWA to display your e-mail account is to provide your user name and password in the URL.

Usually, URLs for Web traffic are formatted like this:

http://<server>/<path>

Note You should be using an *https://* prefix for an SSL connection. In these examples and figures, we're accessing OWA on an intranet and therefore not using an SSL connection.

If you want to connect to your account rather than the account of the person whose computer you are using, format the URL like this:

http://<username>:<password>@<server>/<path>

The problem with using this form of the URL is that it exposes your password to anyone who might be looking over your shoulder, or who might look in the Internet Explorer history. However, if you substitute an asterisk (*) for your password, Internet Explorer will prompt you for the password. For instance, if my user name is *rbogue*, the server is *gemini*, and the path for OWA is the default path of */exchange,* the URL would be:

http://rbogue:*@gemini/exchange

Admittedly, this URL is messy, but it enables you to log on to your mailbox from someone else's terminal, and it doesn't display your password.

One final note: As soon as you log on, OWA will determine which browser you are running and download ActiveX components to it. This might take a while if you have a slow connection. Be prepared to wait a bit the first time you use OWA from a new computer.

Reading Messages

The Inbox is the first screen in OWA. It displays unread messages, which appear in bold, and any previously read messages still in your Inbox. Figure 7-11 shows my Inbox in OWA. I keep only pending items in my Inbox, so the list of items is short. When your list is long, you can move between pages of messages.

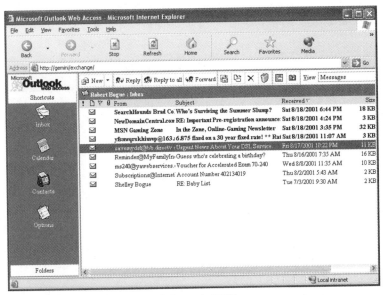

Figure 7-11   *My Inbox viewed through OWA.*

To read a message, double-click it in the pane on the right side. This will open a new window with the message displayed in it. Figure 7-12 on the next page shows one of my messages in its own window.

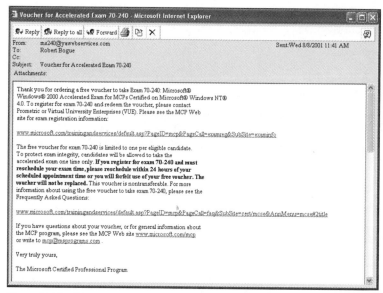

Figure 7-12   *Every message opens in its own window.*

The scroll bar on the right side of the window enables you to read further down in the message. The icons and buttons work the same as in Outlook. For instance, if you click the Move To Folder button, a dialog box like the one shown in Figure 7-13 appears, which enables you to move your message into another folder, just as you would in Outlook.

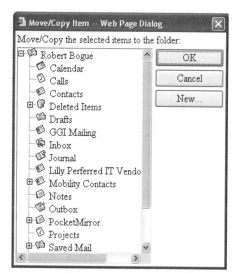

Figure 7-13   *The Move dialog box performs the same function as Outlook's Move dialog box.*

The Reply, Reply All, and Forward buttons work the same way they do in Outlook. They enable you to send the current message either to the originator or to a third party. That's the subject of the next section.

Sending Messages

The easiest way to send a message, as with any e-mail system, is to reply to a message that has been sent to you. This can be done with the Reply, Reply All, and Forward buttons. You can also send a message by clicking the New Message button on the main OWA screen, shown earlier in Figure 7-11.

After you have a new window open for your message (as shown in Figure 7-14), you need to make sure that the message is addressed correctly. If you clicked Reply in an existing message, the proper recipient is probably already set up for you. If you're sending a new message, there are two ways to address it. One way is to type the recipient's name or e-mail address directly into the To, Cc, or Bcc fields. You can also click the To, Cc, or Bcc buttons to display the Find Names dialog box as shown in Figure 7-15 on the next page.

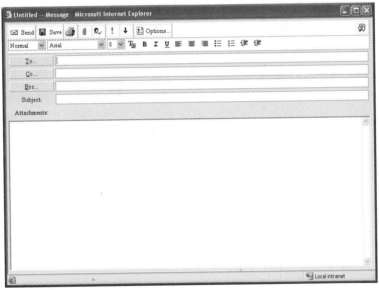

Figure 7-14   *A new message is much like a blank page.*

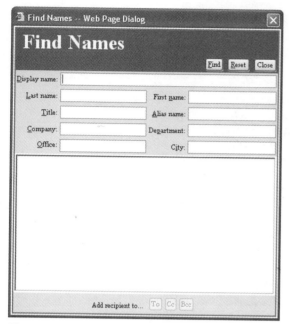

Figure 7-15   *It's easy to search for a contact.*

In the Find Names dialog box, you can search the Microsoft Exchange directory and your Contacts folders for names and e-mail addresses. You'll notice that this differs from the regular Outlook client, which displays your Contacts list automatically when you open it. To conserve bandwidth, OWA doesn't populate this list.

After you've entered search criteria in the text boxes, click the Find button to search all your contacts and display the results. Figure 7-16 shows the results of a search for my own contact record.

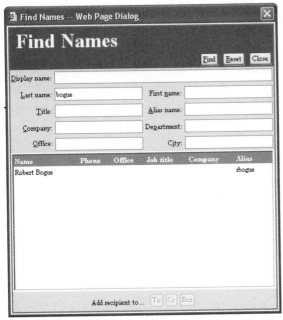

Figure 7-16 *Search for* bogue, *and you find a Bogue.*

To add the results of your search to the To field of your new message, click the name you want in the Results list, and then click the appropriate Add Recipient To button at the bottom of the dialog box.

The second step in creating your message is adding the content of the message. The main text box in the new message form is for your content. In fact, if you started your message by clicking Reply in the original message, the content of the original message appears in the main text box.

The OWA client also supports the addition of attachments. To add an attachment, click the Attachment button on the toolbar at the top of the window. This opens the dialog box shown in Figure 7-17 on the next page.

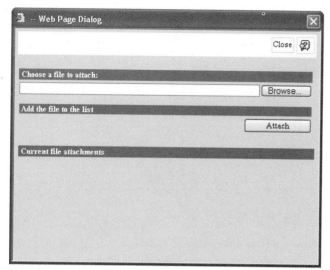

Figure 7-17   *You can add attachments through this dialog box.*

To add an attachment, in the first text box, type the name of the file you want to attach, or click the Browse button to find the file, and then click the Attach button.

When you're done, click the Send button. This will send your message immediately; you do not need to perform a separate send and receive process because you're already connected to Exchange Server.

Using Other Mailbox Folders

Although this chapter is focused on e-mail, it would be a shame not to mention that you can also view your calendar and contacts with OWA. To display your contacts, click the Contacts icon in the Shortcut bar. To change how the main Contacts list appears, click the down arrow to the right of the View box, and then select the view you want from the drop-down list. Figure 7-18 shows the Contacts list sorted by company.

The biggest difference between OWA and Outlook with regard to contacts is that in OWA, the listings are divided into pages, so only so many contacts can be seen on each screen. To navigate between pages, click the double arrows on either side of the Page box, or type a new number in the Page box itself.

Accessing your calendar is also easy: Click the Calendar icon in the Shortcut bar to display it as shown in Figure 7-19. You can choose other views by clicking the buttons corresponding to different calendar views on the toolbar.

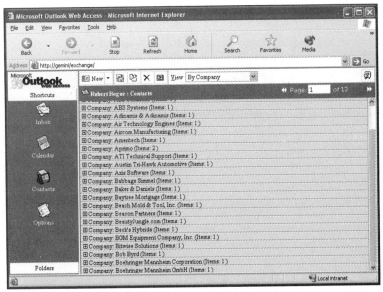

Figure 7-18 *A number of different views are available.*

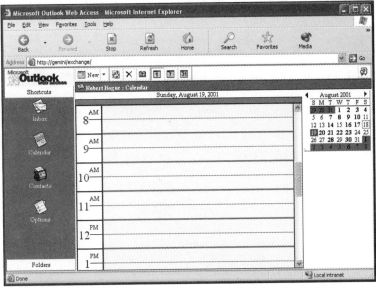

Figure 7-19 *I don't have any appointments scheduled for Sunday.*

In addition to providing a quick way to access your e-mail, contacts, and calendars, OWA makes it easy for you to work with your personal information even when you don't have a digital device available. OWA also allows access to notes, tasks, and all of the other personal information in your Exchange mailbox.

Microsoft Mobile Information Server

People might choose to leave notebooks and even Pocket PCs at home, but most people wouldn't travel today without a mobile phone. Internet-enabled phones aren't great for every need, but they can address some basic information access needs.

Microsoft Mobile Information Server (MIS) provides two basic functions that are critical if you want to use your mobile phone as a digital information access device while traveling. They are:

- **Accessing and translating content**   MIS acts as an intermediary capable of translating information into a form that can be displayed on your mobile phone.

- **Guaranteeing delivery**   MIS can communicate directly with your telephone service provider to guarantee that messages are delivered to your phone.

Let's explore the content features first, because they are similar to those of our previous topic, Outlook Web Access.

Accessing and Translating Content

Compared with a computer or even a Pocket PC, the display capabilities of a typical Web-enabled phone are paltry. With four lines and 20 characters per line, most phones display less information than is displayed in one line on a computer. Still, they have the advantages of their built-in connection and light weight.

Note When I say *Web-enabled phone,* I am not referring to Microsoft Smart Phones. Smart Phones can use MIS, but they don't need it because they are able to read regular Web pages written in HTML. They also have larger screens.

The other challenge with Web-enabled phones is that most of them don't use the Hypertext Markup Language (HTML) that most Web browsers use. They use a language called Wireless Markup Language (WML). This difference, coupled with the differences in screen size, makes developing applications for Web-enabled phones very difficult.

MIS helps to simplify these differences and makes it possible for your Web-enabled phone to display Web sites it ordinarily wouldn't be able to display.

Outlook Mobile Access

The best example of this technology is bundled with MIS. Outlook Mobile Access (OMA) is similar in functionality to Outlook Web Access, but on a smaller scale. Figure 7-20 shows what OMA looks like when viewed through Microsoft Mobile Explorer Emulator. Microsoft Mobile Explorer Emulator is available from the Microsoft Web site (*http://www.microsoft.com*), and it enables you to see what sites look like on your mobile phone without having to use your airtime to look at them.

Logging on to your Exchange mailbox might be difficult, depending on your familiarity with your phone's method for entering text and the complexity of your password. MIS enables you to create a separate account from a Web-enabled phone. This account can have a different password than your main account—one that can be more easily entered on a mobile phone. However, establishing a separate account for logon isn't a requirement of the installation.

Open your Inbox by selecting it from the list. A partial listing of your Inbox messages, their subjects, and their senders will appear on your phone, as shown in Figure 7-21. You'll notice that the subject is greatly shortened, as is the sender's e-mail address. Hopefully, you'll still be able to determine enough about the message to decide whether you want to read it.

To read a message, select it from the list. The options in the lower part of the message enable you to move to another section of the message. Return to the Inbox by clicking the Back button, shown at the top of the message in Figure 7-22.

Figure 7-20   *The Outlook Mobile Access main menu is simple.*

Figure 7-21   *Because of the small screen, not much of the sender's e-mail address or the subject fits.*

Figure 7-22   *It can take a while to view a long message on your phone.*

You can view the other features, including your calendar and contacts, in a way that is similar to the way you review e-mail. These features are skillfully designed, but have little space in which to display information. Some tasks, such as searching for contacts, are difficult to master because of the difficulty most users have entering text on the keypad

Other Content Translation

If your system administrator turns the appropriate option on, you can also use MIS to access corporate intranets and other Web-based applications. Admittedly, the translation isn't perfect; but it does enable you to get some basic functionality out of the corporate intranet from your Web-enabled mobile phone.

Content translation works best with a very simple page that displays only the information that you need. For instance, a page that contains the number of new orders entered that day would be well suited to this technology. Simple informational screens are translated appropriately by MIS without any special work.

MIS is more than just a gateway to your Exchange mailbox from your mobile phone. It's an entire platform to make the development of wireless applications easier.

Guaranteeing Delivery

Most Web-enabled phones also have a messaging feature that enables them to receive short text messages. This service is similar to an alphanumeric paging service. Generally, these messages can't be longer than 140 characters or so, but most providers guarantee these messages will be delivered after they are processed by the system.

Note If you're not interested in the details of how messages get to your phone, you can skip ahead to the next section. I've included this coverage here because most of us have missed a message we wish we hadn't.

Historically, there have been three ways to get messages to a person's wireless phone and alphanumeric pager: the Telocator Alphanumeric Protocol (TAP), Simple Mail Transport Protocol (SMTP), or a proprietary solution.

Of these three solutions, only the proprietary and TAP solutions provide guaranteed delivery to the service provider. Proprietary solutions are difficult to develop, because they require changing internal programs that need to be notified any time you change providers. TAP solutions work relatively well, but they require modems and analog phone lines that can be difficult to set up.

The SMTP transport gets messages to the provider, but because the connection is store-and-forward based, there's no guarantee that a message will be delivered. In other words, the message doesn't need to be delivered to its final destination directly. It can go through a series of relay points, where it is stored until it can be forwarded to the next relay point or the final destination. Further complicating things, there is no standard for how the SMTP messages are converted into mobile messages. Some providers include the sender's information in the message, and some don't. Some providers automatically break up a single long message into multiple messages, and some don't.

One of the goals of MIS is to provide verified and secure delivery of short messages. It does this by coming in two editions: Enterprise edition, which is installed by organizations; and Carrier edition, which is installed by mobile phone service providers. When MIS is installed at both locations, messages between the organizations and providers are verified and encrypted during transit. The messages are, therefore, guaranteed to reach the intended recipient as long as the providers guarantee delivery across their wireless networks. (Almost every provider in operation today does.)

If the service provider you are using doesn't have MIS installed, you can still use SMTP as a message delivery format for your short messages. Delivery isn't guaranteed, but the mechanism for sending messages doesn't change, whether you are using SMTP or communicating directly with a service provider that has Carrier edition installed.

Using Message Delivery

The preceding section focused on how MIS abstracts message delivery and attempts to provide verified delivery. What I didn't cover, however, is what information these messages might contain.

One example of a message you might receive would be a notification about an important e-mail message. MIS enables you to view your Exchange mailbox, but there is no other way to know when new e-mail has arrived.

Outlook Mobile Manager (OMM) uses MIS to deliver messages to your mobile phone based on the types of messages you identify as being important. After OMM is installed, it runs as part of Outlook and prompts you to identify messages when you move or delete them. This information is used to control when OMM will notify you that an important message has arrived. When an important message arrives, OMM prompts you to check your Exchange mailbox to see if the message requires your immediate attention.

Other uses for notification include updates from your corporate systems, including production problems, system processing errors, and any other type of corporate message that might require immediate attention.

Summary

In this chapter, I explained alternate ways of receiving your e-mail. Instead of using Active-Sync connected to a Pocket PC, I outlined how to get e-mail from ISPs, how to get e-mail without any devices, and how to get e-mail on a mobile phone.

It's possible to leave your devices behind and get your e-mail on the road using Internet access points or your Web-enabled mobile phone. With these options, you can stay in touch with your office and keep up with your e-mail.

As always, I'll end with a few questions for you to think about when you're planning your next trip:

- How many e-mail messages do you get that are truly urgent?

- Do you miss any of your messages when you travel?

- Do you feel out of touch while you're on the road?

- Are there private places with Internet connections you could use while traveling?

- Does your organization have systems in place so that when there is a problem, you know about it?

- How closely do you keep track of the orders and production information for your organization?

Instant Messaging

If you're a parent of a teenager, you might have already been introduced to instant messaging. Instead of asking to go over to a friend's house to watch TV, hundreds of thousands of children today are logging on to online services and "chatting" with their friends through instant messaging clients. The big advantage for these kids is that they can talk with half a dozen or so of their friends at the same time, so they don't have to decide whether they like Suzi or Jane better.

In addition to occupying a young adult's mind, instant messaging is useful for business challenges. This chapter is designed to show you when an instant messaging client on your computer or Pocket PC might be beneficial—and when it might not be. I'll start by briefly addressing the different forms of communication and some of their basic characteristics.

Note If you're fairly comfortable in your knowledge of when instant messaging is appropriate and want to get started using an instant messaging client, skip ahead to the "MSN Messenger" section.

Communication and Messaging

There is a very subtle difference between communication and messaging. Communication implies a two-way exchange of information and verification that the information was received. Messaging is one-way—it usually doesn't allow for verification that the message was received.

Speaking with someone face to face or on the telephone is clearly communication. You interact with the other person by answering their questions and indicating that you are receiving their messages by saying "yes" (or the more popular "uh-huh").

Sending a message to a pager, leaving a voice mail message, sending an e-mail, and sending a letter are all, technically speaking, forms of messaging. They transmit information in one direction. There is no confirmation that the person on the other end received the message.

In an attempt to make these messaging forms more useful, many companies have transformed messaging into rudimentary forms of communication. Some pagers now enable people to respond to the message with a few preset options. Other pagers now verify message delivery so that sent messages are not accidentally lost.

E-mail systems such as Microsoft Exchange Server can now provide a delivery receipt when a message is delivered and a read receipt when a message is read. These systems can't confirm that the recipient understood the message, but they can confirm that it was received.

Because messaging forms are becoming more and more like communication forms, you need to be able to quickly see how important a message is, whether you receive it through a traditional communication channel or from a newer messaging form.

Most business communication today is done though e-mail or voice mail. Although there is still a great deal of communication that goes on face to face or on the telephone, we are becoming increasingly dependent on messaging systems to connect with one another.

The challenge comes when we need to communicate an urgent message, and the other party isn't available. Let's say that a pregnant woman goes into labor. She might try calling her spouse on his office phone and not get an answer. She can't go to his workplace, because her first priority is to get to the hospital. What should she do? She could try to leave a message for him on his voice mail or send him an e-mail message, but leaving a message using these messaging systems won't ensure a rapid response.

Back in the late 1980s, when I first started implementing distributed e-mail systems, I told people to expect that their e-mail would be seen within 24 hours. That wasn't because the systems were slower back then; it was because e-mail is a non-urgent method of communication. You can reasonably expect someone to check his or her e-mail once or twice a day.

Voice mail is usually checked slightly more frequently; however, you're not likely to check your voice mail during a long meeting. Most likely, you'll check after the meeting ends.

There are sometimes cases, such as a spouse going into labor, that require an immediate response. For these needs, we have devices like cellular phones and pagers. With these devices, we can be reached instantly.

Although it's become common for business professionals to bring their cellular phones to meetings, cellular phones are necessarily disruptive. Even when set to vibrate, they can't be answered without speaking. Courteous business professionals walk out of the room. This is less intrusive than carrying on a conversation in the meeting room, but it's still distracting.

Pagers are certainly not as disruptive as cellular phones, but in most cases they don't allow any kind of a response to the sender, and delivery can be hit or miss. Some pagers have been known to miss messages altogether or to delay their delivery for minutes or hours. However, the fundamental problem with these devices is that they don't facilitate communication; they only deliver a message. Even devices that provide response options might not provide the kind of response that the recipient needs to send.

When used in a wireless LAN environment, the instant messaging clients offer solutions to many of the problems inherent in communicating urgent messages. Most instant messaging clients provide confirmation of receipt. If the recipient is online, he or she receives it immediately. You don't have to worry that delivery will fail or be delayed.

Note One of the biggest ways that messaging clients differ from each other is how they handle a message sent while the recipient is offline.

Instant messaging clients also offer a mechanism that isn't necessarily disruptive. If the messaging client is used on a Pocket PC with the sound turned off, when a message is delivered, the messaging light on the Pocket PC blinks.

Finally, instant messaging clients enable your recipient to respond. This means you can send information to the recipient and receive the answer you need quickly, without disturbing others.

The key to ensuring that instant messaging clients add value without interrupting important meetings is using them only for truly urgent messages.

Instant Messenger Basics

Although each instant messaging system enables you to do slightly different things and has a slightly different interface, they all have some basic similarities. A few of these similarities are listed here:

- They are designed for short messages. Their input boxes will accept only limited amounts of text. You cannot send *War and Peace* in one message.

- They enable you to choose whether you're visible to other users.

- They enable you to indicate whether you are busy, away, available, and so on. Some of them enable you to set your own status messages. AOL Instant Messenger is an exception; it does not support status messages.

- When you send a message, a window on the recipient's computer opens, displaying your message and a place to type a response.

- A connection to the Internet is required. It enables you to communicate with all users on the Internet, not just those on your local network. MSN Messenger is an exception when it is used with Exchange Server.

In the next three sections, I'll review the three most popular messaging systems available for the Pocket PC: MSN Messenger, Yahoo! Messenger, and AOL Instant Messenger. Each of these messaging systems can run on a desktop computer as well. This means someone can send a message from a desktop computer to your wireless Pocket PC, and you can send a response.

Note For the moment, there are no bridges between these services. Each service runs independently of the others. Although there are some clients for desktop computers that will log into more than one service, there are no similar clients for Pocket PCs. You have to decide which instant messaging clients you want to use. You will be able to communicate only with people who use the same systems you use.

MSN Messenger

Of the three messaging clients, MSN Messenger is uniquely positioned for use in a corporate environment. MSN Messenger enables the user to communicate over the Internet or on a corporate network using Exchange Server's Instant Messaging services. This is perfect for organizations that want to take advantage of instant messaging but don't want employees to send instant messages outside the organization.

The other helpful feature unique to MSN Messenger is that it can be used to send messages to other types of mobile devices. In other words, if someone doesn't have a wireless Pocket PC, you can send a message to his or her cellular phone or pager. In most cases, the recipient won't be able to respond to the message, but it does make it easy to contact him or her if you need something urgently.

Note The Pocket PC client cannot yet send a message to a mobile device; it's limited to sending instant and e-mail messages to an e-mail address. However, the desktop computer version sends messages to cellular phones or pagers.

The next few sections take you through signing in, adding a contact to your MSN Contacts list, and sending a message.

Signing In

MSN Messenger uses the information in your Microsoft Passport to sign you in to the system. The Passport system is an authentication mechanism that Microsoft is encouraging Web sites to use instead of maintaining user information on each individual site. The idea is to have one user name and password for all the resources you want to access on the Internet.

Note At the moment, only a limited number of organizations other than Microsoft are using the Passport authentication method. However, the .NET platform for Web site development encourages the use of Passport authentication information rather than internal authentication systems. It's likely that when Web sites are redesigned to support the .NET infrastructure, they will shift toward using Passport authentication.

If you don't have a Passport already (or don't know whether you have one), sign in to MSN Messenger from your computer rather than your Pocket PC. The MSN Messenger client for the computer enables you to create a Passport if you don't already have one. The following steps show you how to sign in from a computer running Microsoft Windows XP.

Note Windows Messenger is included with Windows XP. This is the MSN Messenger client for Windows XP. If you have an earlier version of the operating system, you might need to download the MSN Messenger client. The easiest way to do this is from Windows Update. You can select Windows Update from the Tools menu of Internet Explorer, from your Start menu, or by entering the URL *http://windowsupdate.microsoft.com* in your browser.

---

1. On your computer, start MSN Messenger. You'll see a screen similar to the one shown in Figure 8-1. It's essentially the "Welcome to the Wizard" page that more and more applications are using.

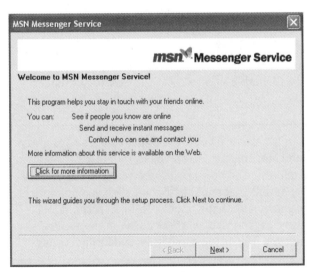

Figure 8-1 *Welcome to MSN Messenger.*

2. Click the Next button. The Get A Free Passport page is shown in Figure 8-2 on the next page.

   If you already have an MSN Internet or Hotmail account, you also have a Passport. Because having a Passport is still relatively uncommon, I'll go through the steps of creating one here.

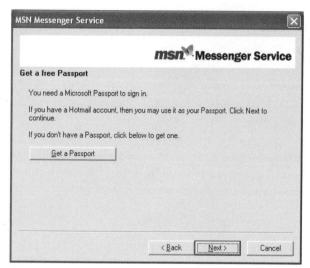

Figure 8-2   *You must have a Passport to use MSN Messenger.*

3. Click the Get A Passport button. The window that appears enables you to create a Hotmail account and a Passport, as shown in Figure 8-3.

4. If you don't want to create a Hotmail account, click the Try This Instead link. This will take you to a similar page that will enable you to use your existing e-mail address as the basis of the Passport.

Tip It's wise to create a Hotmail account to conceal your real e-mail address. This gives you another level of anonymity—a good idea, particularly if you routinely enter chat rooms. You can give out your Hotmail address, and no one will know where in the country you live, what ISP you use, or any other details that might help them steal your identity or stalk you. The amount of information you must provide to get a Hotmail account and a Passport is relatively small. You can also clear the last two check boxes on the account signup page. Clearing these will prevent you from being listed in the public directories.

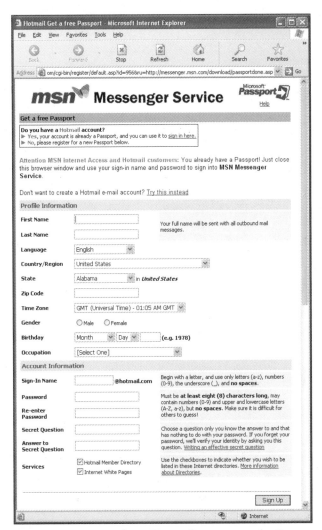

Figure 8-3   *Sign up for a Hotmail account and a Passport at the same time.*

5. When you're finished filling out this form, click the Sign Up button to create your Hotmail account and your Passport. After a few seconds, a window that confirms your Hotmail and Passport account appears. Close this window and return to the MSN Messenger Wizard. A prompt for your Passport information appears, as shown in Figure 8-4, on the next page.

6. Select the Remember My Name And Password On This Computer check box so that you won't be prompted for your password every time you log on to MSN Messenger.

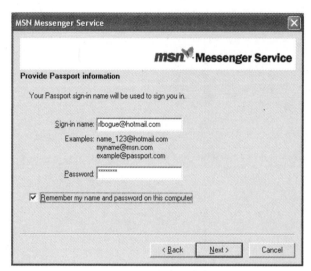

Figure 8-4   *Your Passport ID is your e-mail address.*

7. When you're finished entering your Passport information, click the Next button to move to the final page. This page is your confirmation that you have set up the MSN Messenger service.

8. Click the Finish button to start MSN Messenger and log on with the Passport ID you entered in the previous page. Your MSN Messenger screen will look similar to Figure 8-5.

Figure 8-5   *MSN Messenger displays your name as well as your contacts, if any.*

After you have completed these steps on your computer, you can move to your Pocket PC:

1. On your Pocket PC's Start menu, tap Programs. On the Programs menu, tap MSN Messenger. As soon as you start MSN Messenger on your Pocket PC, you'll see a screen similar to the one shown in Figure 8-6.

2. Tap the Tap Here link on the screen to display the logon screen, shown in Figure 8-7. This screen, like the one for the desktop computer, is where you enter your Passport ID.

3. Enter your Passport ID and password, and then tap the Sign In button. There will be a brief delay during which the Pocket PC logs on to MSN, and then a screen similar to the one you saw for the computer will appear. Figure 8-8 shows the MSN screen on a Pocket PC.

Figure 8-6 *The Pocket PC MSN Messenger client has an appealing interface.*

Figure 8-7 *Signing in is as easy on the Pocket PC as on the computer.*

Figure 8-8 *The MSN Messenger screens for the computer and the Pocket PC are similar.*

Note You can be logged on to MSN from only one location. If you log on from your Pocket PC while you are still logged on to MSN from your desktop computer, your computer will be disconnected, unless you have a separate Passport account for your Pocket PC.

The next step is adding contacts to your MSN Contacts list.

Note If you're interested in add-ons to MSN Messenger, you might want to check out *http://www.patchou.com/msgplus/*.

Adding Contacts

If you know the e-mail address your colleague uses for his or her Passport, the process of adding a contact is relatively simple:

1. On the Tools menu, tap Add A Contact to display the Add A Contact screen, shown in Figure 8-9.

2. Enter the contact's e-mail address, and tap Next. If the contact information is added successfully, a screen like the one shown in Figure 8-10 appears. If the addition fails, a screen like the one shown in Figure 8-11 appears.

Figure 8-9   *The Add A Contact screen requires only the Passport ID.*

Figure 8-10   *A successful contact addition screen.*

Figure 8-11   *A failed contact addition screen.*

After you have added a contact, his or her name and status appears on the main screen, as shown in Figure 8-12. Regardless of whether the contact is online or offline, his or her name always appears in your Contacts list.

Figure 8-12   *Contacts appear in the Contacts list whether they are online or offline.*

Sending Messages

Sending a message to a contact is easy. Click his or her name in the Contacts list, and a screen like the one shown in Figure 8-13 appears. You need only type your message and click the Send button. The message will be displayed immediately on the recipient's screen.

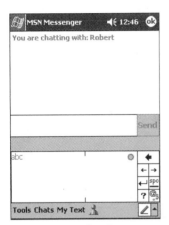

Figure 8-13   *The chat screen is not complicated.*

If someone sends you a message on your Pocket PC, a message box appears from the title bar, as shown in Figure 8-14. If you ignore the notification long enough, the message box will disappear; however, as is shown in Figure 8-15, the MSN icon will remain on the title bar to let you know there is a pending message for you. You can retrieve the message by tapping the MSN Messenger icon.

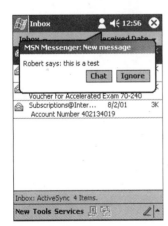

Figure 8-14   *Messages sent to you appear over whatever application you are running.*

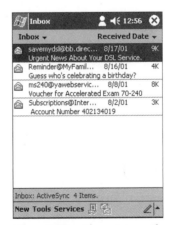

Figure 8-15   *If you ignore the message long enough, the message box disappears, but the icon stays.*

Tip To change how MSN Messenger notifies you when you receive a message, on the Start menu, tap Settings, and then tap Sounds And Notifications. In the Sounds And Notifications dialog box, click the Notifications tab. By default, MSN Messenger displays an icon but does not turn on the message notification light. For more information on changing sounds and notifications, refer to Chapter 11.

To ignore the message, click the Ignore button. To initiate a chat session, click the Chat button. The chat screen appears as shown in Figure 8-13. (Yours will contain the message that you received.) Further messages will be displayed in the chat screen, and the MSN Messenger icon won't appear as long as you keep the chat screen open.

Using My Text to Send Messages

Pocket PCs don't have keyboards, so it's difficult to send even short messages quickly. To combat this, MSN Messenger includes a feature called My Text that enables you to send one of ten preset messages by selecting it from the My Text menu. Tap the message that you want, and the text is transferred to the Send box. Then all you need to do is tap the Send button.

To change your text messages, on the Tools menu, tap Edit My Text Messages to open a dialog box in which you can edit the messages.

Changing your Status

To change your status so that it indicates that you're not available, tap and hold your name at the top of the MSN Messenger screen. A status menu appears, as shown in Figure 8-16. From this menu, you can set your status, and it will be visible to other users of MSN Messenger. You can also set it to appear offline to other users. When you appear to be offline, you can see other people who are online, but they will not send you messages.

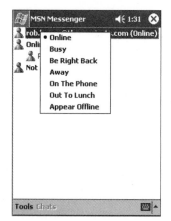

Figure 8-16 *A number of status settings are available.*

Conscientious use of the status setting can help you maintain your accessibility for critical messages and discourage frequent use of it for non-urgent issues.

Blocking and Inviting Users

Two other features of MSN Messenger bear mentioning. The first is the ability to block people you are chatting with from sending you any more messages. This isn't as powerful as limiting who can send you messages in the first place, but it can help you deal with annoying people who don't understand that you don't have time to chat.

The second feature is the ability to add someone to the conversation at any time. By tapping Invite on the Tools menu, you can add anyone else in your Contacts list to a conversation. This is useful when you need multiple people to see what you're saying, or when an associate asks you a question that you don't know the answer to and you want to consult a third party. You can add the appropriate person to the conversation, indicate what the problem is, and then bow out quickly by closing the messaging window.

Yahoo! Messenger

Yahoo! is probably as recognized a name as Microsoft, particularly in terms of Internet presence. One of the first Internet darlings, Yahoo! has diversified from its core search business into many other services, including a messaging client.

Yahoo! was one of the first messaging systems to store your Friends list on its server rather than on your local computer. Although today all three of the major messaging clients store your Friends list on a server, doing so wasn't popular when the messaging clients first came out. Yahoo!'s messaging client was also one of the first ones to work consistently behind firewalls. (Corporations use firewalls to protect corporate information and resources on their networks from unauthorized access from the outside.) Other clients had spotty coverage behind firewalls, but Yahoo! excelled in this capacity.

In addition to providing instant messaging services, Yahoo! Messenger enables you to view stock quotes, news, sports scores, and weather without leaving the messenger client. If you want more detail, tapping the appropriate link takes you right to the Yahoo! page and the information you're looking for. In this way, Yahoo! Messenger is more like a Web portal than a messaging client. It comes in handy when you want to make sure you're up-to-date with the latest news, or if you just want to make sure you won't need an umbrella.

In the next several sections I'll walk you through the process of downloading Yahoo! Messenger, creating an account, adding friends, sending messages, changing your status, and ignoring messages you don't have time for. These steps are similar to those for MSN Messenger, but they are different enough to warrant a detailed description of how to do them.

Downloading the Yahoo! Messenger Client

The first step is downloading the Yahoo! Messenger client. Unlike MSN Messenger, the Yahoo! Messenger client isn't installed by default on your computer or your Pocket PC. You must go to *http://messenger.yahoo.com* to download it. The upper left corner of the Web page has links to the download pages.

Yahoo! doesn't require a lengthy process for getting the downloads. After you click the link for your desired platform, you go immediately to a page where you are given instructions for the download and a link to download the files.

You should download both the computer version and the Windows CE (Pocket PC) version, even if you only intend to use the Pocket PC version. As was the case with the MSN Messenger client, it's easier to set up the client on a Windows computer first and sign in on the Pocket PC after the account is set up.

Creating Your Yahoo! Account

The Yahoo! Messenger client for Windows will walk you through the process of creating an account the first time you run it, but you might want to create your account while the client is downloading. Here are the steps:

1. Go to *http://edit.yahoo.com/eval_register*, and enter all the information necessary to create your Yahoo! account in the one-page form, shown in Figure 8-17.

   Unlike MSN Messenger, Yahoo! requires you to open an e-mail account. You can use this address as you would a Hotmail address—to maintain additional anonymity when surfing the Internet.

2. When you've entered all the information on the form, click the Submit This Form button. The next page that appears should be similar to the page shown in Figure 8-18, confirming the creation of your Yahoo! ID.

3. After the Yahoo! Messenger clients are downloaded, install them to the computer and Pocket PC. After you've installed the computer version, a wizard appears in which you can create a new ID.

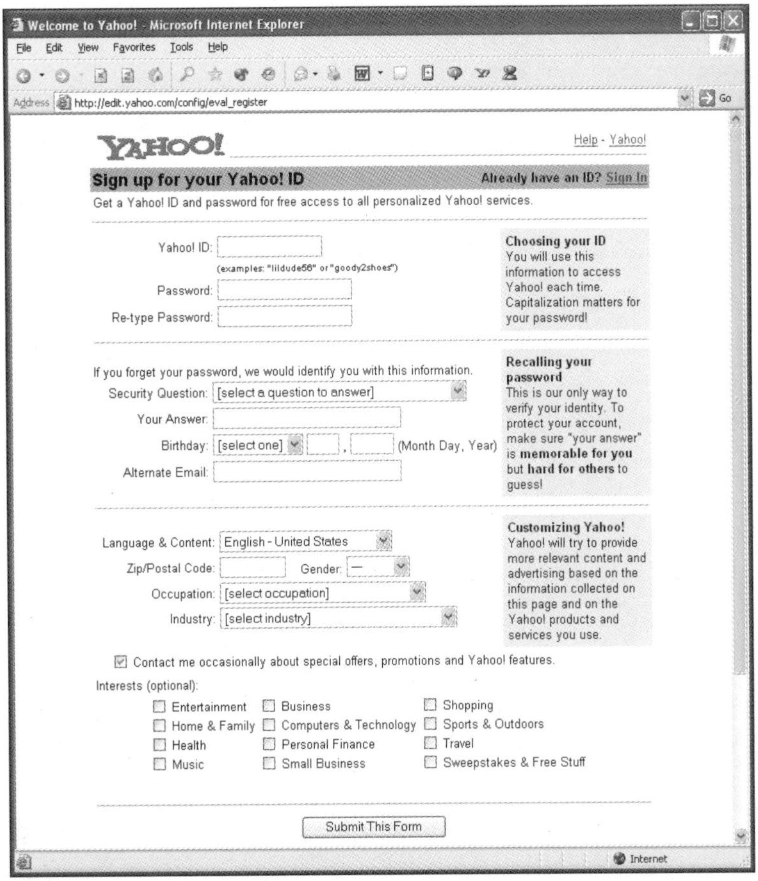

Figure 8-17   *Yahoo! requires less information than MSN to create an account.*

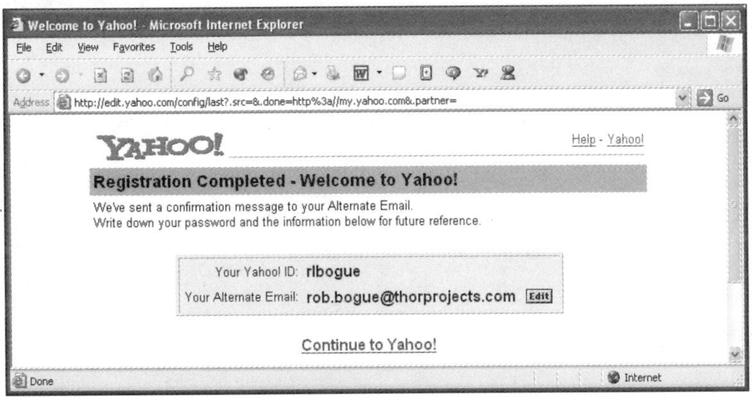

Figure 8-18   *Success is sweet.*

After you are signed in, you'll see a screen like the one shown in Figure 8-19.

Figure 8-19   *Yahoo! Messenger on a desktop computer always displays a contact you can message for help.*

The next step is adding friends to your list.

Adding Friends

Friends in Yahoo! Messenger are the equivalent of MSN Messenger's contacts. They appear in your main Yahoo! Messenger window. Unlike MSN Messenger, however, the list of names isn't divided into those who are online and those who are offline. You can tell which of your friends are logged on to the system by viewing the icon to the left of his or her name. When the icon is dimmed, the friend isn't online. When the smiley face to the left of a friend's name is yellow, he or she is online and available.

The process of adding a contact is similar for the Pocket PC and the desktop computer, with one exception: The Pocket PC does not enable you to search for the Yahoo! IDs of your friends. For this reason, let's walk through the process of adding friends from your computer:

1. Click the Add button located at the far right end of the toolbar. This displays the Add A Friend dialog box, shown in Figure 8-20.

2. Enter the Yahoo! ID of the person you want to add to your Friends list, and the group to which you want to add him or her. You can also search for people to add by clicking the Search For Friends button, which displays the Search For Friends window shown in Figure 8-21.

Figure 8-20 *Add a friend.*

Figure 8-21 *Find a friend, or make a friend.*

After you've added a friend, that person's name will appear in the list. Figure 8-22 shows a Friends list with drbogue in it. On the Pocket PC, the icon is yellow, which means drbogue is online.

Figure 8-22 *All friends are listed. Friends who are online have smiley-face icons to the left of their names.*

The next step is sending a test message to your friend.

Sending Messages

We're going to send a message from the Pocket PC, because the Yahoo! Messaging client has a feature that is quite helpful on systems that don't have keyboards. This feature enables you to send short, predefined messages. This is similar to the feature in MSN Messenger, but you cannot change the messages with Yahoo! Messenger as you can in MSN Messenger. However, you can follow along on your computer if you would like:

1. On the Start menu, tap Programs. Scroll down to the end of the Programs submenu, and then tap Yahoo! Messenger.

2. When you start Yahoo! Messenger for the first time, a sign-in screen similar to Figure 8-23 appears. Enter your Yahoo! ID and password. You might also want to select the Remember My ID And Password check box, so you don't have to enter it the next time you sign in.

3. After you're signed in, you'll see a screen that is almost identical to the one for the computer, except that there's no option for YahooHelper. To send a message to a friend who is online, double-tap his or her name in the list. This opens a chat screen for that person. Figure 8-24 shows a chat screen with drbogue.

4. If you're in a hurry, tap the down arrow to the right of the message box, and select one of the predefined messages in the drop-down list, as shown in Figure 8-25. Tap the message in the list to move it to the Send Text box, where you can edit it before you send it. These predefined messages are handy when you want to send someone a standard message (such as "Where are you?"), or you need to reply quickly.

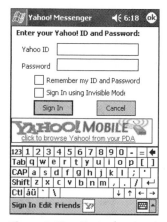

Figure 8-23   *Even the sign-in screen has an ad banner.*

Figure 8-24   *Chatting with drbogue.*

Figure 8-25   *Predefined messages make it easy to send a quick note.*

The messages your friends send you are displayed at the top of the screen, as you might expect. You can close your communication session by tapping the OK button in the upper right corner.

Changing your Status

With MSN Messenger, you are limited to a small number of predefined status settings. With Yahoo! Messenger, you have a larger list of predefined status settings and the ability to apply a custom message to your status. This is helpful if you want to transmit information other than just whether you are available.

For instance, let's say you're in a planning meeting in the H-105 meeting room. You might set your message to "H-105 Plan Mtg." This would let anyone who saw your status know what you're doing. Similarly, if you were performing employee reviews in your office, you could set your message to "Emp Rev/DND." That way, your co-workers will know not to disturb you unless the building is on fire. (Maybe you should just log off while you are doing employee reviews.)

To set your status, tap the down arrow to the right of the status box, and select a status setting in the drop-down list. Figure 8-26 shows the expanded status menu.

If you select Custom Message, the dialog box shown in Figure 8-27 appears, prompting you to specify how your status should be displayed. The computer version of Yahoo! Messenger enables you to display a busy icon instead of a regular icon, but the Pocket PC version does not.

Figure 8-26 *I'm always "Out to Lunch."*

Figure 8-27 *Your status message can be anything you like, but remember that everyone can see it.*

Note The Pocket PC version of Yahoo! Messenger has more than a few bugs when it comes to custom status messages. Be aware that your custom message might be missing or truncated when displayed on another user's screen. Hopefully, Yahoo! will resolve this problem soon.

Try to keep your status messages up to date and reflective of what you are doing.

Ignoring People

One of the less virtuous things we learn in business is how to politely ignore people. There is always a particularly troublesome person we must work with but don't generally have time for, so we often delay our responses to him or her until the last possible moment. Unfortunately, the more accessible you make yourself, the harder it is for you to politely ignore someone.

This is particularly true of people who are not co-workers but who continually harass you through instant messaging. Because instant messaging is designed to be accessible, it's difficult to prevent people from sending you messages you don't want—that is, it was difficult before the Ignore list.

To open Yahoo! Messenger's Ignore list, on the Edit menu, click Ignore List. The screen that appears is shown in Figure 8-28. With this feature, you can make sure only people in your Friends list (or another list you specify) can send you a message.

Figure 8-28   *You can ignore anyone.*

If you want to receive messages only from a very specific group of people, such as your immediate colleagues and boss, it might be appropriate to limit the people who can send you messages to those on your Friends list. However, if you want everyone by default to be able to send you messages and only those who are troublesome to be excluded, select the Ignore The People Below check box, and enter the names of the people you want to ignore in the box provided.

The beauty of the Ignore list is that you won't even be aware that people on the list are trying to reach you. Their messages are simply discarded. You don't have to delete an e-mail message or skip over a voice mail message; you simply won't see or hear anything about the message. I can't wait until this feature is available for my voice mail!

AOL Instant Messenger

AOL Instant Messenger (IM) is the largest messaging client network. Most of the teenagers who log in each night to chat with their friends do it through AOL's instant messaging client. Everyone with an AOL account is automatically signed in to the instant messaging system the moment that they log on to AOL. This means that the largest base of Internet users already has this messaging client.

However, most of my colleagues do not use AOL IM for their business instant messaging needs. Because AOL IM isn't a frequently used business instant messaging client, I'll limit this topic to a few of the points that are important when you're deciding whether to use AOL IM in a business environment.

Perhaps the greatest advantage of AOL IM is its ability to temporarily block someone on your Buddy list. This comes in handy if your colleagues don't get the hint that you don't want to be disturbed. You can unblock them later so that they can send messages to you again.

The greatest disadvantage is that you can't specify your current status, making it impossible for the person sending you a message to determine whether it's a good time to chat or to specify that a message is very important.

If you decide that you want to use AOL IM on your Pocket PC, you can download it from *http://www.aol.com*. Be aware that the Pocket PC version does not enable you to block or unblock Buddies; however, you can permanently ignore anyone you want.

Summary

Instant messaging can have a place in the corporate office if used wisely and appropriately. The use of instant messaging system status messages can help guide users toward understanding when messaging is appropriate and when it isn't.

MSN Messenger is included on your Pocket PC and has native support for Exchange Server's instant messaging server, enabling it to be used on the Internet, the local network, or both. This flexibility makes it a good choice when you don't necessarily want every user on the Internet to have access to you.

Yahoo! Messenger has been innovative in its solutions to common problems and implementation of technology. Although MSN Messenger has caught up with it, Yahoo! Messenger is still a strong player for business instant messaging.

Although AOL IM enjoys the largest installed base, its lack of basic features to inform others of your current status makes it a poor choice for business instant messaging.

You have a lot of choices to determine what instant messaging system you will use. The following are a few questions to prompt your thoughts about which solution might be right for you:

- Do you run Exchange Server for e-mail? Would it make sense to only enable instant messaging between employees?

- What messaging clients do the people you need to communicate with run?

- How important is minimizing meeting disruptions?

- Do you trust yourself and your peers to use instant messaging only when it's appropriate?

Personal Applications

Part III explores solutions to some of the problems you face while traveling, from opening and editing the documents from your office to getting driving directions and video surveillance.

Chapter 9 examines the Pocket PC versions of your favorite Microsoft Office applications. I'll cover the basics of editing and reviewing documents created using Office. I'll also review the limitations of moving documents to your Pocket PC.

Chapter 10 covers my personal favorite application. Driving directions always seem to be wrong, whether I get them from the person I'm going to meet or the person at the rental car counter. In this chapter, I show you the tools you can use to create your own directions and maps. I also explain Global Positioning Satellite (GPS) receiver technology and how it can be used to make getting where you want to go easier.

Chapter 11 expands your view of the Pocket PC by addressing audio capabilities and how they can be used both to entertain and to get work done from the road. I also show you the voice recognition features of Microsoft Office XP.

Chapter 12 addresses the programs and services that can be used to deliver news, information, and complete books to your desktop computer and Pocket PC.

Chapter 13 covers the options that you have for tracking your expenses and stock portfolio from your Pocket PC. Expenses are one of the tasks least favored by most mobile professionals; this chapter will help make it a little bit easier.

Chapter 14 shows you how digital video surveillance products can help you keep an eye on the office, or the house, while away. Video surveillance allows you to keep a record of who's been through your door, in your parking lot, or in your yard.

Pocket Office

Making information portable has always been a challenge; unless people were willing to cart their notebooks around, they couldn't access the information they created in even the standard Microsoft Office applications, let alone any third-party packages.

Microsoft Windows CE and the Pocket PC have changed that. Your Pocket PC gives you access to most of the documents you create in Microsoft Word or Microsoft Excel. With the addition of third-party software, you can work with your Microsoft Power-Point and Microsoft Project documents as well.

This chapter will cover Pocket Word and Pocket Excel. These two applications are included with the Pocket PC; you don't have to add anything to be able to use your Pocket PC to read the Word and Excel documents you create on your computer.

I'll also cover Pocket SlideShow by CNetX (*http://www.cnetx.com*) and outline how it can be used to display presentations from your Pocket PC rather than from your notebook. Finally, I'll take a look at cyProj and cyStat from cyWren Systems (*http://www.cywrensystems.com*), to see how these applications can be used in conjunction with Microsoft Project to manage project activity.

Pocket Word

As an author, project manager, and consultant, I have a special relationship with Microsoft Word. I spend about 75 percent of my computer time writing, editing, and reviewing in Word. The idea of having a version of Word I can take with me is particularly appealing. Pocket Word does not work well as an editing tool, though; it's primarily a tool for preparing blocks of text and reviewing documents.

> **Note** In Chapter 5, I addressed synchronization and file conversion. You'll remember that documents shouldn't be "round tripped," or sent from the computer to the Pocket PC and back again, because information is lost in the conversions. This is the primary reason Pocket Word doesn't make an effective editing tool, but there are other reasons too. I've listed them here.

I'll break down my exploration of Pocket Word into three sections: The first section addresses creating a new document, including the modes you can use to enter information. Next I'll explain how you can review and annotate existing documents. Finally, I'll explain the specific limitations of Pocket Word.

Creating New Documents

The first time you open Pocket Word, one of two screens will be displayed. If there are documents Pocket Word can read, the first screen will be a list of those documents. The document listing screen should look similar to Figure 9-1. If you don't have any documents on your Pocket PC that Pocket Word can read, the editing screen will be displayed. The editing screen is shown in Figure 9-2. If you have a document list displayed, you can create a new document and enter information by tapping New on the Word toolbar.

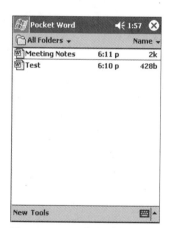

Figure 9-1   *A list of documents on your Pocket PC.*

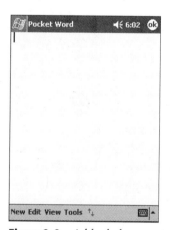

Figure 9-2   *A blank document.*

The blank document shown in Figure 9-2 is in Typing mode, one of Pocket Word's four modes. Typing mode is used for entering text with either an external keyboard or one of the character-recognition features built into the Pocket PC. In other words, you can enter text from the soft keyboard, as shown in Figure 9-2; the transcriber; the letter recognizer; or the block recognizer. Try them all, and see which method of entering data you like best.

Note The most convenient way to enter text is to use an external keyboard like the ones discussed in Chapter 4.

You can select font settings from the Edit menu or the Formatting toolbar. On the View menu, tap Toolbar to display the Formatting toolbar. Figure 9-3 shows the Formatting toolbar at the top of the block recognizer.

You can use the buttons on the Formatting toolbar to make text bold, italicized, underlined, or any combination of these with just a tap. You can also change the alignment of the text. Figure 9-4 shows the effect of changing the settings.

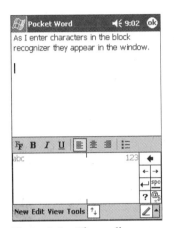
Figure 9-3 *The toolbar appears above your method of input.*

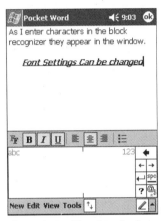
Figure 9-4 *Tapping the buttons on the Formatting toolbar changes the text.*

There are, however, some things that can't be changed from the Formatting toolbar. To change the size, font, or color of the characters you enter, you have to change the settings in the Format dialog box. To display this dialog box, tap the FF button at the left end of the toolbar. The Format dialog box contains all the remaining character-formatting options in Pocket Word, as shown in Figure 9-5 on the next page.

In Pocket Word, there are only four fonts installed by default—Tahoma, Bookdings, Fruitiger Linotype, and Courier New. If you're used to the hundreds of fonts you can have on your computer, having only four might be a bit of a surprise.

To change the formatting of paragraphs, display the Paragraph dialog box shown in Figure 9-6 on the next page. On the Edit menu, tap Paragraph to display this dialog box. Both the character-formatting options and paragraph-formatting options in Pocket Word are small subsets of the options available in Word for the computer.

Figure 9-5   *Font properties are somewhat limited.*

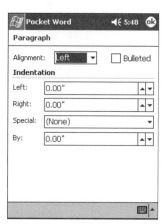

Figure 9-6   *Paragraph properties support the bare essentials.*

Pocket Word is a good tool for creating documents, but it's not always the best tool for finalizing them.

One of the less obvious problems with Pocket Word is the lack of paragraph and word styles. And because there are no styles, there is no Outline view. If you are creating large documents, you might find the absence of styles particularly frustrating. If, however, you work mostly with letters and short reports, you might not even notice.

Pocket Word does, however, have something almost everyone needs—a spelling checker. (You should see my writing before my spelling checker and the marvelous editors get ahold of it!) To start the spelling checker, on the Tools menu, tap Spell Check. When the spelling checker searches the document and finds a misspelled word, it displays a menu with a list of suggested words, as shown in Figure 9-7. When the spelling check is complete, it displays a message to let you know, as shown in Figure 9-8.

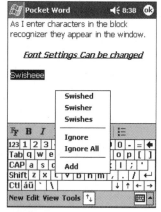

Figure 9-7   *I can't spell* swished *without help!*

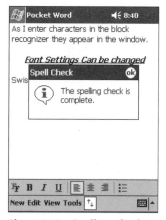

Figure 9-8   *Spelling check is complete.*

Pocket Word offers another feature that is useful if you write articles or columns: a Word Count feature (on the Tools menu, tap Word Count). Authors who write for magazines and some Web sites are often required to write a specific number of words. Many authors can estimate how many words they have written when working in Word, because they can see how many pages they've written, but estimating is much more difficult in Pocket Word. With the Word Count feature, though, there's no need to guess.

The other three modes in Pocket Word are Writing mode, Drawing mode, and Recording mode. In Writing mode, as shown in Figure 9-9, you can handwrite your text on the screen, and Pocket Word will recognize it. Simply write your text, and then on the Tools menu, tap Recognize. Unfortunately, Pocket Word is not particularly good at converting my chicken scratch into meaningful words. Figure 9-10 shows the results of Pocket Word's attempt to recognize the text in Figure 9-9. Because Pocket Word isn't effective at "reading" my handwriting, I rarely use this mode, but if you have better penmanship than I do, you might find it an effective way to get information into your Pocket PC.

In Drawing mode, you can create drawings in your Pocket Word document. This is particularly useful if you can draw and need to communicate something that would be very difficult to express in words.

In Recording mode, you can use the Recording toolbar to add voice annotations to your Pocket Word documents. When you've added a recording to your document, a small speaker button appears where you recorded the annotation. Figure 9-11 shows the Recording mode with a voice annotation at the very beginning of the document.

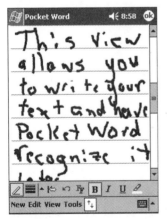

Figure 9-9   *I can't write on my Pocket PC very well.*

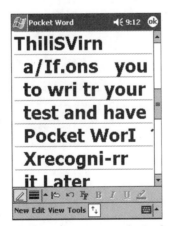

Figure 9-10   *As a result, Pocket Word can't "read" my writing very well.*

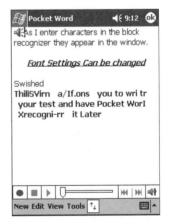

Figure 9-11   *Recording mode is like Typing mode with sound.*

Reviewing and Annotating Documents

Even if you don't use Pocket Word to write new documents, there's a good chance you will use it at some point to review documents. Word offers a wide variety of annotation tools, such as comments, revision marks, and highlighting, but the tools in Pocket Word are limited to highlighting the text you want to mark for later review and entering new text into the document itself. You have to decide whether you want to enter your remarks into the Pocket Word document, or write them down on paper and enter them when you get back to your computer.

There are two ways to annotate text on the Pocket PC. The first is to highlight your remarks so that they stand out; the second is to include voice recordings of your remarks throughout the document.

There are two ways to use highlighting in a Pocket Word document. The first way can be used in either the Typing or Writing mode. Select the text you would like to highlight, and tap the FF button on the toolbar. In the Format dialog box, select the Highlight check box as shown in Figure 9-12, and tap OK. The text you selected will appear highlighted, as shown in Figure 9-13.

Figure 9-12   *Highlighting is a character property.*

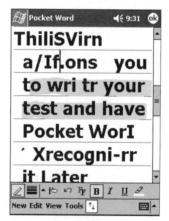

Figure 9-13   *Highlighting appears over the text you select.*

To highlight text in the Writing mode, tap the pen tool button on the toolbar to deselect it, select the text you want to highlight, and tap the Highlight button on the far right side of the toolbar.

Highlighting is very useful if you have a small amount of text to call attention to or if you want to enter a brief annotation and make it easy to see; however, it's not a good way to call attention to a lot of text, particularly when you don't have an external keyboard. In situations like this, you might want to use Recording mode and embed recorded messages in the document.

On the View menu, tap Recording to switch to Recording mode. At the location where you want to place an annotation, tap the screen to move the insertion point to that location. Then tap the Record button on the Recording toolbar. Record your message, and tap the Stop button. Repeat this process until you've placed annotations everywhere you feel it's necessary.

One concern with embedding recorded annotations is that the person to whom you send them must have a sound card and be willing to listen to them. Another concern is the potential for your remarks to be overheard by others. The fact that the recipient might not listen in complete privacy should encourage you to be diplomatic about what you record.

Using Pocket Word—What You Can't Do

Word is a great tool, but fitting it on a smaller platform necessitated some limitations. Some of Pocket Word's limitations are as follows:

- **No styles**   Large documents that use styles can be created with Pocket Word, but the styles have to be added to the document from a computer. You also might not be able to send larger documents with styles in them to and from Pocket Word, because the style information will be lost.

- **No Outline view**   Outline view requires styles, which Pocket Word doesn't support.

- **No pagination**   Because Pocket Word works on a small screen, you can't view a whole printed page on one screen. As a result, Pocket Word doesn't plot what will end up on what page.

- **No headers or footers**   Because you can't print a document directly from Pocket Word, neither headers nor footers are supported.

- **No automatic numbering**   If you're used to Word automatically numbering the items in your numbered list, you'll be disappointed to find that you must number your lists by hand in Pocket Word. You can, however, create bulleted lists (with the default bullet only).

- **No revision marks**   If you want to use revision marks to edit documents someone else created, you have to do it in Word. Pocket Word doesn't support revision marks.

- **No comments**   Comments are another way you can annotate a document without disturbing its contents. Pocket Word doesn't support comments, though—you'll have to go to Word to add comments to a document.

- **No tables**   Tables are converted to normal text when a Word document is converted to Pocket Word format.

Pocket Excel

The spreadsheet—another personal productivity application created at the beginning of the personal computer revolution—is an invaluable tool that performs "what-if" analysis, navigates through complex formulas, and produces accurate results. Pocket Excel doesn't have all the graphing features of its computer counterpart, but it can still display and calculate information like any other spreadsheet application.

Pocket Excel's formatting options are also limited. Gone is the option to have text appear vertically, as is the ability to merge text across cells. However, what is left is a very stable—if not flashy—spreadsheet application that you can use on your Pocket PC.

Pocket Excel is used for small, relatively simple spreadsheets like the one shown in Figure 9-14. This spreadsheet calculates the estimated payout from the sale of a home, taking into account the anticipated sale price, the mortgage payoff amounts on an offer, and transaction information such as the commission rates and anticipated taxes. It also calculates the total charges and the anticipated amount of cash that will be returned to the seller at the time of the sale.

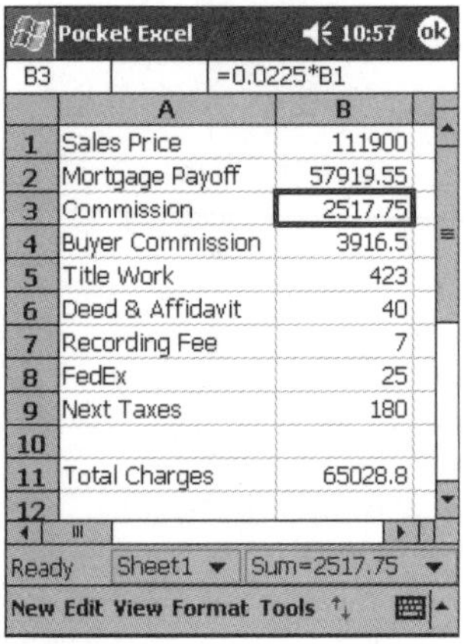

Figure 9-14   *Pocket Excel is perfect for simple spreadsheets that perform basic calculations.*

This spreadsheet has only basic addition and multiplication; however, this is all most of us need—something slightly more sophisticated than a calculator. Essentially, these kinds of spreadsheets contain the formulas, so we don't have to manage them by hand. Spreadsheets also make it easy to do what-if analysis—to see how changing the sale price of your home would affect your profit margin, for example.

Perhaps your spreadsheets calculate your commission on the deal you just closed or the number of items you have to sell to meet your sales quota. These calculations—simple multiplication, addition, and subtraction—are perfect for Pocket Excel.

Pocket Excel's user interface is almost identical to Excel's. For instance, to add up a set of numbers, tap and drag the insertion point across the cells you want to total. The result is displayed on the status bar in the right corner of the screen. Pocket Excel also is similar to Excel in that typing an equal sign (=) signals the beginning of a formula.

Because the Pocket PC has such a small screen and no keyboard, if your spreadsheet is more complicated than the one in Figure 9-14, prepare it on Excel for the computer, and then convert it to Pocket Excel.

Pocket SlideShow

Many people who travel to give Microsoft PowerPoint presentations know how problematic carrying a notebook computer *and* a projector can be. The notebook can weigh 10–15 pounds or more including the case; a projector and its case are another 10–15 pounds.

Although many people rely on projectors provided by the facility, sometimes carrying your own projector is unavoidable. In that situation, it would certainly be nice to eliminate some of the weight. That's where your Pocket PC, a VGA card, and a slide show viewer fit in.

Microsoft doesn't have a Pocket PC version of PowerPoint, but several other software developers do. The examples in this chapter were created using CNetX's Pocket SlideShow and Color Graphics Voyager VGA PC Card. With this combination of hardware and software, you can completely replace your notebook as a driver for your presentations.

Note CNetX's Pocket SlideShow isn't the only viewer capable of putting on slide show presentations from a Pocket PC. I used Pocket SlideShow, but other similar products are used in much the same way.

The Voyager Video Graphics Array (VGA) PCMCIA card provides you with a standard VGA monitor output capable of an 800 by 600 pixel display at 8-bit color. Color Graphics has recently released a CompactFlash-based replacement for the Voyager VGA in a PC Card form that will support a higher resolution and 16-bit color. In addition, several other vendors have solutions available, including an expansion pack for the Compaq iPAQ called a FlyJacket.

The first step in displaying presentations from your Pocket PC is installing the slide show and video card software. After these are installed, you can copy documents to your Pocket PC just as you would any other file. Refer to Chapter 5 for specific instructions on how to move files to your Pocket PC. ActiveSync will take care of converting the files to a file format readable by the slide show viewer.

Part of the slide show can be edited on the Pocket PC, but most of the editing features available in PowerPoint are not available in Pocket SlideShow. You can reorder the slides in the presentation and hide the slides you don't want to display, but you won't be able to create or change graphics, tables, or other components of the presentation itself.

To run Pocket SlideShow:

1. On the Programs menu, tap Pocket SlideShow. When Pocket SlideShow starts, a screen similar to the one shown in Figure 9-15 is displayed.

2. Tap the name of a slide presentation. Figure 9-16 shows the default view when opening a presentation from the Microsoft Mobile Experience Tour (available from the Microsoft Web site, at *http://www.microsoft.com*). The default view shows a preview of the slide as well as the notes for that slide.

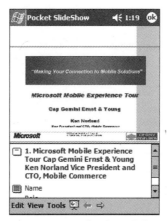

Figure 9-15   *A listing of all of the files on your Pocket PC that SlideShow can open.*

Figure 9-16   *The first slide and the notes.*

This view is designed to give you a chance to make sure you opened the right presentation before you display it to the world. You can also do some basic editing, such as hiding or rearranging the slides.

3. When you're ready to put on your show, start it by selecting View and then Slide Show. Figure 9-17 shows the first slide in Slide Show mode. Because slides normally use a landscape rather than a portrait orientation, the slide will automatically be rotated on the display of your Pocket PC.

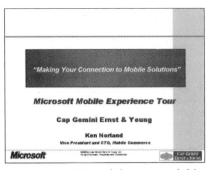

Figure 9-17 *Most slides are readable on your Pocket PC's display.*

If you are using an external VGA adapter, the display will already be in landscape orientation. The external VGA adapter will display the presentation on all external devices on its own.

Note If the VGA adapter has a utility to copy the Pocket PC's display to the external adapter, disable this feature before running your slide show. If you don't, both Pocket SlideShow and the utility will try to take control of the external display, and you could get unpredictable results.

---

4. Move through the slide show by tapping the display of your Pocket PC or by pressing the hardware navigation buttons. If you need to end the slide show before it is completed, tap and hold the Pocket PC screen.

Memory is the biggest challenge when you're presenting from your Pocket PC. You might need CompactFlash cards to provide the space to hold all the presentations. Of course, you have to copy these presentations over to your computer or have a Pocket PC capable of supporting the presentation card and a CompactFlash card simultaneously.

cyProj and cyStat

Although Microsoft Project isn't included with Microsoft Office, many businesses use it to manage their projects. Even if your job description doesn't have "project manager" in it, you might still find yourself overseeing programs, initiatives, or other projects.

One of the challenges for project managers is keeping track of everything while on the road. Often, they must carry their notebooks with them to keep up to date. Project files can be updated in only one location at a time, so if a project manager takes files on the road and makes changes to them, those files won't be synchronized with the files on the corporate network. In addition, it's difficult for project managers to copy their modified files to the network. This makes it hard for anyone else to know whether the files on the network are current.

Two applications for the Pocket PC by cyWren Systems offer a solution to this problem. They also make traveling with data easier, because the application runs on a Pocket PC, not a notebook.

The first application, cyProj, manages a project in much the same way Microsoft Project does. For instance, Figure 9-18 shows a project in Task view and Figure 9-19 shows the same project in Gantt view. (A Gantt chart is the most basic project management tool. It represents tasks and their durations with a series of horizontal bars.) Both of these views are nearly identical to the corresponding views in Microsoft Project, except that they have much less screen space.

cyProj's analysis feature can be a great help to beginning project managers and those who are too busy to look through details all the time. The analysis feature tests your project with guidelines taken from the project's body of knowledge. If a guideline is not met, it is flagged on the analysis screen, as shown in Figure 9-20. In addition, the feature can notify you when data needed for the analysis of certain features is missing.

Figure 9-18   *The Task view of a project.*

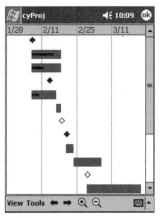
Figure 9-19   *The Gantt view of a project.*

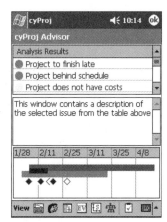
Figure 9-20   *An analysis of a project.*

These tools are all useful for a single project, but if you are a project manager, it's likely that you manage more than one project. One of Microsoft's new tools for use with Project is Project Central. Project Central is a Web-based project management data interface that can consolidate data from more than one project and make the data easier for a non-project manager to read. Another application, cyStat, enables you to look at all the projects in progress and identify which ones are on track (green light), which ones have the potential for trouble (yellow light), and which ones are in trouble (red light). The initial view of cyStat, shown in Figure 9-21, displays each currently defined project and its status. The names of the projects in Figure 9-21 are the same as their current status.

To view details about the project, tap its name in the list. As shown in Figure 9-22, the details displayed include manager information and the basic parameters for the project. To review other details about the project, tap the buttons at the bottom of the screen.

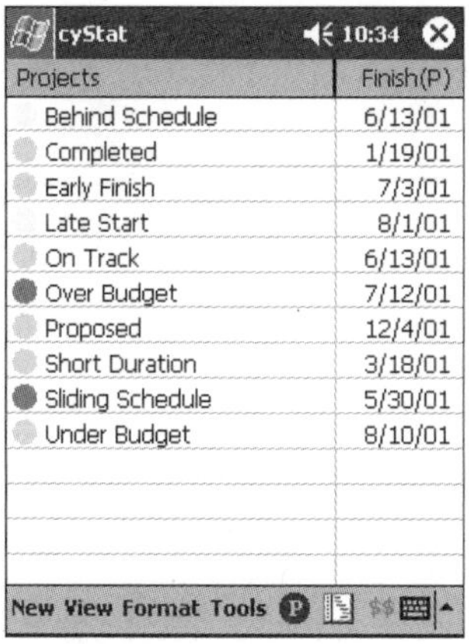

Figure 9-21 *Each project and its status.*

Figure 9-22 *To display details for the project, tap the project's name in the list.*

Like cyStat, Project Central is a good way to get an overall feel for which projects are in good shape and which projects might need more attention, work, and review.

Summary

This chapter addressed the Microsoft Office applications most people use—Word and Excel—as well as a PowerPoint-compatible viewer and a pair of Project-compatible programs for the Pocket PC.

The primary limitation of using these programs on the Pocket PC is screen size, but its primary advantage—portability—means that there are several ways you can use Pocket PCs for work or to keep up with information while you are traveling.

Pocket Word contains the most basic support for documents. Because the Pocket PC doesn't have a built-in keyboard, entering information into Pocket Word can be challenging. Reviewing documents in Pocket Word is difficult for a different reason—Pocket Word doesn't have most of the editing tools that Word does. However, you can highlight text to draw attention to it and embed voice recordings to verbalize your remarks.

Pocket Excel's user interface is very similar to Excel's. Although the small screen makes Pocket Excel useful for only the most basic spreadsheets, you can still perform basic calculations quickly and efficiently.

CNetX's Pocket SlideShow is an effective way to get your PowerPoint presentations to your audience without the need to carry a notebook. Coupled with a VGA card or expansion pack, Pocket SlideShow can display your slide shows almost as effectively as a notebook, and in a much lighter configuration.

The purpose of cyProj and cyStat is to help you manage your projects and review project information. Their ability to work with Project files makes them ideal for project managers who are constantly on the go.

Overall, there is little you can do with your computer that can't be done with your Pocket PC. Admittedly, some of the tasks are more difficult on the Pocket PC, but they can still be done.

As always, I leave you with some questions to think about:

- What kinds of documents do you create with Word—notes, memos, white papers? How many of these could you create in Pocket Word and apply styles to later?

- How large are the documents you review? How much time could you save by reviewing them while you're riding in a cab or waiting for a plane? Do you work in places where it would be inappropriate or inconvenient to use your notebook?

- How many calculations do you have to do to verify margins, calculate commissions, or compute figures? Could you use Pocket Excel to simplify this process?

- How badly do you want to leave your notebook at home? Would you leave your notebook at home if you could do your presentations from your Pocket PC?

- How do you stay on top of your projects while you are traveling?

- What do you need to do on your trip? Can you get it done with your Pocket PC?

CHAPTER 10

Getting There: Driving Directions

I'm particularly excited about this chapter. It's my opportunity to share with you some of the secrets I've learned to make travel fun and productive. Among the coolest developments of the last five years or so are the improvements made to map and directions applications.

These improvements have resulted in better programs with which to plan trips. Microsoft Streets and Trips 2002, which grew out of the old AutoMap program, has an amazing amount of information and detail. It's easy to use and a wonderful way to plan how you're going to get to your destination. With travel times, advisories on tolls, and other information, it can help make your trips a lot less stressful.

For example, when you are navigating in a new city, there's nothing worse than running into construction detours along the route. Although the various state Departments of Transportation are well intentioned, some of their detour signs require a secret decoder ring to figure out. I've been to several cities where I've missed the appropriate turn because of poor placement of construction and detour signs. With Streets and Trips, you can avoid this problem by downloading current information from the Internet about construction on your route before you get into your car.

Microsoft Pocket Streets 2002 for the Pocket PC is bundled with Streets and Trips 2002. Pocket Streets is great for looking up addresses and finding your way if you don't have your notebook with you. Although pre-planning with Streets and Trips is necessary, Pocket Streets can help you get back on track if you've wandered off the path laid out in Streets and Trips. It is even more helpful when you get the update (from the Microsoft

Web site) that connects Pocket Streets to a Global Positioning System (GPS) receiver. The one limitation to Pocket Streets is that it can't generate driving directions. This means that you'll be able to find your destination on the map, but you'll have to figure out on your own how to get there.

Other vendors create mapping software for the Pocket PC, including Pharos (*http: //www.pharosgps.com*). This company's Ostia program gives dynamic, turn-by-turn directions while you're driving your car. These directions alert you when a turn is coming up, what direction the turn will be, and when you've arrived at the turn location. This can be a great help if you're driving in an unfamiliar city—looking at the map while driving is not a good idea.

The next section begins with an overview of GPS receivers, how the GPS system works, and what you need to know about the system. (If you're confident in your GPS knowledge, feel free to skip this section.) From there, I'll show you how to preplan with Microsoft Streets and Trips; how to use Pocket Streets to find your way; and finally how, with a little preparation, you can use tools like Pharos' Ostia to get driving directions.

Understanding GPS

Technically, what most people call a GPS is a GPS receiver. It's a complicated radio receiver that receives signals sent from 24 satellites in orbit. From the information it receives, it calculates your position on earth. Your position can be determined very accurately from this information—the newer GPS receivers can determine your position to within approximately 20 feet.

GPS works because each GPS satellite contains an atomic clock and a computer that calculates where all the satellites in the system should be. The GPS receiver catches a time-stamped signal from a satellite, determines how long the signal took to reach the receiver, and thus calculates the distance from the satellite to the receiver. With this information from three satellites, the exact position of the receiver on the earth's surface can be determined. If a fourth satellite is added, the GPS receiver's altitude can be calculated as well.

Note Although altitude can be determined, it is difficult to get a precise result. That is why the FAA is working on a supplementary system that would work with GPS receivers to further refine their accuracy—particularly in terms of altitude. The system is called WAAS. WAAS is the abbreviation for Wide Area Augmentation System. (Say that three times fast.)

One challenge of designing GPS receivers is that they rely on a very precise concept of time. This level of precision isn't available in a cheap and compact package. Most GPS receivers use a quartz clock much like the one in your digital watch and your computer. Quartz clocks are usually relatively accurate; they drift only a few seconds in a given month. The error rate of a quartz clock is very small, but it can be problematic in a GPS receiver, because even a small time error can translate into a large distance. A temporal (time) error of just 1 second equals 186,000 miles in distance error.

One way GPS receivers overcome this limitation is by locking on to more GPS satellites. The more satellites the GPS receiver locks on to, the more efficient it can be at correcting the errors in its internal clock. The receivers evaluate the data from the GPS satellites and perform complex calculations to verify the exact time every second.

A variety of other errors must be taken into account as well. If you're interested in the way GPS technology works and the challenges the receivers must overcome, check out Garmin's Web site at *http://www.garmin.com/aboutGPS*. Garmin is a manufacturer of handheld, marine, and aviation GPS receivers.

How the United States Ensures the Accuracy of GPS

The United States Department of Defense (DOD) established and maintains the GPS system for both military and civilian use. Until May 2000, the DOD inserted a small error into the signals generated by the satellites. This error was designed to make the location process a little less precise in civilian applications, in the hope that this would prevent other nations from using the GPS system against the United States. In May 2000, updated software became available for the DOD to control the amount of error introduced into the signal for civilian applications.

The process of adding error to the signal is called Selective Availability (SA). With the updated software, the DOD can reenable SA for any region of the world without affecting other areas. This means GPS signals will be more accurate—as long as there are no threats to the United States or its allies. During times of conflict, it's certainly possible that the DOD will reenable SA for the purpose of national defense.

Types of GPS Information

GPS receivers provide two types of information. The first is the position of the GPS receiver. The second is a side benefit rarely associated with GPS—highly accurate time. In fact, the time information you can get from a GPS receiver is more accurate than what you can get from almost any other source.

Knowing where you are and what time it is can be valuable. However, a GPS receiver can use these two pieces of data to extrapolate information that you will find even more useful.

If you know where you are and where you were a moment ago, you can determine two things: in what direction you're traveling and how fast you're traveling. Of course, it's really your *average* direction and your *average* speed—the calculations are only exact if you were going the same direction and speed during the entire length of time covered in the calculation. These calculations are more accurate with GPS receivers that recalculate the speed and direction a few times per second.

The direction and speed a GPS registers will likely lag slightly behind your current direction and speed. You'll notice it most when you're making a sharp turn or decelerating. Small errors might also occur in gauging speed (generally in the neighborhood of tenths of a mile per hour), and the direction reported from a GPS won't be valid until you've moved.

You can also calculate your estimated time of arrival (ETA) based on your direction, speed, and the distance to your destination.

Note ETAs are notoriously optimistic. This is in part because curves in the roads that add distance to the trip aren't accounted for in the estimates, and in part because of traffic congestion. An ETA is a useful guide; just remember to pad it slightly to be a little more accurate.

Ultimately, GPS receivers are tools we can use to overcome limitations in our ability to navigate. Although I can navigate fairly well, some members of my immediate family are "geographically challenged." They have a hard time keeping track of where they are, let alone determining in what direction they are traveling. GPS receivers are great for people who are prone to getting lost, because they can receive continuous reports telling them where they are, the direction they are headed in, and how fast they are going.

Some GPS programs for the Pocket PC and the computer report all this extrapolated data, but most do not. However, these additional, extrapolated data fields are common for handheld receivers. The next section explains the different types of GPS receivers.

Types of GPS Receivers

Just as there is an array of Pocket PCs and mobile phones to choose from, so too there is an array of GPS receivers. GPS receivers used to vary in the number of parallel channels they had—that is, the number of GPS satellite signals they could receive simultaneously. However, almost every modern GPS has 12 channels, so it can receive all the potentially "visible" satellites at the same time.

Today, the primary difference among the different kinds of GPS units is their display and what information the display can communicate. Almost every unit has a serial connection that can be used to connect the GPS to a computer or Pocket PC. The basic categories are:

- **No display**   These units are designed to be used exclusively with GPS software on a computer, Pocket PC, or other specialized device. The receiver contains all of the receiving electronics and a serial connection to the device that will display all the information. All commercially available packaged GPS solutions for the Pocket PC use this type of GPS receiver hardware.

- **Non-mapping display**   These units contain the receiver hardware and are capable of displaying the longitude and latitude, but they cannot display a map. They also often display the number of satellites from which they are receiving. These units are only slightly more useful than the no-display units in that you could conceivably use the information to plot your location on a paper map, but they are most often used with a computer or Pocket PC.

- **Base mapping display**   These units contain all the receiver hardware and can display moving maps. However, these units do not contain detailed "street-level" maps, only major roads in ROM that cannot be changed. These units are useful without a computer or Pocket PC for navigation, but can't generally be used to look up specific addresses or easily navigate through smaller roads.

- **Mapping display**   These units contain the receiver hardware, can display moving maps, and have onboard memory to which detailed "street-level" maps can be downloaded. These types of GPS receivers are the most expensive, but they can be used for turn-by-turn guided directions without the assistance of other devices, such as a computer or Pocket PC.

Tip Consider using a base mapping display unit. It provides you with an overall reference map that is generally good enough to get you close to where you're headed, and it can be attached to your Pocket PC or notebook if more detailed maps or directions are needed. I own a Garmin GPS III Plus. The unit's base map functionality provides most of what I need.

No matter what kind of GPS you get, you can connect it to your computer or Pocket PC and use it with your navigation software. In some ways, that makes getting a mapping display GPS receiver a bit like overkill. Although these units are very nice, they are also quite expensive—usually more expensive than the value they add. That is, unless you *really* don't want to carry a Pocket PC or notebook on those occasions when you need better navigation assistance than the base mapping units can provide.

Preparing to Travel

For me, the biggest factor in having a stress-free trip is preparation. If I'm pushed up to the wire before I travel, it will be a stressful trip—at least until I can make the time to plan whatever I have left to do.

Before I leave on a trip, I like to gather all the necessary confirmation numbers, telephone numbers, and contact numbers so that they're easily accessible. Often, the numbers are printed on my itinerary from the travel agent, but I don't always use a travel agent. Sometimes I store the numbers on my Pocket PC in a note, which I can pull up at various counters. I do this more often these days, particularly because I can get an e-mail message from the travel agent with this information. I just move the message to a folder I keep synchronized on my Pocket PC, and it makes life easy.

The other major issue with preplanning is getting directions to and from the places I need to go. Although I have a fairly good sense of direction, looking at a map helps me figure out where I am and how to get to my destination.

Microsoft Streets and Trips 2002 is a great way to get driving directions. In addition to providing turn-by-turn route information, these driving directions also give you an overview map that can be used to familiarize yourself with the area. Let's look at how to get directions from Las Vegas McCarran International Airport to a nearby health care clinic. To create a set of directions:

1. Start Microsoft Streets and Trips 2002. Streets and Trips opens with a window similar to the one shown in Figure 10-1.

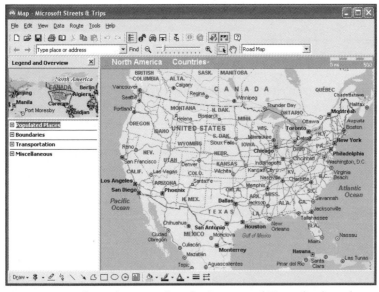

Figure 10-1   *The opening window for Streets and Trips displays the entire United States.*

2. If you haven't updated your construction information lately, on the Route menu, click Update Construction Information. You may get a prompt warning you that your construction data is up to date and asking whether you want to proceed. In this case, click No, because there's no point in downloading data that you already have. If the prompt tells you that your construction data is out of date, click Yes to proceed with the download. Streets and Trips logs on and update your construction information so that you'll know whether there is construction along the path you must travel. When the process is complete, Streets and Trips displays a dialog box letting you know that the most up-to-date construction information is now available.

3. In the Type Place Or Address box, enter the location where you want your driving directions to start.

4. If Streets and Trips finds an exact match, it displays the map and the location. If no exact match is found, click the down arrow to the right of the Type Place Or Address box. You'll get a drop-down list of potential matches, similar to the one in Figure 10-2.

Figure 10-2   *Often, searching for an airport means searching for a rental car agency.*

From this list, select the exact location where you want your directions to start. The list in Figure 10-2 shows all the agencies at McCarran Airport. In this case, I will select Avis.

5. After you choose your starting location, Streets and Trips displays it as a highlighted icon on a map. Right-click this icon. Next, click Route on the shortcut menu, and then click Add As Start. Figure 10-3 on the next page shows the Avis location at McCarran International Airport as the start of the route, indicated by a green square with the number 1 in it.

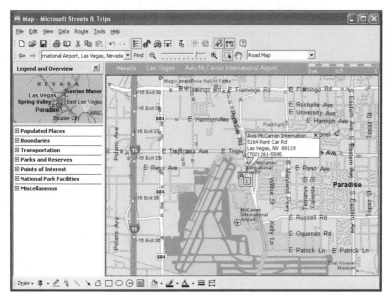

Figure 10-3   *When a location is selected as part of the route, it gets a color-coded marker.*

6. In the box where you entered your starting location, type the destination address. Figure 10-4 shows the results of a search for 2940 N. Tenaya Way, Las Vegas, NV 89128.

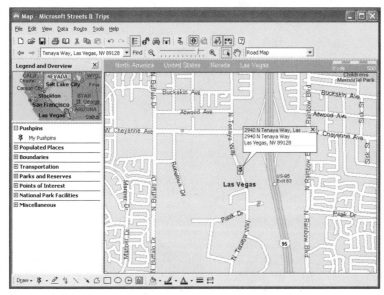

Figure 10-4   *If you search for an address that doesn't have a marker, Streets and Trips will add a pushpin for you.*

7. Right-click the icon selected by the search. Click Route on the shortcut menu, and then click Add As End.

8. Right-click anywhere on the map. Click Route on the shortcut menu, and then click Get Directions. A screen displaying the text directions and the highlighted map appears, as shown in Figure 10-5.

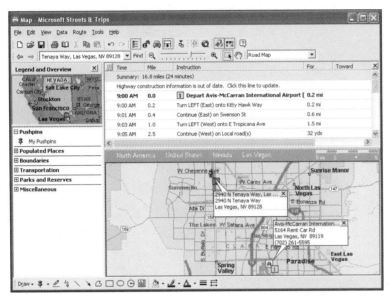

Figure 10-5 *Directions are at the top of the screen, and the map is at the bottom.*

If you can't take your Pocket PC with you, it's a good idea to print the map. There are three printing options. You can print driving directions, turn-by-turn maps (shown in Figure 10-6 on the next page), or strip maps (shown in Figure 10-7, also on the next page).

No matter what type of map you print, you can include an overview map that displays the entire route on one page. You might not need an overview map with a strip map, but it is often a helpful addition to turn-by-turn maps.

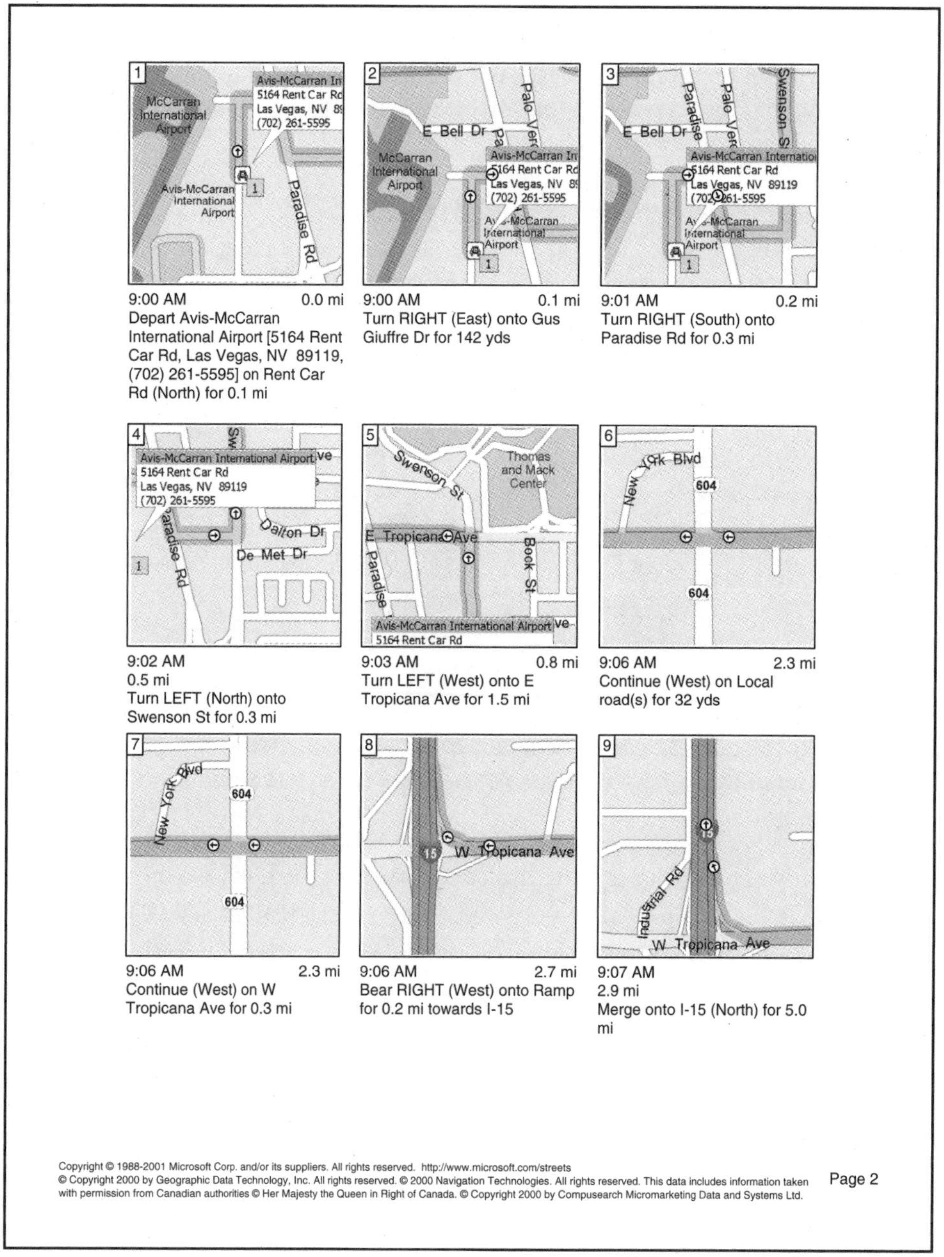

9:00 AM   0.0 mi
Depart Avis-McCarran
International Airport [5164 Rent
Car Rd, Las Vegas, NV 89119,
(702) 261-5595] on Rent Car
Rd (North) for 0.1 mi

9:00 AM   0.1 mi
Turn RIGHT (East) onto Gus
Giuffre Dr for 142 yds

9:01 AM   0.2 mi
Turn RIGHT (South) onto
Paradise Rd for 0.3 mi

9:02 AM
0.5 mi
Turn LEFT (North) onto
Swenson St for 0.3 mi

9:03 AM   0.8 mi
Turn LEFT (West) onto E
Tropicana Ave for 1.5 mi

9:06 AM   2.3 mi
Continue (West) on Local
road(s) for 32 yds

9:06 AM   2.3 mi
Continue (West) on W
Tropicana Ave for 0.3 mi

9:06 AM   2.7 mi
Bear RIGHT (West) onto Ramp
for 0.2 mi towards I-15

9:07 AM
2.9 mi
Merge onto I-15 (North) for 5.0
mi

Copyright © 1988-2001 Microsoft Corp. and/or its suppliers. All rights reserved. http://www.microsoft.com/streets
© Copyright 2000 by Geographic Data Technology, Inc. All rights reserved. © 2000 Navigation Technologies. All rights reserved. This data includes information taken
with permission from Canadian authorities © Her Majesty the Queen in Right of Canada. © Copyright 2000 by Compusearch Micromarketing Data and Systems Ltd.

Figure 10-6 *Turn-by-turn maps display thumbnail maps of each turn.*

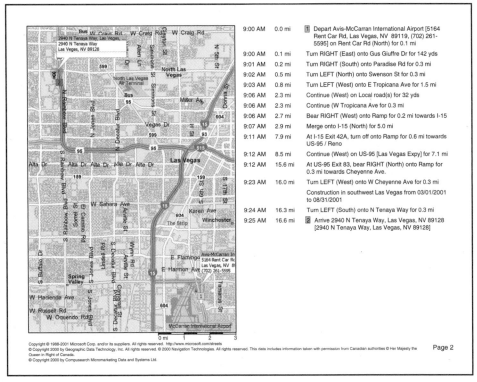

The following is the directions list shown beside the map:

Time	Distance	Direction
9:00 AM	0.0 mi	1 Depart Avis-McCarran International Airport [5164 Rent Car Rd, Las Vegas, NV 89119, (702) 261-5595] on Rent Car Rd (North) for 0.1 mi
9:00 AM	0.1 mi	Turn RIGHT (East) onto Gus Giuffre Dr for 142 yds
9:01 AM	0.2 mi	Turn RIGHT (South) onto Paradise Rd for 0.3 mi
9:02 AM	0.5 mi	Turn LEFT (North) onto Swenson St for 0.3 mi
9:03 AM	0.8 mi	Turn LEFT (West) onto E Tropicana Ave for 1.5 mi
9:06 AM	2.3 mi	Continue (West) on Local road(s) for 32 yds
9:06 AM	2.3 mi	Continue (W Tropicana Ave for 0.3 mi
9:06 AM	2.7 mi	Bear RIGHT (West) onto Ramp for 0.2 mi towards I-15
9:07 AM	2.9 mi	Merge onto I-15 (North) for 5.0 mi
9:11 AM	7.9 mi	At I-15 Exit 42A, turn off onto Ramp for 0.6 mi towards US-95 / Reno
9:12 AM	8.5 mi	Continue (West) on US-95 [Las Vegas Expy] for 7.1 mi
9:12 AM	15.6 mi	At US-95 Exit 83, bear RIGHT (North) onto Ramp for 0.3 mi towards Cheyenne Ave.
9:23 AM	16.0 mi	Turn LEFT (West) onto W Cheyenne Ave for 0.3 mi
		Construction in southwest Las Vegas from 03/01/2001 to 08/31/2001
9:24 AM	16.3 mi	Turn LEFT (South) onto N Tenaya Way for 0.3 mi
9:25 AM	16.6 mi	2 Arrive 2940 N Tenaya Way, Las Vegas, NV 89128 [2940 N Tenaya Way, Las Vegas, NV 89128]

Copyright © 1988-2001 Microsoft Corp. and/or its suppliers. All rights reserved. http://www.microsoft.com/streets
© Copyright 2000 by Geographic Data Technology, Inc. All rights reserved. © 2000 Navigation Technologies. All rights reserved. This data includes information taken with permission from Canadian authorities © Her Majesty the Queen in Right of Canada.
© Copyright 2000 by Compusearch Micromarketing Data and Systems Ltd.

Page 2

Figure 10-7   *Strip maps display the map and the directions.*

If you are bringing your Pocket PC, consider saving the driving directions as an Excel file. That way, you can move the file to your Pocket PC and view it in Pocket Excel before you start your trip. Here's how to save the driving directions in an Excel file:

1. Right-click the directions, and click Copy Directions on the shortcut menu.

2. Start Microsoft Excel.

3. In the blank Excel worksheet, right-click the A1 cell, and click Paste on the shortcut menu. Figure 10-8 on the next page shows the results of pasting the directions into an Excel worksheet.

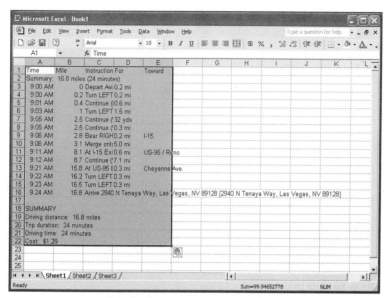

Figure 10-8   *Initially, the directions are a bit messy.*

4. Resize the columns so that they are easier to read, and remove columns you don't need (such as the Time column). When you're done, your spreadsheet might look something like Figure 10-9.

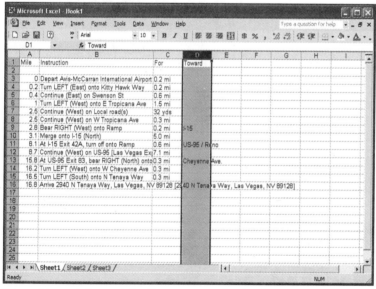

Figure 10-9   *A few quick adjustments make the directions easier to read.*

5. On the File menu, click Save. If you have file synchronization to your Pocket PC enabled, save the file in your Pocket PC My Documents folder. If not, copy it to the Pocket PC manually. For more information about copying files to your Pocket PC, refer to Chapter 5, "Park It in the Garage: Synchronization."

Now that you have a copy of the directions on your Pocket PC, create a map you can use with Pocket Streets 2002. Because of the Pocket PC's limited memory, you must export the maps you want to use from Streets and Trips 2002 on the computer to a Pocket PC file. The only map data in Pocket Streets will be what you export.

Here's how to export the map to a Pocket Streets file:

1. In Microsoft Streets and Trips 2002, close the Directions pane.

2. Click the map to make sure it's selected.

3. To zoom out and display more of the area around your route, press the minus key on the keyboard once or twice.

4. On the File menu, click Export Map For Pocket Streets.

5. In the Create Map For Pocket Streets dialog box, click OK. Figure 10-10 shows this dialog box.

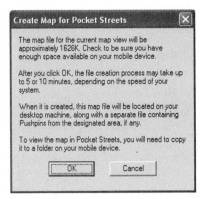

Figure 10-10   *The dialog box contains information about the size of the file and how long it will take to create it.*

6. Give the file an appropriate name, and then save it. If you have plenty of memory available on your Pocket PC, save the file in the Pocket PC My Documents folder. If file synchronization is turned on, the map will automatically be copied to your Pocket PC. If you don't have a lot of memory available, save the file to another folder, and then copy it to a CompactFlash storage card for use in your Pocket PC.

7. In the Completion dialog box, click OK.

If you didn't save the file in the synchronized Pocket PC My Documents folder, you still have to get the map to your Pocket PC. Copy both the *.mps* (map) file and the *.psp* (pushpin) file to your Pocket PC if you want to take your selected addresses with you on your trip.

That's all you have to do to prepare for your trip. In the next section, I explain how to use Streets and Trips 2002 with a GPS while you're traveling.

Taking Pocket Streets on the Road

After you've installed Pocket Streets and downloaded electronic maps to your Pocket PC, you have a tool that can make sure you stay on track or get back on track if you've strayed.

When you open a map in Pocket Streets, an overview of the map you've chosen is displayed, as shown in Figure 10-11.

Figure 10-11   *Greater Las Vegas as seen through Pocket Streets.*

Maneuvering Around a Map

In the overview map, you can draw a box around an area for which you want to see more detail, and zoom in on it. For instance, I drew a box around an area just to the east of I-15 to get a map that represents a segment of the "The Strip," as shown in Figure 10-12.

Figure 10-12 *An area of the Las Vegas Strip, with icons indicating hotels (and casinos).*

Tap the magnifying glass with a plus sign (+) to zoom in and show more detail and less area. Tap the magnifying glass with a minus sign (−) to zoom out and show less detail and more area. Repeatedly tapping the zoom-out magnifying glass eventually returns you to the map shown in Figure 10-11.

If you use the zoom controls instead of drawing a box around the area you want to display, you'll likely have to reposition the screen so that the area you want to look at stays centered on the display. Even if you draw a box around the area you want to look at, you might still miss the area slightly. (It took me three attempts to find "The Strip" for Figure 10-12.) Use the navigation buttons in the lower right corner to move the center of the map.

The navigation buttons function as you would expect. Tap the up arrow to see more of what is to the north of the area you're currently viewing; tap the down arrow to see more of what is to the south. You can use these buttons to move to any point on the map.

Note It probably seems obvious, but you cannot reposition to a place outside the map you exported from Streets and Trips.

Finding Places

Although Pocket Streets can't calculate driving directions, it can search for a place or a specific address. When you exported the map from Streets and Trips, all the points of interest and address information were exported with it.

On the Tools menu, tap Find Place to search for a place. In the Find Place dialog box (shown in Figure 10-13), enter the name of the location, and then tap the OK button.

If the name of the location is unique on the map, that location is displayed. If you enter a common name like *McCarran*, the Las Vegas airport, you receive a list of possible locations. Double-tap the location you want to display on the map. Figure 10-14 shows the McCarran Airport selected.

Figure 10-13   *The Find Place dialog box.*

Figure 10-14   *McCarran Airport in Las Vegas.*

Similarly, on the Tools menu, tap Find Address to find an address. In the Find Address dialog box, enter the location's street address, and tap OK. As with the Find Place dialog box, if the address is unique, it will be displayed. If you don't enter a unique address, you must tap the correct one in a list.

Note No matter what mapping software you're using, you'll probably encounter some addresses that can't be located. For instance, Pocket Streets can't locate my home address, and Pharos' Ostia product, which I'll cover shortly, couldn't locate a business address in Chicago. The cause of this problem might be new streets or just omissions in the data set. One of the biggest challenges for electronic mapping software manufacturers is getting address data that is complete and up to date.

When you've found the destination on the map, you can zoom out, reposition the map, zoom in, and move, until you can determine how to get from your current location to your destination—that is, assuming you know where you are. That's where GPS receivers come in.

Using a GPS Receiver

> **Note** You must download the updated Pocket Streets from Microsoft's Web site to get GPS support in Pocket Streets. The address is *http://www.microsoft.com/pocketstreets/*.

The first step in using a GPS receiver is configuring Pocket Streets. On the Tools menu, point to GPS, and then tap Configure GPS Receiver. Figure 10-15 shows the GPS Configuration dialog box. My iPAQ has three possible COM ports. I selected COM1, which corresponds to the serial port.

Next, on the Tools menu, point to GPS, and tap Track Position. If your GPS is operating correctly, your position is displayed on the map as a large circle, and you'll see your exact location displayed on the status bar. Your position will be updated every 15 seconds. Figure 10-16 shows a GPS tracking map.

Figure 10-15 *You must select the COM port to which the GPS will be connected.*

Figure 10-16 *Driving along in my automobile...*

> **Note** Streets and Trips has the same support for GPS receivers that Pocket Streets has. You can have your position displayed on your notebook screen just as you can on your Pocket PC. Although the screen is bigger, the maps are not any more detailed. If you are "geographically challenged" and don't have a Pocket PC, it might make sense to set up a GPS receiver and your notebook on the passenger seat.

Because of the 15-second delay in reporting your position, the circle on the map will probably lag behind your actual position. This shouldn't be a problem if you're using the map at a stop light or while pulled over—and you shouldn't be looking at the GPS receiver while driving anyway. The GPS receiver functionality in Pocket Streets should be considered basic functionality. For more advanced GPS features, you'll have to go to a specific GPS application.

Note The maps of the United States in mapping applications are good compared to those of the rest of the globe. GPS devices, mapping software, and driving directions are always helpful, but you might find them of less value outside the United States.

Using GPS Receiver Software

Pocket Streets is a good general-purpose mapping software program that finds addresses and locates your current position, but it does not focus on facilitating a GPS receiver's operation. It's a mapping tool.

However, other programs are specifically designed to take full advantage of the GPS receiver. One such program, Pharos' Ostia, is commonly bundled with a GPS receiver. I'll cover that program in a moment. Other programs on the market offer similar features, and new programs are appearing every day. When you're ready to purchase a GPS receiver, check the latest magazine reviews to see which programs are rated most favorably.

Tip Although GPS software for the Pocket PC is useful and sometimes offers more flexibility than handheld GPS receivers, I still prefer a handheld, stand-alone GPS receiver to one that is connected to my Pocket PC. It's easier to deal with one integrated device than to connect multiple devices together. Pharos and others sell their software either separately or bundled with a GPS. You can always buy a handheld GPS and purchase the GPS software separately.

The first screen of Pharos' Ostia software is a warning, as shown in Figure 10-17. The warning is valid for any Pocket PC application, but particularly for applications such as GPS receiver software, because you might be more tempted to divert your attention from driving.

Before you can display a map, you must download the maps to your Pocket PC.

Note You'll need a CompactFlash card on which to store Ostia's maps for your Pocket PC. The maps are so large that it's impractical to download them to the main memory of your unit. You should consider the cost of a CompactFlash card a part of the cost of your GPS purchase.

Figure 10-17 *Do not drive while working with your Pocket PC.*

Downloading Maps

Unlike the simple process of exporting a map from Streets and Trips, the process of down-loading maps for Ostia is much more complicated. Downloading maps to your Pocket PC is difficult in all GPS receiver programs, not just Ostia.

The first step to downloading the maps is selecting the correct CD. Because of the large amount of data involved, the map data is split between several CDs. Each CD is, however, clearly labeled, so selecting the correct CD is just a matter of finding the CD with the picture of the region you want.

After you insert the CD into your computer, a window appears displaying the region of the country you selected and all the different maps that make up the region. Each map is displayed in a different color, as shown in Figure 10-18.

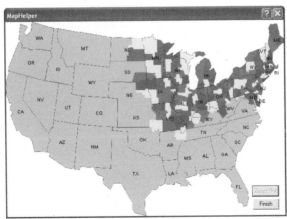

Figure 10-18 *Each map on the CD is displayed in yellow, red, blue, or green.*

The process of unpacking the maps is slightly complicated; you must use File Explorer to extract the map data, because it is compressed on the CD. Here's how to extract a U.S. map so that you can move it to your Pocket PC:

1. Double-click the My Computer icon on the desktop to open a My Computer window.

2. Right-click the CD drive icon, and click Open on the shortcut menu.

3. Double-click the folder labeled with the name of the state you want to open. Each state on the CD has its own folder that contains all the maps for the state.

4. Double-click the name of the map you want to extract.

5. In the WinZip Self-Extractor dialog box, enter the location where you want to store the extracted files. For instance, enter *C:\temp* if you want the map extracted to your temporary directory.

6. Click the Unzip button.

7. In the Confirmation dialog box, click OK.

8. Close the WinZip Self-Extractor dialog box.

9. Copy the map files to your Pocket PC or a CompactFlash storage card for your Pocket PC.

Perhaps the biggest challenge in extracting maps for your Pocket PC is determining which maps you need. On a recent trip to Chicago from Indianapolis, I remembered to get maps for Indianapolis, Lafayette, and Chicago, but neglected to download the Gary map. Ostia worked throughout the trip, but when I got to Gary, I didn't have any map reference data.

Heading Out

After you have the map data downloaded to the Pocket PC, you're ready to use Ostia for basic positional awareness, to navigate, and to get driving directions. Getting started is a simple three-step process:

1. Start the Ostia program, and clear all warnings.

2. Open the map file for your current area.

3. Enable the GPS.

By default, Ostia is stored in the Programs folder on the Start menu. When it opens, a logo screen is displayed briefly. This is followed by the warning message shown earlier in Figure 10-17. After you clear this warning message, you're ready to open the map file.

To open the map file for the current area, on the File menu, tap Open. Ostia displays all the map files on the device and on attached storage cards by default. Tap the map you want to display. The map file displays an overview of the area, as shown in Figure 10-19.

On the Find menu, tap Enable GPS to enable the GPS. Ostia communicates with the GPS and gathers information about the current position. The small icon to the right of the directional arrows is your indicator of GPS status. A red icon means communication failed, or the GPS is not enabled. A yellow icon means the receiver has not yet indicated a position. A green icon means the GPS is operating properly and has determined its position.

Note Occasionally, this icon isn't updated and fails to indicate communication with the GPS when it is occurring. In the following section, I'll show you how to look at other views within Ostia to determine the exact status of the GPS receiver.

After a position has been established, an indicator appears on the map, which is magnified at an appropriate level. Figure 10-20 shows the screen after the signal is found and indicated on the map.

Figure 10-19   *An overview map of Indianapolis.*

Figure 10-20   *Ostia's screen with a GPS position indicated.*

Note You cannot control the zoom level of Ostia's map; the program determines what zoom level to use. If you need control of the zoom level, switch back to Pocket Streets.

Diagnosing GPS Problems

If the GPS receiver indicates a position, it's working, but if you're not getting a position indicator, it makes sense to find out what is going on.

Although Pocket Streets receives GPS position information, it doesn't attempt to check the status of the GPS receiver—how many satellite signals it's receiving, their signal strength, and so on. Also, Pocket Streets has no view that provides information on your current direction and speed. Ostia provides this information.

The Sat Info view displays information on all the satellite signals the receiver is currently picking up. On the View menu, tap Sat Info to display this view, shown in Figure 10-21. The unique satellite numbers are displayed in the upper part of the screen, indicating their current position in the sky.

In the lower part of the screen, there is a series of vertical bars that indicate different satellite signals the receiver is "listening to." A gray bar indicates that the receiver is picking up the satellite, but hasn't yet calculated the distance. When the distance from the satellite has been calculated, the bar turns blue. In either case, the height of the bar indicates the strength of the signal.

You might recall from earlier in this chapter that it takes at least three satellites to determine the position of the receiver, and the more satellites are "locked on," the better the signal.

Note The amount of time it takes a GPS receiver to determine its position depends on both the device itself and when the device was last used. If the device was used recently, the chances are better that its almanac data will be correct and that it will "know where to look" for satellites. This dramatically decreases the amount of time it takes the GPS find a location. However, don't worry about this too much. Most receivers available today can determine their position in less than a minute—less time than you'll spend adjusting the mirrors on your rental car or sitting at a stoplight.

On the View menu, tap GPS Info to access the GPS Info view shown in Figure 10-22. The GPS Info view displays the receiver's position in latitude and longitude, as well as the current time, direction, and speed. If you have a route active, it will also show the distance to the destination. The direction and speed information can't be displayed on the main map screen, but you can access this information through GPS Info view.

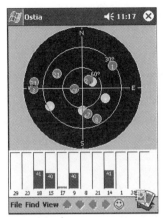

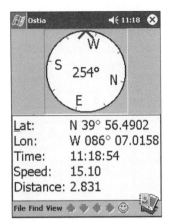

Figure 10-21   *The Sat Info view.*

Figure 10-22   *GPS Info view provides basic travel information.*

Tip If your signals are consistently low or from a small number of satellites, you should reconsider where you are placing the GPS receiver. GPS signals rely on a line of sight to get through, so putting the GPS receiver on one side of the dashboard might put some satellites behind the roof and thus out of reach. The best place is near the middle of the dash and as far forward as possible—as long as that isn't underneath the wiper blades.

Setting a Route

Now that you know the GPS receiver is working, it's time to set a route from your current location to your destination. To set your destination, follow these steps:

1. On the Find menu, tap Address. (You can also tap Intersection or Point Of Interest as a destination, but I won't show you the procedure for selecting the destination using these methods, because they are so rarely used.)

2. In the Street Lookup dialog box, enter the name of the street, and tap the Next button. Note that you're not entering an address the way that you do in Pocket Streets—you're just entering the street name. Figure 10-23 on the next page shows the Street Lookup dialog box.

Note If you tap the Back button while using Ostia, you will have to sort your search over again. Do your best to pick the correct options the first time.

---

3. In the Lookup City dialog box, enter the city, state, and ZIP code of your destination, and tap the Next button. As shown in Figure 10-24, you often need to know
the ZIP code to navigate to the next step.

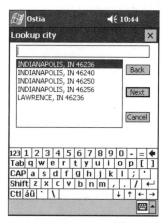

Figure 10-23   *Enter the street first.*   **Figure 10-24**   *Enter the city/state/ZIP*
code combination.

4. Enter the street number, or select it from the list. When you are done, tap the Finish
button. The Address Lookup for street numbers is shown in Figure 10-25.

5. A map of the location displays briefly, and then a dialog box appears asking whether
the address is the destination or the origin, as shown in Figure 10-26. In almost
every case, the address is the destination because the GPS receiver location is the origin. If the address is the destination, tap OK.

Figure 10-25   *Enter the street address,*   **Figure 10-26**   *Ostia confirms that the*
or select the correct range of addresses.   *address is a destination.*

6. A map with the destination highlighted in red appears, as shown in Figure 10-27. If you still have the GPS enabled, the map will quickly display your current location, so you might not see the destination highlighted.

7. On the Find menu, tap New Route to have Ostia calculate a new route for you.

Ostia highlights the route for you in a the color cyan, as shown in Figure 10-28. It also, by default, alerts you audibly when you approach a turn, or when you are off the route.

Figure 10-27   *The destination is highlighted.*

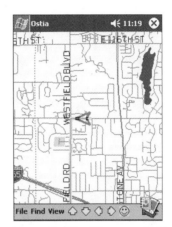

Figure 10-28   *The route is highlighted.*

Putting It All Together

At the beginning of the chapter, I mentioned that I am most comfortable traveling when I've had a chance to plan. It is for that reason that I want to mention a few thoughts about getting all the data you need on your Pocket PC so that you can use a pause in driving (such as a stop light) to refresh your memory.

On my recent trip to Chicago, I needed several pieces of information from different Pocket PC applications. I had Pocket Streets and Ostia running at the same time, because Pocket Streets has a zoom I could control, and Ostia includes GPS support.

In addition, I had the Calendar application running so that I could get the detailed street address of my meeting, and I had the Contacts application running so that I could call the person I was meeting to let him know of my progress.

Finally, I had the directions that I had exported from Streets and Trips open in Pocket Excel. I could have excluded them, because I had Ostia's directions, but Ostia didn't have my destination address in its map database.

Because I had all these applications open and displaying what I needed, it was easy to switch quickly to the Contacts application at a stoplight and call the person I was meeting, and then switch back to review the directions.

Summary

In this chapter, we covered the technologies that can help you get from one location to another. These technologies are useful for people who are "geographically challenged," and even for those who are not.

GPS receivers decode signals from orbiting satellites to determine the receiver's position. GPS receivers determine their position using a time-based method, and therefore also keep very accurate time.

GPS receivers can be used to generate other pieces of information, such as your direction and speed, by evaluating the differences between subsequent position readings.

With or without a GPS receiver, the first step in a successful trip is preplanning with Microsoft Streets and Trips to determine what route you'll follow. The directions and maps you can get with Streets and Trips can be exported to the Pocket PC so that you can bring them along easily.

Pocket Streets can store a portable version of the map you exported from Streets and Trips, including the points of interest and the Address Lookup feature. The biggest difference between Streets and Trips and Pocket Streets is that Pocket Streets won't calculate driving directions.

Other vendors, such as Pharos, offer products for the Pocket PC that provide turn-by-turn driving directions. Pharos' Ostia uses a GPS receiver and the destination information to calculate driving directions and provide audible prompts to indicate when you should turn, when you've arrived, and when you're off track.

In today's fast-paced world, traveling to other cities doesn't need to be stressful. Careful preparation and powerful tools such as GPS receivers can make travel simple and uneventful.

Here are a few things to consider when you're traveling:

- How "geographically challenged" are you? Could you benefit from a GPS receiver?

- If you're not geographically challenged, would it be helpful to get most of what you need from a base map GPS receiver and only connect it to your Pocket PC or notebook for those special circumstances when things are particularly confusing?

- What kind of a checklist might you make when preparing to travel, particularly to cities that you've not been to before or that are relatively unfamiliar to you?

- Are there places where you go repeatedly? Would it be helpful if you could export a map of the entire area to a Pocket Streets map and keep it on your Pocket PC all the time?

- How much has getting lost cost you?

Listen to Me: Recording and Sounds

Ten years ago, industry experts predicted that by now, our personal computers would control everything for us: the lights, the temperature, the channel that we watch on TV, and how our breakfast is cooked. These computers would understand our speech and would respond in our native language to verbal commands.

Although the computer interface we watched on *Star Trek* is still a ways off, today's technology has laid the foundation for conversations with our computers. Specialized speech recognition programs, such as L&H's Voice Xpress and IBM's ViaVoice, have been around for years, giving users who want to invest in the technology the ability to dictate to their computers.

With Office XP, Microsoft moved speech recognition to the mainstream. Now anyone with Office XP has a fairly capable speech recognition engine. Speech recognition also enables users to control the interface of Office applications with just their voices.

Of course, as interesting as speech recognition is, it's only one part of the attempt to communicate with computers. The other part is for computers to be able to speak to us. Great strides have been made in computers' ability to speak since the speech synthesis portrayed in the movie *War Games*, but it is still not perfect. (Do you remember those infamous words— "Would you like to play a game?")

Despite the advances, most of the sounds that come from computers are simple recordings, such as voice mail and previously recorded music or audio books. Very little is done in the way of speech recognition or translating the computer's output into speech.

Tip If your organization hasn't investigated or employed an integrated voice mail system that enables you to access your voice mail messages from Microsoft Outlook and your e-mail messages though a telephone, you should look into it. It makes getting your voice mail and e-mail messages as easy as possible.

In this chapter I'll explain how you can record and play sounds to improve your mobile experience. First I'll address recording and dictation. Then I'll explore these technologies and their drawbacks. Lastly I'll move on to how computers play sounds and music.

Recording and Dictation

In Chapter 9, I explained how to use the recording capabilities of your Pocket PC to record notes for your Microsoft Word documents. In this chapter, I'll explain the Notes application on your Pocket PC. I'll also look at the speech recognition features in Office XP and show you how to use them to navigate through menus or as an alternative to typing.

Pocket PC Voice Notes

If you have a Compaq iPAQ, you probably already know it can make voice recordings. Recorded notes are a great convenience, because you can record them anywhere—while you're walking down the hall or through a busy airport terminal, or driving (that is, at a stoplight).

To see a list of the notes on your Pocket PC, like the one shown in Figure 11-1, tap the recording button. If your Pocket PC doesn't have a recording button, or if you'd prefer to access the Notes screen through the menus, on the Start menu, tap Notes.

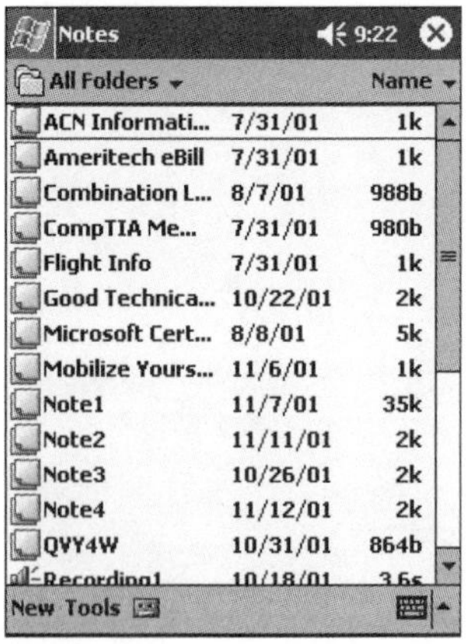

Figure 11-1 *A list of the notes on your Pocket PC.*

If your ActiveSync settings synchronize your notes with Outlook, the Notes folder on your Pocket PC will match the Notes folder in Outlook. Figure 11-2 shows the Outlook Notes folder. Notice that in Outlook the Recording icon is a microphone, but on the Pocket PC, it's a speaker.

Tip   If you don't see a Recording icon, you might need to install the Outlook forms on your computer. To do this, go to the folder where you installed ActiveSync, and double-click the *forminst.exe* file.

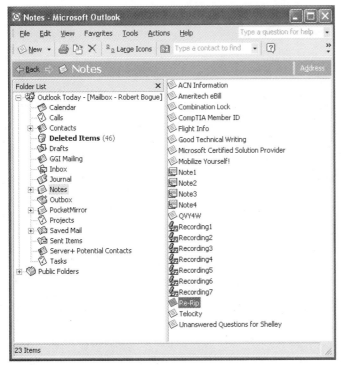

Figure 11-2   *Recordings appear with a microphone icon in Outlook.*

There are three types of notes you can create on your Pocket PC. Text notes are the most common. You can also create a drawing in a note. See Chapter 9 for information on Drawing mode.

The third type of note is a recording. On the Pocket PC, setting the type to a recorded note adds a Recording toolbar to the bottom of the screen, as shown in Figure 11-3 on the next page. Outlook displays the mini-toolbar shown in Figure 11-4 on the next page while the note is playing.

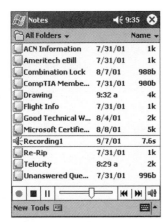

Figure 11-3 *The Notes screen on the Pocket PC doesn't change very much when playing an audio note.*

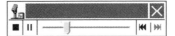

Figure 11-4 *In Outlook, this mini-toolbar appears while an audio note is playing.*

To record a new audio note, in the Notes screen, tap the Record button, or tap the Tape button on the main toolbar to display the Recording toolbar, and then tap and hold the red Record button on the Recording toolbar. To stop recording, release the Record button, or tap the black Stop button to the right of the Record button.

A new recording will be placed in your Notes folder. The recording will be named *Recording* and assigned a sequential number based on how many notes you have on your device at the time. You can play the recordings on your Pocket PC or on your computer, if it has a sound card.

I often use the recording capability of my Pocket PC to make quick notes to myself. This is much more convenient than using the stylus. I've also used my Pocket PC to record important phone conversations (with the other party's permission, of course). The microphone on your Pocket PC probably isn't powerful enough to pick up all the sound in a large meeting, but it might work for meetings in small rooms.

Office XP Speech Recognition

Perhaps you've heard that Microsoft has integrated speech recognition into Office XP, but you haven't been able to find it yet. You can access the feature through the Tools menu, but you might have to hunt down your Office XP CD, because it's not installed by default.

With the speech recognition tools included in Office XP, you can do two things. First you can dictate to the computer so that it can translate your words into text. Second, you can use Voice Command mode to maneuver around the system without using the mouse or keyboard. In Voice Command mode, you can navigate by saying the words associated with menu items and special command keys. The computer isn't perfect at understanding your commands yet, but it's a start.

Tip More than anything else, a high-quality microphone improves the accuracy of speech recognition. This is particularly true of notebooks, because they often use cheaper sound cards. You can buy USB-based headsets and microphones that have their own built-in sound cards. These units are generally best for the highest level of accuracy when using speech recognition.

Using Speech Recognition for the First Time

The first time you use Speech Recognition, two wizards guide you through the process of setting it up. The first wizard sets the volume of the microphone and makes sure your system can use Microsoft Speech. The second wizard starts the training process, which helps Speech Recognition to more accurately understand your words. The process begins with the dialog box shown in Figure 11-5.

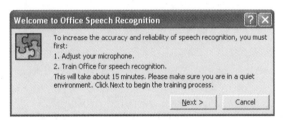

Figure 11-5   *Wizard mania—two wizards get Speech Recognition working.*

The Microphone Wizard isn't particularly complicated—it has only three pages, including the introduction. First you'll read text aloud until the Microphone Wizard can determine the input level for the microphone. Then you'll test that the microphone is positioned correctly so that Speech Recognition can understand sounds like the letter *P*. On the concluding page of the Microphone Wizard, you'll either continue on to the Speech Recognition Wizard or be notified that your system can't perform speech recognition.

Troubleshooting Speech Recognition

If you are notified that your system can't use the Speech Recognition feature, you should try a few things: Turn off any radio, TV, or other sources of noise near the computer. Make the environment as quiet as possible. Try repositioning the microphone to a different location. Then restart the wizard and try again, speaking clearly into the microphone. If the Microphone Wizard still won't continue on to the Speech Recognition Wizard, consider using a different microphone.

In the Speech Recognition Wizard, you read text into the microphone so that the program can learn your speaking style. As each word you speak is registered, it is highlighted on the screen in light blue. When you have finished the sentence, or when the program recognizes the word, it changes the highlighting to dark blue, as shown in Figure 11-6.

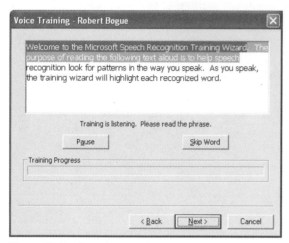

Figure 11-6   *Speech recognition training is an interactive process.*

When you've completed the Speech Recognition Wizard, your personal profile is updated. After you click the Finish button, you watch a short movie that shows you how Speech Recognition works. Then you return to Word, and the Language toolbar, shown in Figure 11-7, appears.

Figure 11-7   *Control how your voice is being used with the Language toolbar.*

When you start dictating, you see ellipses with a blue highlight displayed for a moment, and then your text appears. The ellipses indicate that Word recognizes that you are speaking, but hasn't yet determined what you said. Figure 11-8 shows a Word document with some pending dictation.

It takes a powerful computer to keep up with you while you're speaking, but if you're a poor typist and someone can help clean up your documents, Speech Recognition can save you a lot of time.

Note One of the reasons I'm covering Office's Speech Recognition is that Microsoft Research is working on a demo called MiPad, which can link your Pocket PC to the Speech Recognition feature in Office. Although it wasn't available at the time of this writing, it might be available by the time you read this. For more information, go to *http://research.microsoft.com/srg/mipad.asp*.

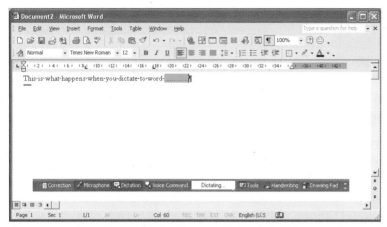

Figure 11-8   *The ellipses stand in for words that Speech Recognition is still working on.*

Sounds and Music

When the Macintosh first came out, it supported sound. IBM-compatible computers could have sound cards added to them, but it was rare to find a computer equipped for sound, particularly in a business environment. That has changed, of course—almost every computer sold today has a sound card. Sound is a part of our computer (and PDA) experience.

Computers and PDAs emit sounds to alert you of a certain event or situation. Lots of other devices do this too, causing varying degrees of annoyance. One type of alert that we're all familiar with is someone's phone going off in a church, movie theater, or restaurant. Worse yet, we've all heard phones that play cute songs to notify people of incoming calls. (I *always* use the vibrate setting to be considerate of others.)

Music is another popular way to use sound on a computer or PDA. The big news in the world of music is the MP3 format that compresses music files so that they can be transferred between computers in a reasonable amount of time and stored on a hard disk. I, for instance, have over 4000 songs on my computer, requiring nearly 20 GB of storage. (For those interested, these are all ripped [created] from CDs that I own and that are stored safely so that they won't be scratched.)

Microsoft has introduced another format—the Microsoft Windows Media Audio (WMA) format—that is the preferred format for Microsoft Media Player. It is slightly better at compressing data, but its acceptance has been negligible, in part because of the proliferation of MP3 players. However, it is the format you'll likely get if you download anything from Microsoft.

Tip For a detailed comparison of the different file formats, you might want to check out *http://www.microsoft.com/mobile/pocketpc/stepbystep/audio.asp.*

In this section, I'll explain two ways you can use sound on a mobile device. The first is customizing the sounds on your Pocket PC. The second is downloading music to your Pocket PC in both MP3 and WMA formats so that you can play music during your flight, while you're waiting in an airport, or just sitting in your hotel room. I'll cover audio books for the Pocket PC in the next chapter.

Changing Event Sounds on Your Pocket PC

By default, your Pocket PC makes certain sounds when events occur. For instance, when you connect the unit to your computer through ActiveSync, a sound is played. A different sound is played when the Pocket PC is disconnected. Each of these sounds is called a notification.

All notifications are controlled from the Sounds & Notifications dialog box in Control Panel. To view this dialog box, on the Start menu, tap Settings, and then tap Sounds & Notifications. On the Volume tab, shown in Figure 11-9, you can control the overall volume and select which sounds are played.

Tip Clear the Screen Taps and Hardware Buttons check boxes unless you really need them. These noises get annoying pretty quickly, particularly to someone who's sitting close to you. Notification sounds might be slightly disruptive, but at least you can prevent them from playing every few seconds.

On the Notifications tab, shown in Figure 11-10, you can control how the Pocket PC notifies you. Make your selections to control what sound (if any) is played, whether an icon is displayed on the title bar, and whether the device's notification light is flashed.

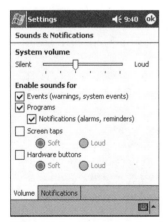

Figure 11-9   *How annoying do you want to be?*

Figure 11-10   *Choose your settings on the Notifications tab.*

Selecting the Display Message On Screen check box briefly displays an icon on the title bar. Similarly, selecting the Flash Light For check box turns on the message light for the period of time you specify. Noncritical events, such as beginning and ending ActiveSync, might not warrant a notification, but you might want the message light to flash when you receive a new Inbox message.

Note The message light doesn't always work properly. The light isn't always turned off when the event has been addressed, which means it might be on for no reason. Specifically, if the message light flashes when you receive a new Inbox message, it doesn't turn off when you read the message—it stays on for the entire length of time you specified in the Flash Light For box.

The Play Sound drop-down list includes all the *.wav* format sound files in the Windows folder of your Pocket PC. I've added my own files to my device, including the Bullwink *.wav* file. This file is Bullwinkle saying "Hello out there in TV Land."

The process of adding a *.wav* file to your Windows folder is long but simple. Open My Computer, double-click Mobile Device, double-click My Pocket PC, and finally click Windows. This opens a window where you can drag or copy additional *.wav* files. After you've put a *.wav* file in this folder, open the Sounds & Notifications dialog box, and select the sound in the Play Sound drop-down list.

Note There are two reasons why you shouldn't use sounds that are very long. First, it will use more precious space on your Pocket PC. Second, the longer the message, the quicker it gets annoying. Even my Bullwinkle notification will be replaced eventually because it's too long.

Playing Music on Your Pocket PC

For the past few years, portable devices that play MP3 files have been available. There are no moving parts—no CD spinning and no tape spooling. This was a godsend for athletes who previously had to use expensive CD players with enough anti-skip protection to absorb the impact of running.

Today, Pocket PCs can do what MP3 players do. A Pocket PC can store music and display what is currently playing, and most have both a speaker and a headphone jack. You'll probably need to add a CompactFlash card with more memory, though, because even a compressed MP3 file requires between 1 and 5 MB.

Understanding Compressed Music Basics

Compression, which grew from encryption technology, enables us to put more data in the same amount of space. Today, most of us are familiar with data compression from working with *.zip* and *.cab* files.

However, one of the limits of traditional compression is that it must return the data to the form it was in before it was compressed. This is very important for spreadsheets, payroll numbers, and programs, but it is less important for subjective data such as photographs and music.

With subjective data, small amounts of information can be lost during the compression process without rendering the entire file useless. The person viewing the end result might not even notice the missing information. This kind of compression, called *lossy* compression, is used in JPG photographs and in compressed music files.

For instance, when a photograph is compressed, a single dot, or *pixel*, might be assigned a slightly different color (one that is easier to represent in a compressed form) than it had originally. However, it's likely that the variation would be so slight that it would be very difficult for the person viewing the compressed photograph to notice the change.

The idea in music compression is the same. There are some sound variations that humans won't hear, or won't miss hearing. Music compression takes advantage of the human ear's natural filtering process.

Note Although I keep referring to music files here, the same concept applies to any sound file. The primary difference is that with alert sounds or a spoken voice, the human ear can tolerate lower sound quality than it does with music files.

For instance, if you're sitting in a room listening to music, there might also be background noise that you're filtering out. As I'm sitting here listening to music now, I'm filtering out the sound of the keys as I'm typing, the fans in my computer, and the sounds of the leaves rustling outside. (I have the door open.) All these sounds are there, but I'm ignoring them because they aren't the music that I'm trying to listen to.

Because our ears are so adept at filtering out unwanted sounds, some of the information in music can be discarded without our noticing it. This is particularly true when we are distracted by another activity such as writing, jogging, or playing a computer game. The same kinds of mathematical tricks that are used to remove unnecessary data in a photo are used to process music files so that they will take up less space.

Another factor with music files is the quality of the device that reproduces the sound. For instance, a Walkman doesn't produce the same sound quality as a $5,000 home entertainment system. The Walkman still produces music, but it doesn't do it at the same level. It's likely that whatever sound is lost during compression, we wouldn't have been able to hear anyway. In a way, losing information we couldn't have heard is helpful—it saves space by making the file smaller.

One of the interesting things about lossy compression mechanisms is that you can often indirectly decide how much data you're willing to lose. The more data you're willing to lose, the more compressed the file can be. You can determine the quality of a file by specifying how much space you're willing to let it occupy.

Music compression is based on *bit rate*. A bit rate is the number of bits per second used to represent the sound file. (You might remember that a bit is a single binary digit, a one or a zero.) Lower bit rates mean lower file quality because more information is discarded— but the file is smaller too.

MP3 bit rates are generally 320, 192, or 128 kilobits per second (Kbps). A 320 Kbps file will sound most like the original. The Microsoft Windows Media (audio) file format (*.wma*) uses different compression algorithms and can produce higher-quality sounds at lower bit rates. A *.wma* file sounds acceptable at a bit rate of 64 Kbps—half the size of a similar-quality MP3 file.

When deciding how much music will fit on your Pocket PC, consider that *.wma* files can lower the bit rate but still play music that sounds largely like the original.

Moving Music to Your Pocket PC

There are two approaches to moving music to your Pocket PC. The first is to simply copy the MP3 files on your computer to your Pocket PC. You can also move music to your Pocket PC by using Media Player to *transcode* the files.

Transcoding is the process of converting the files from one format to another. In this case, transcoding converts the file from MP3 to WMA format. In addition, Media Player can reduce the bit rate of the coding to reduce the overall file size. This, of course, reduces the overall quality of the sound; however, sometimes the additional quality loss is not so excessive as to decrease the value of the music. Often, a 128-Kbps MP3 file and a 64-Kbps WMA file played on a Pocket PC are indistinguishable.

Note If you're interested in more details about transcoding, read the article at *http://www.microsoft.com/mobile/pocketpc/columns/transcoding.asp.*

Using Media Player to transcode sound files for storage on your Pocket PC is easy. Start Media Player, and select a list of files you want to put on your Pocket PC. Figure 11-11 on the next page shows Media Player and a short list of files in the playlist. When your list is complete, click the Copy To CD Or Device button. After a minute or so, a screen like the one shown in Figure 11-12 on the next page appears, showing that your Pocket PC has been found. If you have a storage card in your Pocket PC, click the down arrow to the right of the Music On Device box, and click Storage Card in the drop-down list.

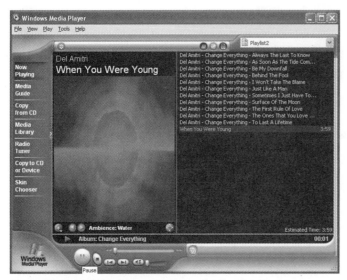

Figure 11-11 *Media Player supports playlists for songs.*

Figure 11-12 *Copy music to any device in this way.*

Windows Media Player will transcode and move to the selected device every song in the playlist with a check mark next to it. To set how Windows Media Player transcodes the files before storage on the device, on the Tools menu, click Options. In the Options dialog box, click the Devices tab. The Devices tab is shown in Figure 11-13. In the Devices area, click the device you are copying to, and then click Properties. The device's Properties dialog box appears, as shown in Figure 11-14.

In this dialog box, you can set the bit rate for the files and thus decide how high the quality will be. Media Player can also set the quality level automatically. My preference is a bit rate of 64 Kbps because it is very clear, and I have a relatively large storage card for my Pocket PC. When you're done, click the OK button twice to return to the Copy Music screen.

Figure 11-13   *A list of currently connected devices.*

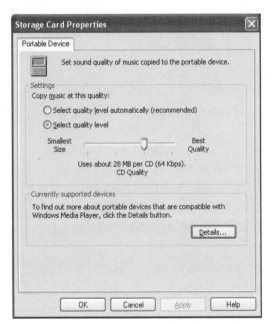

Figure 11-14   *The Quality settings for copying music files.*

Click the Copy Music button, and wait as Windows Media Player converts each file into the file format you selected and copies it to the device. This process can take a little while, particularly if you have a long playlist.

When the process is complete, you can play the songs that you downloaded on your Pocket PC. By default, your Media Player playlist includes all the media files on your Pocket PC. You can, however, edit the playlist if you want Media Player to play only certain songs.

Summary

Speech recognition technology is becoming mainstream. The inclusion of a Speech Recognition feature in Office XP all but guarantees that speech recognition will become widely available. The ability to use this technology with the mobile devices we already have is in development.

In this chapter, you learned how to use voice recordings and dictation to be more productive in the office, in the car, or wherever you might need to record a thought or write a document. Voice recordings and dictation are the foundation for future advances in speech recognition technology.

You learned to how to change the notification sounds the Pocket PC uses to alert you when an event has occurred, and how to control silent notifications. Finally, you learned how to move music files to your Pocket PC and how to use Windows Media Player on the computer to save space with the music files you want on your Pocket PC.

When you're thinking about how to use your voice and your ears to interact with your computer and Pocket PC, there are a few things that you must consider:

- Are you in a place where you can speak freely, like an open street, or are you in a quiet place, like a library, where speaking is inappropriate?

- Will you remember to check the recorded voice notes you made for yourself? How will you retrieve them without disturbing those around you?

- How fast can you type? Does it make sense to dictate to the computer and get help cleaning up that dictation?

- Do you have a favorite audio clip from the movies, TV, or radio? Can you find that audio clip in electronic form? Would it be appropriate for a notification?

- Are you easily annoyed? If so, you'll probably want to stick with very short notification clips.

- Do you go places where you might want to listen to music? An airport? The gym? A hotel room?

- How much space for music files do you have on your notebook or Pocket PC?

Reading Time: eBooks, News Clippings, and Agents

The typical business knowledge worker has to manage a small mountain of paper while traveling. This huge volume of paper greatly increases the amount of weight that he or she carries. Almost all of this paper can be converted into electronic form and carried without any additional weight.

This chapter covers ways to stop carrying paper and start using electronic tools. Admittedly, the solutions aren't perfect. The news you receive on a Pocket PC or a notebook isn't as complete as a typical newspaper, and you might miss an article or two, but the trade-off for this is carrying less paper with you.

This chapter is divided into two sections: eBooks and Agents. eBooks are electronic representations of books. Those books can range from the latest novel to a technical manual or even the latest issue of your favorite magazine. Agents are programs that locate smaller news items and bits of information that are useful to you.

eBooks

Before I explain the complexities and current state of the eBook industry, I'm going to show you why you might want to read an eBook rather than the traditional paper version.

One benefit of most eBooks is that they can be held in one hand. You have to use two hands to turn the pages of even a typical small paperback, but you can advance to the next page on most eBook readers by pressing a single key or tapping a single button on the Pocket PC. In larger book formats, turning pages with one hand necessitates that the book be resting on something. Reading eBooks on a Pocket PC means you don't need any space for the book to rest on.

A subtle benefit of the eBook is lighting: Because the Pocket PC has its own built-in lighting, there is no need to have another light source available. You can comfortably read your eBook in the darkened cabin of an airplane without having to turn on the sometimes blinding and always misdirected reading light. In your hotel room, you can leave the lights on or turn them off while you read.

One reason to read an eBook rather than a printed book is that the navigation tools available in most eBook readers help you locate important information quickly. To illustrate this point, I'll use the book *After the Gold Rush,* written by Steve McConnell and published by Microsoft Press. It's available for free in the Microsoft Reader eBook format on Microsoft's Web site (*http://www.microsoft.com/reader/extreme.asp*).

While reading this book, I highlighted several important passages that I might want to quote in a presentation. I highlight a section by dragging my stylus across it and pausing until the shortcut menu appears, as shown in Figure 12-1. As you can see from the shortcut menu, I can also add a bookmark, note, or drawing. Figure 12-2 shows a highlighted passage.

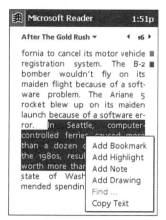

Figure 12-1   *Use commands on the shortcut menu to mark up your eBook.*

Figure 12-2   *This is what the text looks like when it's highlighted.*

Browsing through the eBook, you can quickly locate text you highlighted, much as you would in a traditional book. However, the electronic nature of an eBook opens up new opportunities. On the cover page of an eBook, you'll find a link to the Annotations Index, as shown in Figure 12-3. Tapping the Annotations Index displays a list of the annotations you've made in the book, as shown in Figure 12-4. You'll also see in Figure 12-4 that the selection I highlighted in Figure 12-2 appears as an annotation on the page.

Figure 12-3 *The cover of an eBook is not all that different from a regular book.*

Figure 12-4 *I annotate a lot when I don't have to remember where I put the highlighter.*

Navigating the pages of the Annotations Index enables you to quickly look up any bookmarks, highlighting, or notes. Tapping an entry in the list displays the location in the book where you placed the annotation. By using the Annotations Index, you can locate the place in the book that you want to reference or reread.

You can also find a highlighted passage using the Find feature on the shortcut menu. Use the Find feature to search for a word or phrase. Then jump from reference to reference until you find the passage you need.

The most frequent complaint against eBooks is that the screen size or font size is too small. Without totally discounting these criticisms, I can say that the appearance of the text in eBook readers has improved dramatically. Reading an eBook is probably easier for me than reading a paperback book with poor-quality paper. The contrast is higher and the edges of the letters are much better defined.

If you're interested in eBooks but aren't yet convinced that you want to spend your money on one, go to *http://www.microsoft.com/reader/extreme.asp* and download one of the free Microsoft Reader eBooks. You can copy this file to your Pocket PC and see how you like the eBook experience without installing any new software.

Sorting Out Readers and Formats

Earlier in this chapter, I explained features of Microsoft Reader, which comes preinstalled on your Pocket PC and is available for free for desktop systems. This reader format might be the easiest one to work with on your Pocket PC, but it's not the only one available. There are three eBook readers that you need to be primarily concerned with. They are:

- Microsoft Reader (*.lit*)
- Peanut Press/Palm Reader (*.pdb/.prc*)
- MobiPocket Reader (*.doc*)

There are other readers and formats, but these three will work for most of the eBooks you will find. One item that isn't in this list is Adobe's Portable Document Format (PDF) and its Acrobat program. That's because the PDF format is set up for printed pages, which are too big to display on an eBook reader.

You'll notice that I didn't list Microsoft Word among the important reader formats. It's not because Pocket Word can't be used to read documents, but because Word and Pocket Word are not eBook formats. You can read a Word document on your Pocket PC, but it doesn't have the same ease of navigation and "feel" as reading in an eBook reader. If you're interested in reading Word documents on your Pocket PC, you can review the coverage of Pocket Word in Chapter 9.

Microsoft Reader

For most people, using Microsoft Reader is an easy decision. It's already installed on your Pocket PC, and a significant number of eBooks are available in the *.lit* format that Microsoft Reader uses. Add to this the fact that Microsoft Reader is free for Windows as well, and it's easy to see why it's so popular.

If you're interested in getting Microsoft Reader for Windows, you need to go to *http://www.microsoft.com/reader/download.asp*. Follow the guided steps to download the software and activate the reader. Activation is necessary for some forms of eBook protection that are used to prevent eBooks from being copied. I'll address security after I describe the readers.

Peanut Press/Palm Reader

Peanut Press was purchased by Palm Computing in March 2001. You might think that would mean you can't run a Peanut Press reader on a Pocket PC. However, Peanut Press has a long history of developing eBook reader software for both the Palm platform and Microsoft Windows CE devices, including the Pocket PC. Peanut Press has developed a solid eBook reader for both platforms, called Palm Reader.

Palm Reader supports annotations and bookmarks. However, the interface for adding them isn't as simple as the interface in Microsoft Reader. To perform these tasks, you must select them from the menu at the bottom of the screen. Figure 12-5 shows a free Peanut Press eBook, *The Declaration of Independence*. This book and several others are available from the Peanut Press Web site at *http://www.peanutpress.com*.

Although Palm Reader doesn't have quite as slick an interface as Microsoft Reader, it's certainly workable and easy to use. The big advantage of Palm Reader is that it has an adequate, if not stellar, security mechanism that I'll explain later in this chapter.

Figure 12-5   *The cover page for* The Declaration of Independence *viewed in Palm Reader.*

MobiPocket/MobiPocket Reader

Like Palm Reader, the MobiPocket Reader client isn't as slick as Microsoft Reader, but it's usable. You can tap the right side of the screen to move forward in the book and the left side to go back. Unlike Palm Reader, MobiPocket Reader uses the same library-type interface to manage eBooks that Microsoft Reader uses, eliminating the need to hunt down the books you want to read.

The biggest advantage to MobiPocket Reader is its ability to handle more than one type of eBook. In addition to a proprietary format, it also supports the open eBook formats. This makes it more versatile.

Finally, the MobiPocket Reader client enables you to get electronic news and read HTML and text documents on your Pocket PC. I'll explore these features later in this chapter.

MobiPocket Reader is available for download on the MobiPocket Web site at *http://www.mobipocket.com.*

Understanding Digital Copyright Protection

In the traditional print world, copyright protection is relatively easy. Books are printed without much fear that someone will attempt to copy them, because copying printed books usually takes more time and effort than it's worth. This is not the case with electronic books. Electronic equipment can copy files very easily. Copying an eBook takes almost no effort.

To prevent the reader from viewing the eBook on a device other than the one it was intended for, manufacturers have developed security mechanisms. These mechanisms rely on the encryption methods we looked at in Chapter 3. The eBook is encrypted so that only the correct key can decrypt it into a readable form. The key is embedded in the user's name or in a digital ID on the eBook reader.

There are three levels of protection:

- No protection
- Signed/identified
- Secure

Because there's little to say about the security features of books that have no copyright protection, other than that they can be freely copied, I'll start with signed (also called identified) eBooks.

Signed/Identified

Signed eBooks have information on their cover pages identifying the person to whom the book belongs. This might not seem like much of a deterrent for copyright violators, but most people are more mindful of where they store books that have their name in them. Figure 12-6 shows the identification page from the eBook *The 7 Dirty Words of the Free Agent Workforce*. It was written by Daniel H. Pink and is available for free at *http://www.ipublish.com*.

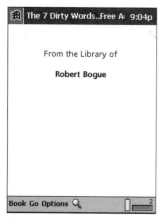

Figure 12-6   *The signed page indicates that this book belongs to Robert Bogue (me).*

Secure

Secure eBooks cannot be moved from one device to another. When you download the eBook, you receive an encrypted copy. The only way to unlock it is to use the device key provided when you purchased the book. This is the greatest level of security for an eBook publisher. Because the key is device-specific, it's very unlikely that someone will be able to forge a key and gain unlicensed access to the eBook. The disadvantage to this is that if you purchase a secure eBook and sign it with the device information from your personal computer, you won't be able to use it on your Pocket PC.

In a bid to provide eBook users with a little more flexibility, Microsoft now allows you to use the same key for up to four devices. This means you can now read the same eBook on your desktop, your Pocket PC, and two other devices. The eBook is still secure, because the activation requires both your e-mail address and password.

Secure eBooks are available in the Palm Reader and MobiPocket Reader formats for the Pocket PC. Secure eBooks are available in the Microsoft Reader format for the personal computer, and for devices running Microsoft's new Pocket PC 2002 operating system. Pocket PC 2002 supports the Digital Rights Management version 5 (DRM5) secure standard—the protocol used to manage digital rights, or secure the book.

Electronic Audio Books

I have so far left out one variation of the eBook. For many years, books have been available in audio form—on cassettes, and more recently on CDs. The audio book is the same as the printed book, except that it is read aloud by the author or an actor, and you can listen to the material while driving a car or when you want to rest your eyes.

Audio books have come into the digital age just as books have. The Web site *http://www.audible.com* offers hundreds of audio book titles in a variety of file formats that fit most portable devices, including the Pocket PC.

Audible.com's AudibleManager software helps you download books from the Web site after you have purchased them and install them on your portable device. This software can break the book into chunks if your device isn't capable of storing the whole book at one time. This is a good thing, because a three-hour book at the highest level of sound quality would consume 43 MB of RAM.

On the Audible.com Web site, you can select from four different file quality levels. The lowest can store a three-hour book in about 7 MB. That's more than a standard eBook would consume, but much more manageable than 43 MB. The other file formats fall between these two extremes. In my sample book, the other formats weighed in at 11 MB and 22 MB.

The lowest-quality format available from Audible.com is too low-quality for my ears; I'm not comfortable listening to it. The second lowest format is passable, and the second highest is good enough for most users. The highest-quality file format is nearly indistinguishable from a good tape or CD.

If you like to listen to audio books, you'll love the flexibility that AudiblePlayer and AudibleManager will give you. Instead of carrying a CD player and a few CDs, you can download an entire book or library to your notebook computer. Then you can move a few hours of audio books at a time to your mobile device.

Audible.com has more than books. It offers subscriptions to newspapers and magazines in electronic audio format. These subscription services help you keep up with the latest news while driving, instead of missing out on news articles because you don't have time to read them.

Web Sites for eBooks

One of the biggest challenges associated with eBooks is finding them. The following Web sites offer eBooks in various formats:

- **Blackmask Online:** *http://www.blackmask.com/Books_for_MS_Reader*
- **DotLit:** *http://www.dotlit.com*
- **EBookWeb:** *http://www.ebookweb.org*
- **Elegant Solutions Software and Publishing Company:** *http://esspc-ebooks.com*
- **Free-ePress:** *http://www.free-epress.com*
- **Chris De Herrera's Windows CE Web site:** *http://www.cewindows.net/scripts /linkman/linkmat.cgi*
- **iPublish:** *http://www.ipublish.com*
- **Learning Network:** *http://learningnetwork.ebrary.com*
- **MemoWare:** *http://www.memoware.com*
- **MobiPocket:** *http://www.MobiPocket.com*
- **University of Virginia Electronic Text Center:** *http://etext.virginia.edu/ebooks*
- **XC Publishing:** *http://www.xcpublishing.com*

This isn't an exhaustive list, but you can find links to other eBook providers on most of these sites.

Agents

If you have read any science fiction in the last 20 or so years, you've probably run across the idea that eventually we'll all have our own digital "agents"—essentially, sophisticated software designed to solve our information needs. They will scour the information land-scape, gathering information we might find useful. When we come to work in the morning and start our computers, the agent will gleefully tell us about new articles it has found that it thinks might interest us.

There's rarely any mention of how these agents got to know what we want to hear about. The agents just seem to work endlessly, searching for whatever information we want, even before we know we're going to want it.

The agent technology of today is much less sophisticated and more complicated than the agents in science fiction. For the most part, we are limited to identifying which Web sites, and sometimes what sections within them, we find interesting. The agents of today don't search the entire Internet for any scraps of information we might want. They search for and download only what we tell them to, and only in the locations we specify.

The agents of today come in three varieties:

- **Search engines**   These agents search for a set of keywords only when you tell them to.

- **Saved searches**   These agents are a slight variation on the search engine. The engine runs the same search for you over and over. It notifies you, normally via e-mail, when the search yields something new.

- **Gatherers**   These agents gather information from a predetermined list of sites and put it all together in one place.

Later in this chapter, I'll explain AvantGo, a content-caching program that enables you to view Web pages offline. This program is included on your Pocket PC and is an invaluable tool for taking the information with you.

Because I assume that almost everyone has used search engines, I'll skip them and address saved searches and gatherers.

Saved Searches

When you're searching for information, you probably need it right away. However, there are times when you might just be looking to see if something is out there. For instance, you might be searching for your own name on the Web. I keep a saved search on Northern Light (*http://www.northernlight.com*) to notify me any time my name is used on a Web page.

Admittedly, part of the reason for this is "ego surfing," looking for places where my name is used because it strokes my ego, but I also want to make sure my character isn't being attacked without my knowledge. This is also my "insurance policy" against someone stealing my identity on line.

To show you how easy it is to set up a saved search, let's create a search for *BattleBots* on Northern Light. *BattleBots* is a show on Comedy Central on which robots fight each other. It's something I have an interest in and would like to keep up with. Here is how I would set up the search:

1. Start Microsoft Internet Explorer.

2. Enter *http://www.northernlight.com* in the Address bar of Internet Explorer, and press Enter.

3. Enter the text you want to search for in the Search box, and click Search. A results page similar to the one in Figure 12-7, on the next page, is displayed.

4. On the Results page, click Save This Search As An Alert. This displays the Create New Alert page, which looks similar to Figure 12-8, on the next page.

5. On the Create New Alert page, enter an alert name, and select the Create An Additional News Alert For This Search check box if you want Northern Light to search newsgroups in addition to the Web.

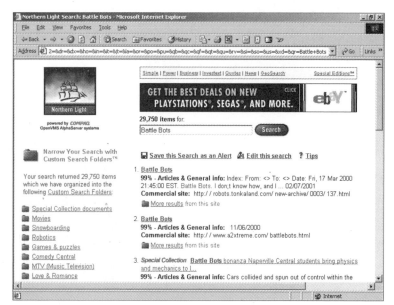

Figure 12-7   *At NorthernLight.com, your results are sorted by relevance and contain both an abstract and a description of the link.*

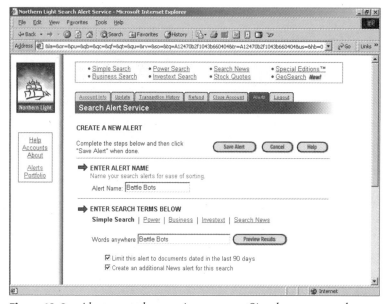

Figure 12-8   *Alerts must have unique names. Simple names are best.*

6. Click Save Alert when you're done. This displays the Search Alert Service Login page, which looks similar to Figure 12-9.

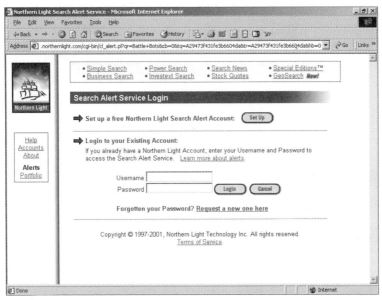

Figure 12-9   *Northern Light's alert service requires that you set up a free account.*

7. On the Search Alert Service Login page, enter your user name and password, and proceed to step 9 if you already have an account, or click Set Up to create a new account. The form to create a new login is shown in Figure 12-10. (Because I already have an account on Northern Light, I created one for my dog, Ashley, also a *BattleBots* fan.)

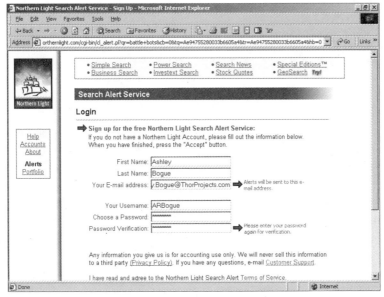

Figure 12-10   *Creating a new account requires only basic information.*

8. On the next page, you'll be prompted for the information to create a search account. Enter your first and last names, e-mail address, and a user name and password. When you're done reading the agreement, click I Agree. A list of your agent searches is displayed, as shown in Figure 12-11.

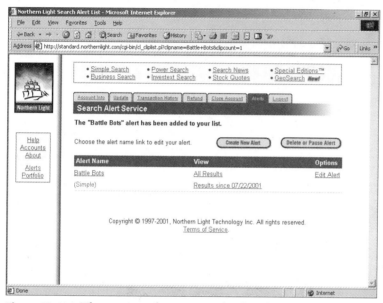

Figure 12-11   *The new search you created is listed.*

9. Review the Search Alert Service page to ensure that your alert was added correctly.

After you've created your search, you'll periodically receive e-mails containing links and abstracts for all the new Web pages that have your search terms in them. If you also created a news agent, you'll receive notifications whenever a newsgroup article is posted on the topic as well. Although search engines crawl the Web every day, it might take some time after a page is posted for it to be indexed by the search engine, and thus for you to receive a notification.

Northern Light is one of several search engines that offer saved searches. If you have a different favorite search engine, look around the site to see if it offers saved searches. They are a powerful way to keep track of topics that interest you.

More specifically news-targeted alert services such as *http://NewsGuard.com* can offer faster turnaround time, sending you daily updates on information you're interested in, but the drawback is that NewsGuard searches only news sites, so it might miss other references. Unlike general alert services, NewsGuard can be set up to notify you immediately when a news story is posted.

Gatherers

The true realization of a personal agent is a piece of software that goes out across the Internet and grabs articles and information of interest to you. We're a long way from having a service that keeps track of the types of news stories you are interested in and filters the news for you, but there are sites available today where you can gather different types of stories from all over the Internet.

These gatherers, when Web-based, are often touted as home pages or Web portals. They are designed to show you all the information you might be interested in on a few pages. The following sites offer customized views of the Internet in which you can choose your own stories or elements:

- **MSN.com**   Everyone who uses Internet Explorer gets MSN as a home page. Many people don't realize that they can change the content according to their tastes. Use the My MSN tab to change the content, the layout, and even the colors.

- **My.Yahoo.com**   Yahoo! is one of the classic Internet companies. Its Web site can be customized to fit your preferences, just as MSN can. Yahoo! even enables you to maintain several different home pages to fit your moods.

- **My.Netscape.com**   If you started your Internet browsing experience with Netscape Navigator (now Communicator), you might have used *http://www.netscape.com* as your home page. My.Netscape.com features the same news and information as *http://www.netscape.com*, but it enables you to customize the information you see.

There are several other sites around the Internet where you can customize your page so that you're getting all the information you want to see and none of the things that aren't useful to you.

The problem with gatherers is that you don't have the content with you when you travel. Because these sites only gather the information for you, it won't be available to you when you are disconnected from the Internet. However, there are ways of taking Web content with you. That is the subject of the next section.

Offline Web Pages

Because most gatherers don't send you an e-mail message with the content you might be interested in, you have to download your Web portal's pages to your notebook or Pocket PC so that you can take them with you while traveling. In this section, I'll explain how you can do this using your notebook and your Pocket PC.

Internet Explorer Offline

Internet Explorer has a feature that enables you to work offline. When you work in this mode, Internet Explorer doesn't fetch new content from the Internet when you visit a page it has cached. It just displays the content it has saved.

Internet Explorer can cache content in two ways. The first way is possible only if you have visited the page recently. Internet Explorer automatically makes copies of pages when you surf them, in case you want to come back to them. If you go back to the page before Internet Explorer has deleted the page from its cache, and it appears that the content hasn't changed, Internet Explorer uses the cached page on your hard disk, rather than downloading the page from the Internet again.

Caching pages you've visited is helpful because it reduces the amount of time it takes to load Web pages the next time you look at them, but it does little to help you get new information for your review while you travel.

The other way Internet Explorer can cache pages is to make a Favorite available offline. You can do this when you save the page as a Favorite, or you can change it later by right-clicking the entry in the Favorites list and clicking Properties on the shortcut menu. On the Web Document tab of the Properties dialog box, select Make This Page Available Offline to make the content available when you are not connected to the Internet.

But that's getting a bit ahead of the game. First, let's set up a favorite that will cache content so that you can work offline. The following process shows how to do that:

1. Open Internet Explorer.

2. Go to the Web site you want to make available offline. Figure 12-12 shows *my.yahoo.com* after I signed in.

Figure 12-12 *My Yahoo! gathers news from many sources.*

3. On the Favorites menu, click Add To Favorites. The Add Favorite dialog box shown in Figure 12-13 appears.

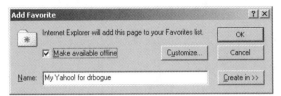

Figure 12-13   *There isn't much to creating a favorite.*

4. Select the Make Available Offline check box.

5. Click Customize to choose how Internet Explorer will make the page available.

6. If the Offline Favorite Wizard's introduction screen appears, click Next to start the wizard. The next page in the wizard is shown in Figure 12-14.

Figure 12-14   *I've never thought of most of the links on the Web as "deep," but Internet Explorer does.*

7. Determine whether you want to cache only the current page or pages linked to the current page as well. In most cases, you'll want to cache pages linked to the current page. This is because your gatherer page rarely includes the content. Most of the time it will contain only the headlines, and in some cases, abstracts of the stories.

8. Select the number of levels from the page that you want to have cached. Start by selecting 1 Links Deep to minimize the amount of time it takes to download the content for caching. You can always change this setting later if you find you didn't download enough information.

9. Click Next to display the wizard's next page, shown in Figure 12-15 on the next page.

10. Decide how you want to synchronize, or cache, the content. In most cases you'll want to set up Internet Explorer to synchronize on a schedule. That way, you won't have to remember to cache the content yourself.

Figure 12-15   *I like to manually synchronize before I leave on a trip rather than letting Internet Explorer do it for me.*

11. Click Next to set a schedule for the synchronization. The wizard's schedule page is displayed, as shown in Figure 12-16.

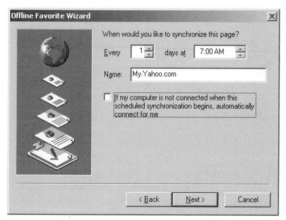

Figure 12-16   *You can set the frequency and time of day for synchronization.*

12. Set the number of days between synchronizations and the time to perform the synchronization. If you usually leave the office at 5:30 in the evening, you might set synchronization to happen at 5 P.M. If you think you'll have your computer plugged in every morning, you might select early morning.

13. Type a name for the synchronization. This can differ from the name of the favorite link, but it doesn't have to.

14. If you want your computer to connect to the Internet when it's time to synchronize, select If My Computer Is Not Connected When This Scheduled Synchronization Begins, Automatically Connect For Me. Most mobile users won't want to select this option. This might cause an unexpected long-distance charge on your hotel phone bill.

15. Click Next to show the authorization page of the Offline Favorite Wizard. Figure 12-17 shows this page.

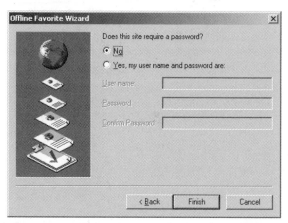

Figure 12-17   *Yahoo! uses cookies, so no authorization is required.*

16. If the site you've selected requires that you log in, rather than leaving a cookie on your system, you must select the Yes, My Username And Password Are option, and enter the information in the boxes provided. (Cookies are small bits of information stored on your computer by a remote Web site. They are used to identify you or store your preferences.)

17. Click Finish to complete the wizard.

18. Click OK to complete the addition of the offline favorite.

19. On the Tools menu, click Synchronization to synchronize the content immediately. When prompted, make sure that your new offline Web page is selected, and click Synchronize.

If at any point you find yourself without a connection to the Internet, on the File menu, click Work Offline. This will switch Internet Explorer into Offline mode, and you will be able to see the pages you have cached.

AvantGo

Pocket Internet Explorer doesn't support offline Web pages; however, there is a solution for Pocket PCs when you want to take content with you. AvantGo works well with the Pocket PC, because the company works with content providers to create special PDA-friendly content.

In AvantGo-speak, the Web sites you want to make available offline are called channels. You subscribe to the channels you want to have on your device. When ActiveSync synchronizes your device, the updated Web content is downloaded and copied to your device.

By default, AvantGo's Mobile Link application is installed as a conduit and turned on. (For more information about installing conduits, refer to Chapter 5, "Park It in the Garage: Synchronization.") To customize the channels you subscribe to, go to the AvantGo Web site (*http://www.avantgo.com*). Sign up by clicking the Sign Up button on the lower right side of the page, below Mobile Internet Service. (The location of this button might have changed since this book was written, so look around for it if you don't see it.)

After you've started the signup process, click the New Users link to confirm that you are a new user. This takes you to a screen where you can specify the mobile platform you have. This should be a Pocket PC device. Then click Next.

After you've selected your Pocket PC device, download the AvantGo client to your Pocket PC. To do this, connect your Pocket PC to your computer, and click Download. When you are done, run the downloaded program.

Your Pocket PC already has AvantGo installed, but downloading the client from the Web page ensures that you have the latest version. It won't hurt anything if you reinstall the same version.

To set up and synchronize AvantGo Mobile Link, on the Active Sync menu, tap Mobile Link. From this point you'll be led through a couple of steps that set up the AvantGo Mobile Link client to synchronize. This is as simple as selecting the Mobile Link option in the ActiveSync options. (See Chapter 5 for more details on how to change synchronization settings.)

Next you need to enter your account information, including your e-mail address and ZIP code. This information enables AvantGo to localize content for your area and to send you notifications of updates. When you've entered your account information, click I Accept to accept the usage agreement.

On the next page, click Click Here To Configure to configure the connection settings for AvantGo and make sure the AvantGo Mobile Link client is working properly. When you've verified the connection options, click Next to move to the next page.

On this page, you'll be told how to manually synchronize your Pocket PC with AvantGo so that it can download the initial content. After the initial synchronization is complete, proceed to the final step of the setup process, in which you choose your channels.

On the final page of the AvantGo setup, click the Channels link to choose the Web sites that will be synchronized to your PC. You can browse the AvantGo channels and add to your account the ones that are interesting. After the channels are added to your account, they will appear the next time you synchronize.

Don't go hog wild with the channels you choose. Each channel consumes precious space on your Pocket PC. Although you can selectively delete channel content from your Pocket PC, you can't do it during a synchronization, so it's possible that you could run out of memory on your Pocket PC if you try to synchronize too much.

Caution Your AvantGo channels have a limit of 2 MB per day. This can be frustrating if you try to synchronize too much.

To use the AvantGo channels you've synchronized, open Pocket Internet Explorer, and open the Favorites folder by clicking the Favorites icon on the toolbar.

Tip You may want to go take a look at Mazingo (*http://www.mazingo.net*). It is an alternative to AvantGo that offers the ability to synchronize any kind of media.

MobiPocket Reader

As I mentioned earlier, MobiPocket Reader enables you to get news as well as eBooks. MobiPocket Reader works similarly to AvantGo in that the reader downloads and caches information from content providers. It differs, however, in that the downloaded content is read in the MobiPocket Reader program, not in Internet Explorer.

The interface for selecting content for MobiPocket Reader runs as an icon in the system tray, and by double-clicking it, you can choose which sites and what content from those sites you want to download. In this way, MobiPocket Reader provides you with more control of the content you download to your Pocket PC. MobiPocket Reader also doesn't suffer from the sometimes odd behavior of Internet Explorer when accessing AvantGo channels.

Summary

Today's eBooks are a pleasure to read, and there's already a wide variety of titles. After you choose one of the many formats now in use, you'll want to read eBooks for a long time.

If you want to stay up on current events, rather than reading the latest novel, you can synchronize Web sites to your notebook or Pocket PC. Synchronizing news Web sites will give you a steady stream of current topics to feed your hunger for news.

Any way you cut it, information is yours for the taking...with you. As you've probably come to expect, I leave you with some questions to ask yourself:

- How much time could you save if everything you highlighted in reference works was indexed for you?

- How much paper do you carry on an average trip? How much weight does this add to your checked or carry-on luggage?

- How much more would you read while traveling if a book didn't weigh anything or take up any room?

- Do you ever feel out of touch with the news back home while traveling? Do you miss the local newspaper?

Show Me the Money: Expenses and Stock Watching

I've never met a business professional who actually liked doing expense reports. I recently ran into a business acquaintance at a coffee shop. She had picked the location so that she would have a comfortable place to be while she worked on the unpleasant task of putting together her expense report.

Although I won't be able to make putting your expense report together a pleasant task, I can show you some techniques that will at least make it more tolerable. From techniques that track expenses when you incur them to techniques that make generating your expense reports easier, this chapter will help.

In the second part of this chapter I will address another side of money management—stock watching. In some markets, keeping track of your investments might be a painful process as well. However, the money-management tools available through Microsoft Money 2002 and the online-banking options of most investment houses make keeping track of your holdings while you're on the road as painless as possible.

I'll show you how to use Money and Money for the Pocket PC to review your holdings. I'll also show you techniques you can use to find out when there are important changes in the value of your holdings.

Expenses

Although every company has different ways of handling expense reports, they all have some practices in common. One such practice is recording the date and type of each expense incurred.

Most companies also request a copy of the receipt for the transaction. Some accept a credit card statement in lieu of a receipt, but this is not always the case. Figure 13-1 shows a sample expense report for the fictitious company Northwind Traders.

Northwind Traders
Expense Report

Name: _____   Department   _____

Period of: _____ to _____   Purpose of Travel: _____

Date	Location From	To	To	Total Miles	Airfare	Brkfast	Lunch	Dinner	Enter-tainment	Lodging	Car Rent Cab Fare	Phone	Parking Fees	Baggage/Laundry	Misc
1/1/2000															
1/2/2000															
1/3/2000															
1/4/2000															
1/5/2000															
1/6/2000															
1/7/2000															
1/8/2000															
1/9/2000															
1/10/2000															
1/11/2000															
1/12/2000															
1/13/2000															
1/14/2000															
1/15/2000															
Totals				0	0.00	0.00	0.00	0.00	0.00	0.00	0.00	0.00	0.00	0.00	0.00
Mileage @ 0.345 /mile			0.00												

Detail Of Business/Miscellaneous Expenses

Date	Persons	Company	Place	Purpose	Amount

Employee Signature _____ Date _____   Total Gross Expenses   0.00   Advance   0.00
                                                       Less Advance Taken   0.00   Total   0.00
Manager Approval _____ Date _____   Less Co. Billed Airfare 0.00
                                                       Net Expenses   0.00

Figure 13-1   *Northwind Traders' expense report form.*

There are two basic problems with creating expense reports: keeping the receipts and entering the information on the expense report form. Keeping the receipts organized is an important part of the process, but one for which there's very little support at the moment. You can use a handheld scanner to scan the receipts into your notebook, but that process is inconvenient and means you have to carry another device.

Both Hewlett Packard (HP) and Casio used to sell scanners that stored the image in the scanner itself. This was ideal, because you could scan in your receipts and download them to your computer when it was convenient. The devices were a great way to manage your receipts quickly and easily. Unfortunately, neither company saw enough sales of this kind of product to keep the products around.

There are, however, techniques for filling out the expense report itself. You can use technology to simplify this process in two ways. The first way is to use Microsoft Money to capture and report your expenses. You enter your credit card expenses and cash expenses such as tips, vending machine costs, and other costs that you wouldn't normally put on a credit card. With a Pocket PC and Money for the Pocket PC, you can even do all of this from your Pocket PC and have it synchronize to your copy of Microsoft Money. Then you use an account transaction report to record all of the expenses you've entered so you don't forget about any of them.

The second thing you can do to make your expense report easier is to create a custom report in Microsoft Money that mimics the format used by your organization. This method enables you to transcribe your expenses easily into the format that the organization needs.

Note If you create a particularly good copy of the expense report the organization uses, you might ask to submit your copy rather than the form everyone else is using.

In this section I'm going to show you all of the steps to track expenses and generate an expense report. Specifically, you're going to learn how to:

- **Create a cash account** You need a cash account to record the cash transactions you make. As I mentioned earlier, these might be tips, vending machine purchases, or other purchases too small to be charged on a credit card.

- **Create new categories** If you're going to create a report in Microsoft Money that mimics your organization's expense report, you have to create the necessary categories.

- **Enter transactions in Microsoft Money** You must enter the transactions and categorize them appropriately so that Microsoft Money can generate a usable report.

- **Enter Transactions in Money for the Pocket PC** An alternative to entering transactions in Microsoft Money is to use Money for the Pocket PC and synchronize those transactions to your computer.

- **Create a Microsoft Money Expense Report** This is the report you use to make it easier to enter your expenses into the organization's expense report.

When you put all these pieces together, you have a solution you can use to make expense reports easier. Please note that I will not walk you through the initial setup of Microsoft Money, nor will I show you how to install Money for the Pocket PC. You can do both of these with the assistance of the online help files.

Creating a Cash Account

By default, Money doesn't create a cash account for you. When it sets up your file, it creates accounts typical of a normal consumer: checking, savings, brokerage, and retirement accounts. This might be appropriate for a vast majority of the people on the planet, but you need a cash account to track your cash transactions for eventual inclusion in your expense report. As I previously mentioned, when you travel, you often make cash transactions that aren't large enough for you to justify charging them to a credit card, but that you nonetheless want to track.

The process of creating the account isn't complex, but admittedly it is rather long. This is how you create a cash account:

1. On the Accounts & Bills menu, click Account List. The Account List window appears, as shown in Figure 13-2.

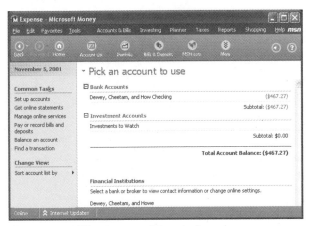

Figure 13-2   *The Account List window shows current accounts and lists common tasks.*

2. In the Common Tasks pane on the left, click Set Up Accounts.

3. Click Add A New Account. The New Account Wizard appears, as shown in Figure 13-3.

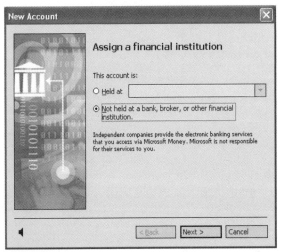

Figure 13-3   *The New Account Wizard starts by asking where the account is held.*

4. In the New Account Wizard, select Not Held At A Bank, Broker, Or Other Financial Institution.

5. Click the Next button.

6. In the list on the left, select Cash.

7. Click the Next button.

8. Type the name you want to assign to your cash account—or accept the default name of Cash.

9. Click the Next button to display the wizard's What's The Opening Value Of This Account? page, as shown in Figure 13-4.

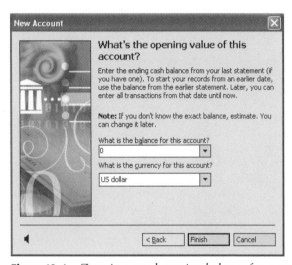

Figure 13-4   *Zero is a good starting balance for a cash account.*

10. Enter the balance for the account. Because this is a cash account and it's unlikely that you're going to track every penny that you spend, enter *0* for this number.

11. Confirm the currency selection. My cash is in U.S. dollars.

12. Click the Finish button.

That is all there is to it. Now, when you have a cash expense such as a cab fare, you can capture it in the cash account so that you don't forget it. This doesn't help you categorize the expense so that you can find it; it only helps you to track cash expenses. The next step is to set up the necessary categories so you can capture expenses in the manner in which your organization wants them captured.

Setting Up Categories

By default, Money creates two subcategories below the Job Expenses category: Reimbursed and Non-reimbursed. This works well enough if all you want to do is determine whether you've remembered to put everything on your expense report. However, it's not really useful for organizing the information that goes on the expense report itself.

To be able to use Money to facilitate the creation of your expense report, you need to capture the information about your expenses using the kind of breakdown in which your organization wants to see the information. For instance, you might need to record phone charges separately from meals or airfare. These different kinds of expenses often get charged against different accounts in the accounting system and must be reported separately.

Although Microsoft Money doesn't ship with a default set of subcategories for job expenses, adding the ones you need—and deleting the generic ones—is not a difficult task. Let's start by creating a new category, and follow that by deleting a generic category.

Creating New Subcategories

Before you create your new subcategories, you should take a look at the rows and columns on your expense report. One of these (either rows or columns) will list the dates of travel, depending on how your organization orients its expense reports. The other will list the subcategories you should add to the Job Expenses category.

When you're entering these subcategories, you might want to precede the subcategory with a number so that the categories appear in the same order on Microsoft Money reports and on the organization's expense report. For instance, if your organization's expense report lists Breakfast, Lunch, Dinner, and Airfare as four separate columns, you might want to create them as 01-Breakfast, 02-Lunch, 03-Dinner, and 04-Airfare. This will keep them in the same order on Microsoft Money reports as on the expense report. If you don't do this, the categories will be sorted alphabetically and appear as Airfare, Breakfast, Dinner, and Lunch.

Here's how to create your subcategories:

1. Click the Categories icon on the toolbar.

2. Click the New button to display the Create Category Wizard, as shown in Figure 13-5.

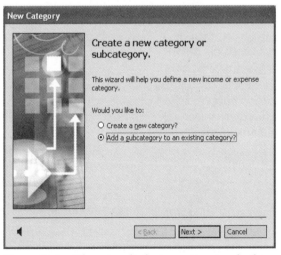

Figure 13-5   *The wizard's first question is whether or not this is a subcategory.*

3. Select Add A Subcategory To An Existing Category.

4. Click the Next button to display the Define The Subcategory page, as shown in Figure 13-6.

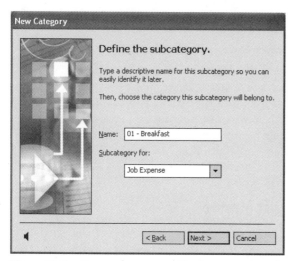

Figure 13-6 *Remember to specify the numeric order when you create the subcategory.*

5. Enter the name of the subcategory in the Name box. As I previously mentioned, you'll probably want these names to match the categories on the organization's expense report form, and you might want to prefix each name with a number indicating its order on the report.

6. In the list box, select Job Expense.

7. Click the Next button.

8. Select Reimbursed Job Exp. from the list. This will ensure that the subcategory is treated appropriately on Microsoft Money's reports, even if the name is different than Money expects.

9. Click the Finish button.

10. Repeat steps 2 through 9 for each category you want to add.

Now that you have the categories you need to create your expense report, it's time to remove the subcategories Microsoft Money created by default.

Deleting Existing Subcategories

Although having the Reimbursed subcategory under Job Expenses doesn't prevent you from exporting data into an expense report, it might get in your way when you enter transactions. In the interest of cleaning up the subcategories, you'll probably want to delete it.

The procedure below shows you the process of deleting a subcategory. You should use it now to delete the Reimbursed subcategory from the Job Expense category:

1. Go to the Categories page by clicking the Categories icon on the toolbar. (If you followed the previous procedure, you'll already be there.)

2. Select the subcategory you want to delete from the list.

3. Click the Delete button.

I suggested deleting only the Reimbursed subcategory, because the categories you added in the previous section are in essence a finer breakdown of the items that you would have previously recorded in the Reimbursed category, and they make it redundant. However, you didn't define new subcategories to organize the non-reimbursed items. If you have any job expenses for which your employer won't reimburse you, you'll need to record them in the Non-reimbursed subcategory so that you can claim them on your tax return. (See your tax adviser to determine what you can deduct on your tax return.)

Entering Transactions in Microsoft Money

Setting up categories and accounts is great, but it's the detailed work of entering the data that will eventually be translated into the expense report that really causes the headaches. Thankfully, Microsoft Money makes the data entry process painless.

In Microsoft Money, it's helpful to organize your receipts according to the accounts to which they belong. This will minimize the number of times you need to change accounts while entering information into Microsoft Money. Let's take a look at the transaction entry process:

1. Start Microsoft Money.

2. Click the Account List icon on the toolbar to display the list of accounts.

3. Click the link to the account into which you want to enter transactions. This brings up the account register.

4. Press the Enter key, or click the New button to start a new transaction. This changes the display to look something like Figure 13-7.

5. Enter the date of the transaction. If you need a calendar to remember what the date was, you can use the calendar that appears when you display the Date box by clicking the arrow on the right.

Tip You can use the Tab key to move between fields. The tab order matches the order in which we cover the fields in this step-by-step procedure.

---

6. Enter the name of the person or organization to whom the transaction was paid. For instance, airfare expenses might be paid to an airline company. You should be conscious of how you enter the name, including capitalization, spacing, spelling, and

punctuation. This is the name that will appear on reports and will be displayed to simplify entry when you enter future transactions with similar payees.

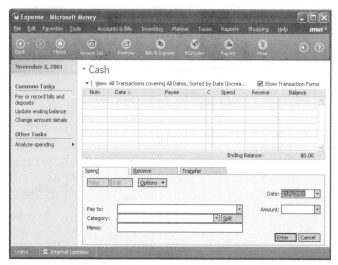

Figure 13-7   *Entering a transaction is a bit like filling out a check.*

7. Enter the amount of the transaction. You can open a mini-calculator program by clicking the down arrow at the right end of the Amount box.

8. Select the category and subcategory of the transaction. If this is a job expense, Job Expense should be the first part. After that, you must decide the appropriate subcategory based on the type of transaction you're entering. (For example, the Airfare category for airfare transactions, Meals for meal transactions, and so on.)

9. Enter a memo describing the transaction. (If you're using the Tab key, press it twice to skip over the Split button.) The Memo box helps you record specific details about the transaction, such as the reason and attendees for a business lunch.

10. Press Enter to complete the transaction.

11. Repeat steps 4 through 10 for every transaction in the same account.

12. If you have other accounts to enter transactions for, click the down arrow to the left of the name of the account, and select the account for which you have transactions to enter.

You'll use the preceding process often, because it is the process you must go through for every transaction you enter into Microsoft Money.

Entering Transactions in Money for the Pocket PC

Entering transactions in Microsoft Money might be the quickest way to record them, but it might not be the easiest to remember or the most efficient. Money for the Pocket PC can capture your transactions and synchronize them with the version of Money on your computer.

Note With online banking, you can download transaction records from your bank; however, these transaction records don't generally list the funds' recipient, nor do they categorize the expense for you. Your Pocket PC is the best way to capture expenses and their categories.

Money for the Pocket PC is particularly useful when you want to capture a transaction and you don't have your computer handy to enter the information. For instance, when you pay a cab driver, you might want to put that information into Money for the Pocket PC right away. Otherwise, you might forget the cab ride, fail to report it on your expense report, and not get reimbursed for the expense.

As I've mentioned throughout this book, the Pocket PC isn't the best tool on which to enter large amounts of information, but entering the occasional transaction is not like trying to write *War and Peace* on your Pocket PC.

Note If you haven't already downloaded and installed Money for the Pocket PC, now would be a good time to do that. You can download a copy of Money for the Pocket PC at *http: //www.microsoft.com/mobile/pocketpc/downloads/money.asp*.

If you haven't synchronized your Pocket PC since you created the cash account and changed the categories, now would be a good time to drop your Pocket PC into its cradle and synchronize all of the changes from Microsoft Money to the Pocket PC.

Entering transactions on your Pocket PC is very similar to entering transactions in Microsoft Money on your computer. Here's how:

1. Tap the Money for the Pocket PC section of your Today screen, or on the Start menu, tap Programs, and then tap Microsoft Money. This starts Microsoft Money or brings it to the foreground of the display if it's already running.

2. Tap the account for which you want to enter a transaction on the Account Manager screen. (You can select any account. You'll be given the chance to select the account into which you want to enter transactions when you create the transaction.)

3. Tap the New button to start a new transaction. The screen changes to enable you to enter a new transaction, as shown in Figure 13-8.

4. If you weren't viewing the account into which you want to enter the transaction, select the correct account from the Account box.

5. Enter the payee name in the Payee box. Money for the Pocket PC will locate the correct payee and display that complete name in the box. When the correct name is displayed, you can move on to the next box.

6. If the date of the transaction isn't the current day, enter the correct date for the transaction in the Date box.

7. Enter the amount of the transaction in the Amount box. Unlike Microsoft Money for the PC, Money for the Pocket PC can't display a mini-calculator when entering data into this box.

8. Tap the Optional tab so that you can add details, including a category, subcategory, and memo. Additional transaction boxes appear, as shown in Figure 13-9.

Figure 13-8 *The required transaction fields are Account, Payee, Date, and Amount.*

Figure 13-9 *The option fields include the important Category and Subcategory fields.*

9. Select the category for the transaction. If you're entering a business transaction, you should select the Job Expense category.

10. Select the appropriate subcategory from the list. In the case of a job expense, set the appropriate subcategory that you added earlier.

11. Enter a memo in the Memo box to explain the reason for the transaction if it is required for business or tax purposes, or if the transaction's purpose is not clear.

12. Tap the OK button.

13. Repeat steps 3 through 12 for each transaction you wish to enter.

When you're ready to create an expense report, you'll need to synchronize your Pocket PC with your computer. After you've done that, you can use Microsoft Money to generate an expense report.

Creating a Microsoft Money Expense Report

Creating an expense report from Microsoft Money isn't as easy as it might seem. The built-in report generator in Microsoft Money won't create an expense report for you; however, Microsoft Excel can take the data from Microsoft Money and turn it into a mock expense report.

There are two approaches you can take to generating reports. The first approach is simply to make a list of all transactions and enter it into your company expense report. This provides an organized way to enter information into your organization's expense report form and helps to ensure that you don't forget any expenses.

The second approach is better. It involves converting the raw data into a format similar to that of your organization's expense report. Excel's PivotTable feature can create a report format that is similar, if not identical, to your organization's expense report.

Getting the Raw Data

The first step in either approach is getting the raw data into a report in Microsoft Money. The following process creates a report that lists all of the job expense transactions you have entered. After you've completed the process once, you'll be able to retrieve the saved report and change the dates, so you won't need to complete the entire process again. Here are the steps:

1. Start Microsoft Money on your computer.

2. Click the Reports icon on the toolbar.

3. Double-click the Account Transactions option to open the Account Transactions report, as shown in Figure 13-10.

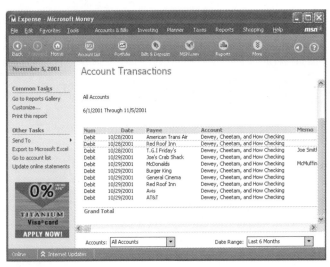

Figure 13-10   *The Account Transactions report is a quick view of recent activity.*

4. Click the Customize link in the Common Tasks bar on the left.

5. In the Include Fields area of the Rows & Columns tab shown in Figure 13-11, select Memo.

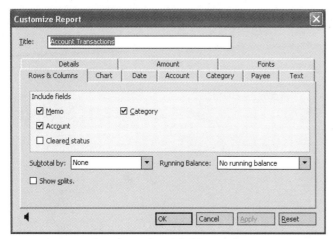

Figure 13-11 *The report detail fields are shown on the Rows & Columns tab.*

6. Select Account.

7. Verify that the Category option is selected.

8. Set the Subtotal By combo box to None.

9. Set the Running Balance combo box to No Running Balance.

10. Click the Date tab, which is shown in Figure 13-12.

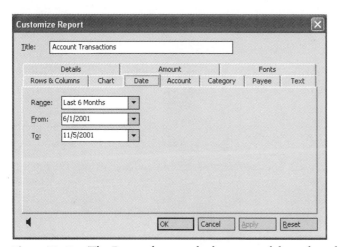

Figure 13-12 *The Date tab controls the range of dates for which transactions will be displayed.*

11. Enter the date range you want to cover in the From and To combo boxes. You do not need to worry about the Range combo box. It will automatically change to Custom Dates. Each time you run the report, you can change the date range to reflect only the transactions you have not submitted on an expense report.

12. Click the Category tab to display the category options, as shown in Figure 13-13.

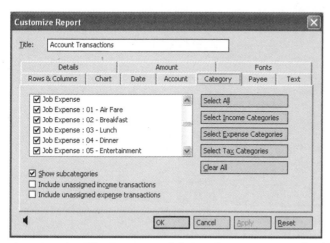

Figure 13-13 *The Category tab limits the transactions displayed to the list of selected categories and subcategories.*

13. Click the Clear All button.

14. Select the Job Expense category and all of the Job Expense subcategories except for the Non-Reimbursed Job Expenses subcategory.

15. Click OK to generate the report.

16. On the Favorites menu, click Add To Favorites.

17. Enter a name for this report, such as Expense Report Transactions.

The report is now ready to use. You can either print the report or export it to Excel. If you want to access the report later and alter it for a new date range, you can follow these steps:

1. On the Favorites menu, click Favorite Reports, and then click the report name you entered above. In my example, I used Expense Report Transactions.

2. Click the down arrow to the right of the date range box in the lower right corner of the screen.

3. Click Custom Dates in the list that appears. This displays the Customize Report dialog box, with the Dates tab preselected for you. (Do not click Custom Dates in the combo box itself. Doing so does not open the Customize Report dialog box.)

4. Enter the new date range in the From and To combo boxes.

5. Click OK to close the Customize Report dialog box.

To run your expense report again for a new set of expenses, just complete the previous steps. You can then print this report as a guide for creating your new expense report.

Creating a Report That Looks Like an Expense Report

Using Excel, you can convert the raw data you created in the previous section into a format that closely resembles your organization's expense report. Excel's PivotTable feature can convert the data in the Money report into the cross tab format of most expense reports. A cross tab report is a summary of information with two different criteria, categories, or dimensions. In the case of an expense report, one of the dimensions is the date and the other is the expense category.

To generate your expense report using Excel, you'll first need to export the data from Microsoft Money to Excel. You can do this by opening the report you want to export and selecting the Export To Microsoft Excel link on the left side of the report. In the previous section, you learned how to retrieve the transaction report format you saved and reset the date range. When you click the Export To Microsoft Excel link, you are prompted to pick a file name and location. With that done, Money saves the file and launches Excel automatically.

The following steps walk you through the process of converting the spreadsheet created by Money into something that looks like an expense report:

1. Select the row containing the Grand Total line by clicking the number to the left of the row.

2. Right-click the row to display the shortcut menu, and click Delete. This deletes the Grand Total line.

3. Select a range of cells that includes all the columns of the report, the column headings, all the data in the report, and a large number of empty rows after the end of the data. For instance, you might select all the cells from column G, row 7, through column A, row 100. Selecting this range indicates to Excel which data range to use. The empty rows at the end will be helpful if you want to copy and paste future reports into the template you're creating.

4. On the Data menu, point to PivotTable, and then click PivotChart to display the PivotTable And PivotChart Wizard, as shown in Figure 13-14 on the next page.

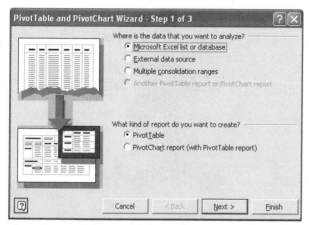

Figure 13-14   *The wizard first asks where the data is.*

5. Accept the default settings by clicking the Next button.

6. The second page confirms the data range you want to use. Because you've already selected this range in step 3, continue by clicking the Next button.

7. Click the Finish button on the third page to confirm that you want the PivotTable placed in a new worksheet. Excel displays a new worksheet with an area for the PivotTable, as shown in Figure 13-15.

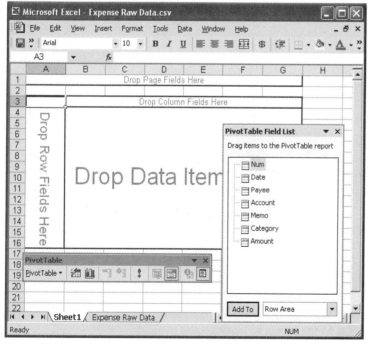

Figure 13-15   *An empty PivotTable looks more intimidating than it is.*

8. Drag the Category field from the PivotTable Field List into the part of the PivotTable that says Drop Column Fields Here.

Note If your organization uses an expense report format in which the dates go in the columns of the report rather than the rows, switch the fields in steps 8 and 9 so that the dates are in the columns and the categories are in the rows.

---

9. Drag the Date field into the part of the PivotTable that says Drop Row Fields Here.

10. Drag the Amount field into the part of the PivotTable that says Drop Data Items Here.

11. Double-click cell A3.

12. Select Sum in the Summarize By list box.

13. Click OK to display the completed but unformatted expense report, as shown in Figure 13-16.

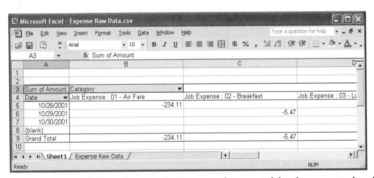

Figure 13-16 *Other than variation in column width, the report should look very similar to your organization's expense report form.*

14. Select row 4 (the column header row) by clicking the number to the left of the row.

15. Right-click the number to display the shortcut menu, and click Format Cells.

16. Click the Alignment tab.

17. Select the Wrap Text check box.

18. Click OK.

19. Resize the columns according to your preference.

20. Right-click the worksheet with the data on it, and click Rename.

21. Enter *RawData* as the name of the sheet.

22. On the File menu, click Save As.

23. In the Save As Type combo box, select Microsoft Excel 97-2002 & 5.0/95 Workbook.

24. Select a location, and enter a file name for the file.

The report you just created will be similar to the expense report your organization uses, allowing you to print and copy the numbers directly. This is substantially easier than trying to sort out where the amount of each transaction belongs.

You should save this initial report as a template for future reports. The process of updating the PivotTable for new data is very simple. The process below shows you how:

1. Run your Microsoft Money report as described in the earlier section titled "Getting the Raw Data."

2. Click the Export To Microsoft Excel link, and enter a name for the exported report.

3. Select the range of cells that represents the data returned from the report. This starts at column G, row 8 and continues to column A in the last row of the report.

4. On the Edit menu, click Copy.

5. On the File menu, click Open, locate the expense report template you created earlier, and double-click it.

6. Select the RawData sheet in the Expense Report template workbook by clicking it.

7. Place the insertion point in column A, row 8.

8. On the Edit menu, click Paste.

9. Select the Sheet1 worksheet in the workbook.

10. Click anywhere in the PivotTable.

11. Right-click the PivotTable, and click Refresh Data.

Save the workbook in a separate file by clicking Save As on the File menu, or print the report for transcription onto your organization's expense report form.

Note It's possible to populate an Excel expense report form directly with raw data from Money, but this process requires some Microsoft Visual Basic for Applications programming and the specific form. As a result, it's beyond the scope of this book. If you're interested in this topic, you can read *Microsoft Excel 2002 VBA for Applications Step by Step,* by Reed Jacobson (Microsoft Press, 2001).

Stock Watching

During the 1990s, people seemed to turn the bird-watching hobby popular in the 1890s into a new stock-watching hobby. It was not uncommon to go into an office and see a stock ticker running across the bottom of a computer screen or a financial Web site up in the Web browser.

Note If you haven't watched your investments much in the past or don't think of yourself as an investor, don't be scared away from this section. If you have a 401(k) account, you're an investor. Even if you're not comfortable with investing, I encourage you to read this section. Investing isn't nearly as scary as it appears to be, when you know a little bit about it. You might also want to visit *http://moneycentral.msn.com*. You'll find numerous stories, tutorials, and examples to help you learn more about investments and money.

In prosperous times, it's fun to watch the stock market, but not many people enjoy watching their stocks when the market is doing poorly. Still, there are many people who feel the need to be in constant touch with the state of the market. This section is for those people. In this section, I will show you how to watch your stocks using Microsoft Money and Money for the Pocket PC.

Note I chose the stock symbols for these examples more or less at random. They don't indicate my or anyone else's suggested stock purchases. Please don't select stocks based on the figures in this book.

There are essentially four steps to creating and monitoring investments on your computer and your Pocket PC. The first three steps set up the appropriate accounts and investments and make sure the prices are current. The fourth step is for Pocket PC users only; it updates the Pocket PC Today screen so that it can show both account balances and investment values. The steps are:

- Create an investment account
- Add a new investment to a brokerage account
- Update prices
- Set up the Pocket PC Today screen for Money for the Pocket PC

The next four sections walk you through each of these processes.

Creating an Investment Account

When you initially set up your Microsoft Money program, you were given the opportunity to create a brokerage account. Even if you didn't create a brokerage account, you can still track investments, but they will be tracked through the Investments To Watch account. This account works if you just want to track a few things but has disadvantages when you manage investments instead of just watching them.

Tip If you're interested in learning more about online financial planning using Microsoft Money, pick up a copy of *Online Money Management,* by Karin Price Mueller (Microsoft Press, 2001).

The steps below show you how to create a new investment account:

1. On the File menu, point to New, and then click New Account.

2. Enter the name of the institution or broker that holds the account.

3. Click the Next button.

4. Select the name of your institution from the list, or select (Not Listed). This list configures Money to use online banking options. If you want to use online banking, it's essential that you select the correct option here.

5. Click the Next button to display the What Kind Of Account Would You Like To Set Up? page of the New Account Wizard, as shown in Figure 13-17.

6. Select Investment from the list of accounts, and then click the Next button.

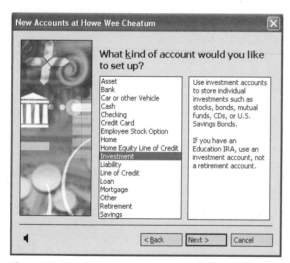

Figure 13-17   *You can set up many different kinds of accounts, but on this page you should select an Investment account.*

7. Enter the name by which you would like to refer to the account.

8. Confirm that the currency selection for the account is correct.

9. Confirm the tax status of the account. In most cases, the account will be taxable.

Note If you want to create a brokerage account that will contain any form of IRA contributions, you will probably want to add a retirement account rather than an investment account. This type of account typically has a tax-free status.

10. Select No, I'll Do This Later from the list.

Note You could add investments now, but to avoid complicating the account setup process by setting up individual investments now, I'll cover setting up individual investments in the next section.

11. Click the Next button.

12. Enter the amount of money in investments using current values.

13. Enter the amount of cash in the account.

14. Click the Next button.

15. Click the Next button again, and then click the Finish button.

    Your new investment account is ready to accept investments.

Adding a New Investment

Now that you have an account to put investments into, you can add investments. When you're adding investments to an investment account, you are essentially indicating your purchases of investments in the account.

The most confusing part about adding investments is determining the symbol of the investment. Each investment option has a symbol associated with it. The symbol is a short mnemonic code that represents the name of the investment. For instance, FFIV is the symbol for the company F5 Networks, Inc.

The first time through, you might add the investment to the Investments To Watch account. Adding it to the Investments To Watch account allows you to play with Money without worrying that you'll disrupt your reports. Follow these steps:

1. Click the Portfolio icon on the toolbar.

2. Click the Add An Investment link in the Common Tasks section.

3. Select the account to add the investment to. You can select the Investments To Watch account if you only want to watch a particular investment option and don't want to indicate that you've purchased it.

4. Click the Next button.

5. Enter the name of the investment. You should enter an easily understood name in this space, not the stock's symbol.

6. Click the Next button to display the wizard's Type Of Investment page, as shown in Figure 13-18.

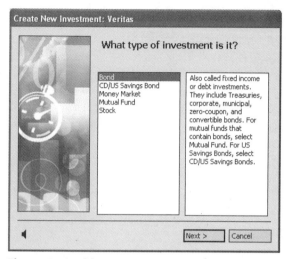

Figure 13-18   *Money supports several common types of investments.*

7. Select the type of investment you want to add. In most cases, this will be a mutual fund or stock.

8. Click the Next button to display the page that prompts you for the investment's symbol, as shown in Figure 13-19.

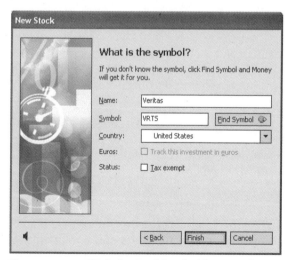

Figure 13-19   *Click the Find Symbol button if you're not sure you know the correct symbol.*

9. Enter the Symbol name, or click the Find Symbol button. If you click the Find Symbol button, Money searches for the stock symbol that matches the information you entered in the Name field.

10. Click the Finish button.

11. Enter the number of shares you purchased. If you are just watching this investment, enter *1* in this field.

12. If you did purchase the investment, you can also indicate the date you acquired it, the price you paid for it, and the commission or fee you paid for the transaction.

13. Click the Next button.

14. Click the Finish button.

The investment you just added will appear on your Investments screen. It will not, however, show the current price until you update the prices. The next section shows you how to update prices.

Updating Prices

Updating the prices of your investments can become an obsession. As I mentioned before, during the 1990s, many people were mesmerized by the prices of their stocks. Even if you are still mesmerized by the prices of stocks, Microsoft Money isn't the best way to stay on top of them.

If you want to see continual updates of stock prices, you should open the CNBC Ticker. You can find a link to this stock ticker at the bottom of the Money Central home page (*http://moneycentral.msn.com*). If you just want to update your stock prices in Microsoft Money, periodically follow this procedure:

1. If you're not already looking at the Portfolio page, click the Portfolio icon on the toolbar to display it.

2. On the Update Prices menu, click Update Prices Online to update your investment properties.

Note If you aren't connected to the Internet, Microsoft Money will attempt to connect at this point.

---

3. Click OK if you receive a message about using background banking.

4. Click OK to close the Call Summary dialog box.

The prices of all of your investments should now be updated. You can update them any time you like; however, all quotes are delayed by 20 minutes.

Setting Up the Pocket PC Today Screen

Most people, myself included, find it difficult to find time for everything. Keeping track of my investments is one of those things I never seem to have time for. Money for the Pocket PC enables you to display the values of your investments and the balances of your accounts on the Today screen of your Pocket PC.

Caution If you decide to set up Money for the Pocket PC to display investment and account balances as I describe here, you will definitely want to set a device password. In Chapter 3, I explained how to set a password on your Pocket PC.

The Today Screen plug-in included with Microsoft Money allows you to view two different kinds of information: account balances and investment values. The procedure below shows you how to turn on the Money for the Pocket PC Today Screen plug-in and turn on display of accounts and investments:

1. On the Start menu, tap Settings to open the settings window.

2. Tap Today to go into the Today settings.

3. Tap the Items tab. This displays a screen similar to Figure 13-20.

4. Tap the check box to the left of Money to display the Money plug-in.

5. Tap the Money option itself. You can use the Move Up and Move Down buttons to control where Money will appear on the Today screen.

6. Tap the Options button to display the options for Money, as shown in Figure 13-21.

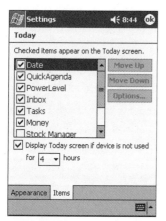

Figure 13-20   *The Items tab of the Today settings dialog box enables you to control what plug-ins are visible and in what order they appear.*

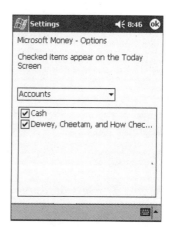

Figure 13-21   *Money anables you to quickly display account balances.*

7. Select the check boxes to the left of the accounts for which you want to display balances on your Today screen.

8. Tap the drop-down list containing Accounts, and select Investments. This changes the display to something similar to Figure 13-22.

9. Select the check boxes to the left of the investments for which you want to display values on your Today screen.

10. Tap the OK button to close the Money plug-in options.

11. Tap the OK button to close the Today settings.

12. On the Start menu, tap Today to show your Today screen with Money information displayed, as shown in Figure 13-23.

Your Today screen can now keep you up to date on your account balances and the status of your investments.

Figure 13-22   *You can decide which investments you want to show on the Today screen.*

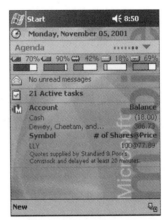

Figure 13-23   *Money displays the account balances and investments at the bottom of my Today screen, as I requested.*

Summary

Managing money is one of the skills at which we must all become at least passably proficient in our lifetimes. More than any other skill, knowing the basics of managing your money controls whether you are wealthy and happy or poor and struggling.

In this chapter, I addressed two aspects of money management. First, I explained how you can use Microsoft Money and Money for the Pocket PC to track and report your expenses so that you can turn them in on your expense report—and get reimbursed for them.

In the second half of the chapter, I explained how to use Microsoft Money to track your stocks and display those investments on your Today screen. You can use Microsoft Money to track your entire financial position.

As has become customary, I leave you with a few questions:

- How much do you loathe sitting with a stack of receipts, trying to figure out which section of your expense report they belong in?

- How much money do you lose each year in transactions you forget to turn in for reimbursement?

- How much time do you waste putting expense reports together each month? How much of that time could you recover if you recorded your expenses while you had down time at an airport or in a cab?

- How many of your expenses are in cash?

- How many times have you wanted to check on your investments but didn't have a newspaper to check the stock quotes?

- How does the market affect your portfolio's value? How closely do you feel you need to monitor this?

Digital Video Surveillance

Just saying the words *video surveillance* conjures the feeling that Big Brother is watching. None of us wants to be watched without our knowledge, but there are situations in which it makes sense to watch what is going on.

Most shops and large buildings have video surveillance. This surveillance is designed to keep people or materials safe. However, there are other reasons for surveillance. Imagine you're traveling and you've arranged to have someone pick up your mail. If you set up a camera on the front porch or behind a nearby window, you can tell when a package has arrived. You can ask the person responsible for picking up your mail to stop by and get it. Similarly, if you have a gated area at your home, a camera pointed at the gate can help you see whether someone has entered without your permission.

Historically, security cameras operated only with video recorders. This significantly limited the ability to communicate motion or activity to people. Using one of today's completely self-contained cameras, you can access images from your personal computer or Pocket PC. These cameras can upload pictures to your FTP server or send you e-mail messages when something moves within the image. You now have complete access to the images through electronic means.

In this chapter, I'll explain how to set up digital video surveillance at your home or office. I'm using Axis Communications' 2120 network camera for this chapter. Cameras from Axis Communications can be directly attached to your network and set up quickly. If you want to know more about Axis' products, visit their Web site at *http://www.axis.com*.

There are dozens of alternatives available if you're willing to connect the camera to a computer to digitize the output and enable viewing across your network. However, there are a limited number of network-attached cameras like the Axis 2120.

Why a Network-Attached Camera?

You shouldn't use network-attached cameras if you need a lot of cameras for your security system. The additional cost involved in the manufacturing of network-attached cameras makes them more expensive than a traditional security system. For this reason, you'll probably want to investigate network-attached cameras if you need only a few cameras.

Consider your wiring costs. In some buildings, there is network cable almost everywhere. Buildings prewired for network and telephone connections frequently have extra cables available that can be used to connect to network-attached cameras. In contrast, you'd need a coaxial cable to connect to a traditional camera. If you have network cable available, but not the coaxial cable for a security system, it might make sense to use network-attached cameras.

Check your ability to view the images from any computer in the building. Unless you have a large security department in your organization, you might not have the resources to have someone sit in front of the video camera every day. Traditional security systems require a single location where all the videos can be viewed.

Finally, you might want to consider network-attached cameras if digital logging is important to you. Most security systems record information on analog videotapes, which don't hold up to continued reuse and deteriorate over time. You can store digital images indefinitely without any quality degradation.

Connecting the Camera

The most difficult part of using the camera is getting it connected to your network. After you've performed the setup process once, you'll be able to view the output of the camera even if you've turned the camera off (and back on) or moved it to another location.

The process of setting up the Axis camera requires three steps. The first step is getting the unit's 12-digit serial number from its underbelly. The second step is to open a command prompt on your computer and type in two commands. The first command is:

```
ARP -s <cameraip> <serialnumber>
```

In this command, `<cameraip>` will be the camera's IP address. The serial number should be entered with a dash between each pair of digits, and `<PCIPAddress>` will be that component's IP address. A blank command prompt will appear.

> **Tip** If you're unfamiliar with TCP/IP and don't know how to figure out what IP address you want for your camera, look at the IP address of your computer by typing the command *IPCONFIG*. Then add 1 to that number to get an IP address for your camera. Most of the time, adding 1 will work if there isn't another system on your network with that IP address. If you still can't get it to work, call the camera manufacturer's technical support. They can help you create a setting that will work in your environment.

The second command is:

```
PING -t <cameraip>
```

The camera's IP address is the same as in the previous command. The PING command will display a series of Request Timed Out messages.

The final step in the process is to connect the camera to the network and plug it in. Shortly after this, the PING command will notify you that it's getting a reply from the camera's IP address. From this point forward, you can interact with the camera using its IP address.

Configuring the Camera

The Axis camera is configured through your Web browser. Type the camera's IP address into your browser to start the camera's interface and display its output.

When you open the page, a dialog box appears, as shown in Figure 14-1, prompting you to install the control that receives the video stream from the camera and displays the moving images. Click Yes to enable this control.

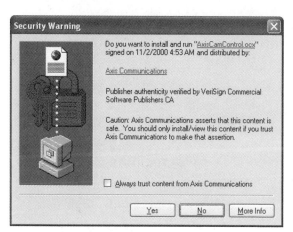

Figure 14-1 *The ActiveX control that Axis uses comes with a security warning.*

After you have installed the control, the images picked up by the camera appear, as shown in Figure 14-2.

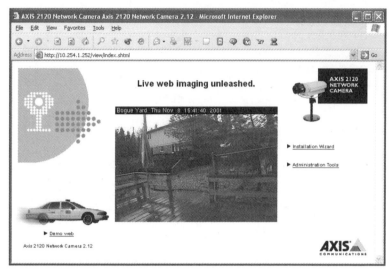

Figure 14-2   *My yard, in the afternoon.*

Click the Installation Wizard link to begin the steps to configure the camera. After the introduction, you'll be prompted to set up user names and passwords to enable other people to access the camera. After user accounts are set up, no one without a password can view the images from the camera. I recommend that you set up new user accounts and change the root password. (Do this by selecting the Root user from the user list, changing the password, and clicking the Save button.) When you're done, click the Next button.

In the next step, choose whether you want to synchronize your computer's time using a Network Time Protocol (NTP) server or through a setting that you select. Setting the camera to an NTP server ensures that the clock is right. When you're done, click the Next button.

> **Note** I use the NTP server *ntp2.usno.navy.mil*, which has the IP address 192.5.41.209 at the time of this writing. This is one of the atomic clocks run by the Navy.

On the Image Settings page of the Installation Wizard, set the picture size and type, as shown in Figure 14-3. The camera has two basic settings: single (or photograph) and motion (or movie). There are two size settings as well: 704 by 480 and 352 by 240.

The higher the image's resolution, the more bandwidth will be required to download it or keep up with its motion. On a local network, it probably doesn't make much difference how you change these settings; however, if you dial in through a modem to view these images, consider keeping the resolution in its lower setting.

Figure 14-3 *The image settings can be confusing at first.*

A Pocket PC cannot display motion video; it's limited to displaying single images. The Pocket PC platform doesn't support the ActiveX control or Java applet required to view the camera's motion output.

Note By being a little tricky with Microsoft Terminal Server, you can display motion pictures on your Pocket PC. I'll show you how in the next chapter.

Now choose how compressed you want the image to be. The settings range from Very High to Lowest. This option can help you reduce the bandwidth required to see the camera's output when it's in motion mode. Choosing a higher level of compression means a smaller amount of data is sent from the camera to the computer, but the compressed images are not as clear as they would be if they were less compressed. Conversely, lower compression sends a larger amount of data, but picture quality is higher. You'll probably have to play with the compression settings to find something that works for you.

You'll also find controls on this page for brightness, white balance, and color. These can usually be left at their default settings. White balance, if you're curious, is a setting that helps the camera define what hues to interpret as white. Our eyes can adjust to the differences in different lights, but the camera needs a little help.

In the Heading area of this page, you can add some details to the image. The heading will be displayed at all times on the image. It might not be necessary to display heading text if you are receiving images from a single camera, but it is useful if your images come from multiple cameras and you need to distinguish between them. The date and time can also be displayed on the image, which can be helpful if you are using motion detection to send the images to yourself, or if you want to store images on an FTP server. When you're ready to move on to the next step, click the Next button.

The next step is focusing the camera. You can use the focusing assistant in the wizard or focus the camera manually. I recommend manual focusing if you want the most accurate focus. Rotate the zoom to the tightest setting—in other words, until it is zoomed in as far as it will go, showing the least amount of the overall area, but the most detail. Next, rotate the focus ring until the image is in focus, and then return the zoom to the level you want. Click the Next button to move on to the next step.

Tip Rotating the zoom to its highest level before attempting to focus is an old camera trick. Because focus is most sensitive when zoomed in, you can focus quickly even on difficult subjects.

The final two steps—if, as I recommend, you skip the motion detection settings—will prompt you to enter the type of connection you're using and the TCP/IP settings. You can leave the TCP/IP settings alone if you're not familiar with them. The final step in the process is to click the Finish button.

After you've completed the wizard, your heading, output size, and compression settings will be in effect. These changes will probably be so subtle that you won't notice them unless you're looking for them—unless, of course, you changed the size of the output to 704 by 480. That is quite an obvious change. Figure 14-4 shows the camera image after the settings have been changed to 704 by 480.

Figure 14-4   *The larger image is easy to spot.*

To further customize the camera's images, click Administrative Tools, and then on the left-hand menu, click Layout to display the Layout page shown in Figure 14-5.

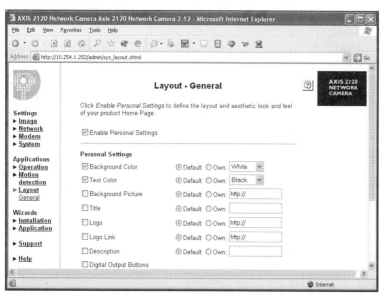

Figure 14-5 *Customize the appearance of the images with the settings on the Layout page.*

To apply your customization settings, select the Enable Personal Settings check box, and then select the check box for each setting you want to enable. To save the settings so that you'll have the page you want when you access the camera's home page, click the Save button.

Tip If you accidentally remove the Admin button by deselecting the Show Admin Button check box on the Layout page, add */admin* after the IP address to access the administrative tools.

Note You can customize the page even more, but it requires some work with the Software Development Kit (SDK). If you're implementing the camera for public use, you'll want to work through the kit. The camera can support only about 10 concurrent users; you'll have to use a separate server to support additional users. The details on how to do this are in the SDK.

Using the Camera

When you configured the camera, you used a Web browser pointed at the IP address of the camera. Now you can use the same address to view the output of the camera.

Viewing with Your Computer

If you've performed the steps outlined so far, you have your camera configured for use with your computer. Simply pointing your Web browser to the IP address of the camera displays the images you selected.

Occasionally, the image you are viewing freezes. This happens most frequently when you are watching the video from a remote location and on a less-than-reliable network. Sometimes a momentary disconnection will freeze the motion video, but refreshing the page almost always restarts it. If refreshing the page doesn't restart the video, close and reopen your browser.

Viewing with Your Pocket PC

Your Pocket PC can display the output from the camera, but it can do this only when the camera is configured for single images. Neither the ActiveX control nor the Java applet runs correctly on the Pocket PC. However, the single image view can be refreshed as often as you like.

Figure 14-6 shows a view of my back yard on the Pocket PC. I turned on the Fit To Screen option; the image is compressed, but it's still large enough for you to see what is going on in the back yard (in this case, nothing). I've scrolled over because by default the image is centered on the page—a page that's much larger than the default view on a Pocket PC.

Figure 14-6   *My back yard looks good in the daylight, even on a Pocket PC.*

You might be wondering what the benefits of still pictures are. They can be useful when you want to check who is at the door before you head that way. If it's your friendly FedEx driver dropping off a package, you probably don't need to rush out. Similarly, if you're at work, you can use still pictures to see who's in the front of the shop while you're in the back. If it's an employee walking in, you might not have to respond; if it's a delivery person or client, you might have to.

Getting connectivity to your network is probably the biggest challenge when you are using your Pocket PC to view the output of the camera. An 802.11b wireless LAN connection is appropriate for most applications with which the network-attached camera is useful.

Configuring Logging

The real benefit of the network-attached camera is its ability to keep you informed of what is going on while you're away. Traditional security cameras record events, but that won't help if you're miles away and can't view the tape. The benefit of the network-attached camera is that the information—in this case a stream of still photographs—can be recorded digitally. These photographs can be e-mailed to you directly or stored on an FTP server until you return—or for your perusal while you're away.

> **Note** There are ways to store a complete stream of photographs from the camera on your hard disk, but it's not something the average user will want set up. If you're interested, refer to the documentation for the camera, and contact Axis about their SDK.

There are two ways you can receive the images. When you receive the images through sequential upload, the camera uploads a copy of the current image at an interval you define. This is used most frequently with an FTP server to create a permanent log of the activity in front of the camera; however, it can also be used with e-mail notification.

The other way you can receive information is through the camera's built-in motion detector. You can specify which parts of the image should be monitored for motion and how much motion is acceptable before you want to be notified.

> **Note** The motion detection system used by the Axis 2120 detects motion through visible light, not through infrared as a typical motion detector alarm would. The problem with this is that even shadows cast by leaves on trees will cause the motion detector to go off. If the lighting is very low, as it is at night, it might not be as effective at detecting motion.

Rather than describing every conceivable way you might want to configure the camera, I'm going to focus on configuring the camera to send e-mail messages when motion is detected. This is the option most people want, because it ensures that they are notified when motion is detected, and they can pick up the messages from anywhere. The first step is to enter the camera's administration from the Administrative Tools link on the right side of the window, from the Admin button at the lower corner of the window if you're using personalized pages, or by entering the IP address followed by *'/admin'*.

There are six steps that need to be completed before notifications can be sent. In these steps you specify the mail servers, the messages you want sent, where you want the mail sent to, and what you want to consider motion.

The first step is to set up the Simple Mail Transport Protocol (SMTP) servers. These are the mail servers the camera will send e-mail to. To do this, click the Settings heading, and then click the Network link. From the Network link, click the SMTP link. A page similar to the one shown in Figure 14-7 appears, in which you supply information about the primary and secondary mail servers. If you have only one mail server, leave the Secondary Server box blank. Click the Save button to save your settings.

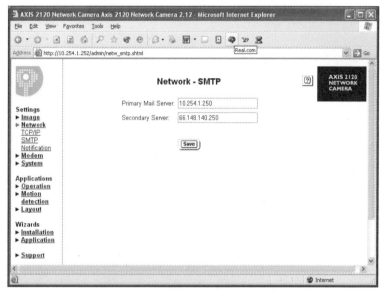

Figure 14-7   *Enter the IP addresses of the mail servers, rather than their names.*

Next, click the Operation link to display a page in which you can select how the camera will operate. Because you want to receive an e-mail message containing the images when motion occurs rather than at a periodic interval, select the Alarm Mode option button, and then click the Save button.

Click the Operation link, and then click the Scheduler link to display the page shown in Figure 14-8, in which you can specify when you want to receive e-mail notifications. You can specify that you want to be notified only if motion is detected within a certain time frame or that you want to be notified any time motion is detected. A good reason to use specific times might be that you want to monitor a rear entrance outside normal business hours. You could specify that you want to be notified of motion detected only after normal business hours so that you aren't notified every time an employee comes in or out.

I recommend that you initially set the primary time in the notification settings to Always, at least while you're testing, so that you won't have to worry about the motion not being detected because you're not in the right time range. You must also select the check boxes to trigger an alarm event when motion starts or stops in the default window. You can select multiple windows or areas of the image to watch for motion. When you're done selecting your settings, click the Save button.

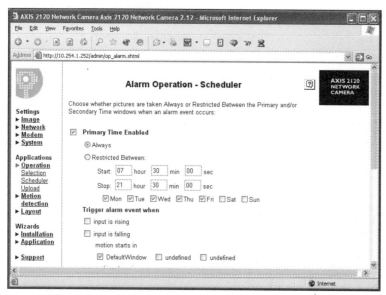

Figure 14-8   *The notification settings are flexible but complex.*

Next, configure how the images will be uploaded. Click the Operation link, and then click the Upload link to display a page in which you can specify how the upload is accomplished, how many images are sent, and other details.

Select SMTP as the upload protocol. Next, determine how many images you want to upload and how often. Select the Pre Alarm Buffer check box to upload images from before the event. I suggest you set this to one image per second, and only one alarm image. There is rarely anything useful in the pre-alarm images. The Post Alarm Buffer should probably be set to one image per second as well. I like about 10 seconds' worth of images, so I set the number of images to 10.

To confirm that you have specified the correct mail servers, click Network, and then click SMTP. Most likely, you will not have to change these settings.

Next, specify the details of the notification message—who the message is to and who it is from. You can also specify the subject and text of the message. You are not limited to specifying e-mail addresses for the message to be sent to. Any entity or object (such as a public folder) that has an address can be sent the message. This is useful if you want multiple people to be able to review the images. Setting up the message's From field is a bit tricky. If your e-mail server verifies that e-mail is sent from an address that is supposed to be internal, it might reject the sender as invalid and you'll never see the message. To avoid this problem, I use my Yahoo! account as the sender and my Exchange e-mail address as the recipient.

In the final section of the page, choose a file name. If you have multiple cameras, you might want to change the base file name—particularly if you're uploading the images to an FTP server rather than sending them through e-mail. Changing the base file name is a quick way to identify which images came from which camera. I also recommend that you use a date/time sequence as a suffix for the name so that you can quickly see when the images were created. When you are done with the settings, click the Save button.

The final step is configuring motion detection. To configure the motion detector, click the Motion Detection link to display a page similar to the one shown in Figure 14-9.

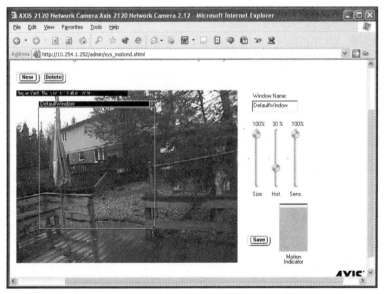

Figure 14-9   *The motion detection screen.*

The motion detection page is by far the most complicated, and the hardest to get set right. The default window can be resized by dragging the lower right corner and repositioned by dragging the title bar. This enables you to exclude areas of the image from motion detection. For instance, in my back yard, I try to exclude the wooded areas, because the movement of the trees trips the motion detector.

After you have positioned the window, change the three controls for size, history, and sensitivity. Under these tools is an indicator that changes to red when motion is detected so that you can test your settings. After you move one of the slider tools, click the Save button to reactivate the indicator.

As for setting the sliders, the three indicators are supposed to indicate the size of the motion, how much history is retained for determining if there was motion, and how sensitive to changes the camera will be. However, my experimentation has shown that you have to call a psychic hotline to get the values you want the first time around—or you have to play with the settings until the motion detector indicator does what you want it to do.

After you've saved your settings, you'll start receiving messages with your images. Actually, you should have been receiving them throughout your testing. As a result, you might end up with quite a few in your mailbox.

Note The Axis 2120 also enables you to connect regular stand-alone motion detectors, rather than using the built-in image processing-based motion detection. Discussing this is beyond the scope of this book, but it's an option if you can't get the image motion detector working as you want.

Summary

Whether you want to feel more comfortable about your home, watch for packages, or keep a log of people who enter your building, digital video surveillance is a good solution. By using a power connection and a network connection, you can view the video camera's images and receive alerts when motion is detected.

You can view the images from the camera through any Web browser. You can even view still images from a Pocket PC, which makes it easy to see what is in front of the camera from wherever you are in the building.

Here are some questions you can answer to help you decide whether digital video surveillance is right for you:

- Do you need only a few cameras?

- Do you have a network cable near where you need the camera, but no coaxial cable near the same spot?

- Do you need to be notified when motion occurs, even if you're not at your desk?

- Do you need to capture and retain large numbers of images for security purposes?

- Have you ever missed a package delivery because you didn't realize someone was knocking at the door?

- Is it difficult to know when someone is at your door?

- Do you ever want to check on the kids at home while you're at work?

Enterprise Applications

Part IV closes the book by examining enterprise applications for your Pocket PC device and ways to get enterprise applications to work on your Pocket PC.

Chapter 15 addresses Microsoft Terminal Services and how it can be used to access almost any application that can be run on Microsoft Windows from your Pocket PC. In this chapter, I show you how to use the Microsoft Terminal Services client from both your desktop computer and your Pocket PC. I'll also explain why you might want to use a Terminal Server in your organization.

Chapter 16 explores some of the ways that mobile technology is already being used. I focus on two areas: Sales Force Automation (SFA) and Enterprise Resource Planning (ERP). In addition, this chapter covers some applications that are specific to a few industries, but are interesting implementations of technology none the less.

Terminal Server

The first computer systems were monolithic—everyone had to share the same processor, memory, and applications. These systems were restricted to business functions such as accounting and inventory control. When people started transitioning to personal computers (PCs), users could run personal productivity applications such as Microsoft Word, Microsoft Excel, and Microsoft PowerPoint. Not long after the rise of the PC, users started connecting PCs to networks and sharing this personal productivity information. Recently, the trend has been to integrate the network back into a single system that provides all the resources users need in a single box.

With a Terminal Server, multiple users can access one computer. Each user gets his or her own window to the Terminal Server that emulates a complete Windows computer. The window has the user's own Start menu and Task bar, and runs applications independently of the applications being run on the local computer. We're heading back to the days when we all shared one monolithic computer—or are we?

A Terminal Server enables multiple users to share a single computer just as the monolithic computers of the past did, but without limiting what those users can do. Instead, a Terminal Server reduces the administrative burden of managing a large number of personal computers.

Note You might have heard about TCO—Total Cost of Ownership. Personal computers are very expensive, but most of their cost isn't in hardware. It's wrapped up in training, and particularly in support. The awareness of these high costs is one of the drivers pushing the IT industry in the direction of using monolithic servers again.

In this chapter, I'll explain what a Terminal Server is and how you can use it. I'll also cover under what circumstances you might—and might not—want to use a Terminal Server.

Tip A Terminal Server is an "ace in the hole" for many problems. Although I don't want to encourage overuse of this technology, it is an excellent tool.

What a Terminal Server Is and When to Use It

A Terminal Server can be set up as part of Microsoft Windows 2000 Server and Microsoft Windows XP Server to enable multiple users to share a single computer. Individual users get their own sessions and can work more or less without any knowledge that other users are sharing the system. Each session behaves as if it were a Windows computer. The user opens a connection to the Terminal Server with the Terminal Services client. A Terminal Services client window resembles a complete Windows desktop, including the Start menu.

Multiple users sharing one server necessitate that the server be powerful. Terminal Servers use the fastest processors available, and as many processors as the server can handle. They also have much more memory—up to 2 GB of RAM, as opposed to a typical server, which might have 512 MB of RAM.

Terminal Servers are based on a simple but powerful idea: Using a Terminal Server, you can run any standard Windows application on a computer other than your own. The client-side hardware (the hardware sitting on users' desks) can be ignored and low-powered computers or terminal devices are deployed at user desktops. It is easier to control the installation of applications on a centralized server rather than on each of the computers on the end users' desktops.

Caution Here we are talking about how the Terminal Server is used on a high-speed local network. Although it can be used when you're not on a high-speed local network, you must pay particular attention to the bandwidth that is available between the client and the Terminal Server. Sending all of the screen updates across a slow connection can significantly slow your response time.

Mobile professionals can reap many of the same benefits from Terminal Servers that system administrators do. A Pocket PC has a small processor and not very much memory, but if you connect it to a Terminal Server, the Pocket PC can have access to the same resources as a desktop computer.

Terminal Servers run Windows applications, but Pocket PCs run only Microsoft Windows CE applications. Using a Terminal Server can be a great benefit to Pocket PC users because so many more applications become available. There are benefits for corporations, too, because developers don't need to learn how to program for a new environment. By using Terminal Server, they can develop regular Windows applications for a smaller screen size and avoid the need to learn how to program for the Windows CE platform.

Terminal Servers are a quick way to use mobile devices for custom corporate applications. The applications are written using the tools that the programmers are already familiar with, eliminating very costly retraining.

Regular corporate users can connect to a Terminal Server and run all their corporate applications, from Enterprise Resource Planning (ERP) to Sales Force Automation (SFA). (ERP systems manage almost every aspect of a business, including manufacturing, distribution, and accounting. SFA systems focus solely on the sales process and improving sales effectiveness.) If you work in such an environment, you will be able to run your regular desktop applications on a Terminal Server and access them on your Pocket PC.

Using a Terminal Server is also a way to get applications from your desktop computer to your Pocket PC. For instance, in Chapter 14, you learned that the Pocket PC can't display motion video through Pocket Internet Explorer. However, if your Pocket PC is connected to a Terminal Server, you're not using Pocket Internet Explorer—you're using the full version of Microsoft Internet Explorer installed on the Terminal Server. Start Internet Explorer on the Terminal Server, and point Internet Explorer to the camera. The motion video will be displayed because it can be displayed on the computer. A Terminal Server enables your Pocket PC to receive motion video images.

When Performance Is a Problem

One of my clients was having a serious problem with a file-based accounting program running across their network. They had many performance problems with creating sales orders, processing invoices, and trying to find information. Sometimes they would wait three minutes or more just to create an invoice. This was starting to affect not only performance, but morale as well.

I looked for the cause of the problem in how the system was set up. I checked the network performance, server performance, and a variety of other potential causes, but I couldn't locate the cause.

The solution was to install a new dual-processor server with a fault-tolerant disk array and a serious amount of memory. I installed Terminal Services on my client's server so that all users could run the accounting program through the Terminal Server. The long waits for transactions were eliminated and overall responsiveness improved.

The response time dramatically improved. This is an excellent example of how a Terminal Server can solve problems. I probably could have diagnosed the cause of the performance problems given enough time, but I might never have found a way to improve them. A Terminal Server solved the problems quickly and cleanly.

Terminal Servers can also be used to run resource-intensive applications, which often don't perform well over the network. File-based network applications such as Act!, Quick-Books, and hundreds of custom applications that need high-bandwidth communications might run substantially faster on a Terminal Server.

Another reason to use a Terminal Server is to run long batch processes. Suppose you have a process, such as month-end report processing, that needs to run for several hours, and you don't want to wait for it. If you have a Terminal Server, you can start the process in the office and connect at home later to check its status.

You can disconnect from your Terminal Server session, and the session will continue to run the batch process. You can connect to the same session later by logging in again. Once you've reconnected, you can review the output of the process just as if you had sat in front of the computer the entire time.

When Not to Use a Terminal Server

Thus far, I've been singing the praises of Terminal Servers, and they are a great solution for many problems. However, Terminal Servers won't solve every problem. Here are a few situations when a Terminal Server isn't necessarily the best solution:

- **As a substitute for installing or upgrading Microsoft Office on individual users' PCs**   A Terminal Server can run Microsoft Office applications, but the resources that Office consumes make a Terminal Server an inappropriate solution for those situations where you have a large number of users who use Office all day long. For instance, you should not use a Terminal Server for the needs of a secretary and office assistant. They usually spend a lot of their day working in Office applications.

- **For use by complex applications**   Applications that would normally strain the resources of a personal computer are poor choices for a Terminal Server. Such applications would include three-dimensional modeling software, digital photograph manipulation, and a host of applications that need huge resources throughout the day.

- **As an excuse not to replace aging computers on users' desktops**   In theory, you can put together a Terminal Server and not worry about what users' desktops are like, because they're using resources from the server. However, the reality is that eventually the hard disks, monitors, keyboards, and other components of the users' computers will fail and need to be replaced. Adding a Terminal Server only delays the inevitable in these circumstances.

Setting Up the Server

This isn't a book for administrators, and it would be inappropriate for me to take you completely step by step through the process of installing the Microsoft Terminal Services component of Windows 2000 and Windows XP. Nevertheless, it's important that you understand just how easy it is to install Terminal Services as a viable option for your business problems. The basic process requires four steps:

1. Installing Windows 2000 on the server hardware.

2. Turning on Terminal Server and Terminal Server Licensing through the Add/Remove Programs applet.

3. Entering the licensing information into the Terminal Server Licensing application.

4. Installing the Terminal Services client on the computers that need access to the Terminal Server.

None of the preceding steps is difficult or complicated. Your IT department should already know how to set up Windows 2000. In the second step, you need only select two check boxes and answer one question to get Windows 2000 to install the Terminal Server.

The one question you must answer is whether the Terminal Server will be used in remote control or application server mode. In remote control mode, a Terminal Server allows for two connections. This mode is designed to help server administrators work with servers that are not easily reachable. This mode doesn't require client access licenses for the Terminal Server clients. Select this mode only if you intend to use Terminal Services to remotely administer your server.

In application server mode, the server can have as many connected clients as you are licensed for. For the first 90 days, the Terminal Server doesn't require any licensing. After this time period, the server will deny any attempts to connect until a license server is set up and the Terminal Server can communicate with it.

The third step requires that you fill out an online licensing application or call Microsoft to receive the activation codes for the license codes that you have. Getting the activation codes is a relatively trivial process; you'll have plenty of time to accomplish it within the 90-day time period.

The fourth step will enable the Terminal Services client software to be accessed by any client that can connect to the server. When the Terminal Server is installed, it creates a directory called %WINDIR%\SYSTEM32\CLIENTS\TSCLIENT\WIN32\DISKS, which contains the client installation software for Microsoft Windows 95/98/Me/2000/XP. By sharing this folder from the server, any client that can connect to the server can install the Terminal Services client software.

Connecting from Your Computer

The first step to connecting to a Terminal Server from your computer is installing the Terminal Services client software. This software is automatically put in a directory on the server that the administrator should make available to you. That directory is %WINDIR%\SYSTEM32\CLIENTS\TSCLIENT\WIN32\DISKS. Alternately, the administrator can make a set of installation disks for you.

After you run the setup, a dialog box appears, as shown in Figure 15-1, in which you can select an installation directory. To accept the default installation location, click the big, square button. In the next dialog box, shown in Figure 15-2, click Yes *only* if you want everyone who uses that computer to have the same initial settings. I recommend that you click No, so that each person can have his or her own unique protocol. Then all you need to do is acknowledge that the setup was completed successfully.

Figure 15-1   *The Terminal Services Client Setup dialog box.*

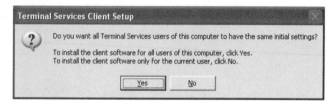

Figure 15-2   *You probably don't want everyone to have the same settings, so click No.*

To run the Terminal Services client, on the Start menu, click Terminal Services Client. A dialog box similar to the one shown in Figure 15-3 will appear.

Most people find this dialog box confusing at first. Fortunately, there's another entry in the Terminal Services Client submenu, called Client Connection Manager, from which you can create icons that bypass this dialog box altogether. However, the dialog box isn't all that complicated once you understand it.

In the Server box, click the down arrow to display the list of server names, and click the one to which you want to connect. If the server you want isn't included under your domain in the list, either the list isn't expanded or no Terminal Servers were detected. Make sure the Expand By Default check box is selected. (You might want to clear this check box if there are so many Terminal Servers in your domain that it takes a long time for this dialog box to appear).

In the Screen Area box, you can specify the size of the Terminal Services client window. The session can be established with any screen size you want, since the session with the Terminal Server is virtual. (It's virtual because it isn't tied to the hardware on the server or on the client computer.) This is particularly useful if you plan on opening multiple terminal sessions to different Terminal Servers, because you can arrange a series of smaller windows on your computer screen. Terminal Services sessions run like any other application on your computer, and multiple sessions can be run as easily as opening two documents in Microsoft Word.

Figure 15-3 *The Terminal Services Client dialog box can be a bit confusing.*

Selecting the Enable Data Compression check box helps reduce the impact of bandwidth limitations. It does, however, require some CPU time on both the client and on the server to do this, so if you're using the Terminal Services client over a high-speed local area network (LAN), you might want to make sure this check box is cleared.

When you select the Cache Bitmaps To Disk check box, the Terminal Services client caches some bitmaps that might come up frequently on the client. Whenever the client display needs to be repainted (for example, when you close or minimize a window), the graphics device interface can use these bitmaps instead of repainting the entire display from scratch. This too saves bandwidth, but it's probably not necessary for high-speed LAN connections.

After you've chosen all the settings, click the Connect button, and a window the size you specified appears, as shown in Figure 15-4 on the next page. The logon screen you see in this window is the logon screen for the Terminal Server. After you log on, a view of your desktop appears, as shown in Figure 15-5 on the next page.

You might have noticed that the window has scroll bars. When you first open the window, it will be the exact size you specified when you set up the Terminal Services client. The problem with this is that it doesn't take into consideration the additional space required by the title bar. If you have room on your screen, expand the window as you would any other, and the scroll bars will disappear.

Figure 15-4 *This logon screen looks exactly like the screen on the console.*

Figure 15-5 *The full screen of your desktop as displayed through the Terminal Services client.*

However, if you specified a window size equal to the size of your monitor's display, you won't be able to expand the window and remove the scroll bars. You can either work with the scroll bars or put the Terminal Services client in full screen mode. To switch to full screen mode, press Ctrl+Alt+Break. This key combination toggles between full screen and windowed mode for the Terminal Services client.

Tip There are a lot of useful keyboard commands for the Terminal Services client. If you want to learn more about them, click the icon in the upper left corner of the Terminal Services client window (the System menu), point to Help, and then click Terminal Services Client Help.

Telling One from the Other

One of the biggest problems people have when using a Terminal Services client is navigating between the Terminal Services client window and the local computer's own desktop. It can be difficult to figure out which things are happening on the local computer and which are happening on the Terminal Server, and to determine which scroll bars and keys to use.

I've learned from experience that it's a good idea to create worksheets and guidelines for how to run the Terminal Services client. If you don't do this, you'll probably wind up with a slew of disconnected sessions and frustrated users.

Make sure you recognize the difference between the Start menu on the local computer and the Start menu on the Terminal Services client. The Terminal Services Start menu displays the name of the operating system followed by the word *Terminal* as shown in Figure 15-6.

Log off of a Terminal Server session through the Start menu just as you do from your Windows computer. Figure 15-6 shows the Start menu complete with the Log Off command and the vertical text indicating that it's the Start menu from a Terminal Services client.

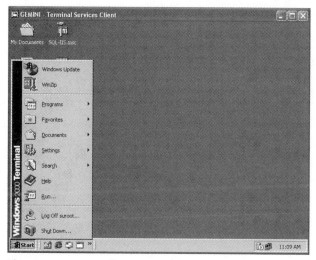

Figure 15-6 *Log off a Terminal Server session the same way you would log off a Windows computer.*

If you want to disconnect the client but continue your Terminal Server session, click the Close box. A message box appears, as shown in Figure 15-7, informing you that the client will be disconnected, but the Terminal Server (Windows) session will remain active.

Figure 15-7   *A message box informs you of your options for disconnecting.*

If you do disconnect from your session, you can resume it later by connecting to the Terminal Server again with the same user name and password.

Warning Although a Terminal Server is supposed to reconnect with the last session, there are times when this doesn't work. The system administrator can change settings to force each user to receive only one session to the Terminal Server to solve the problem, or he or she can show you how to use Terminal Services Manager to reconnect to a previous session.

Whether you close your session or just the window, the connection dialog box appears so that you can connect to another server or close the Terminal Services client.

Connecting from Your Pocket PC

Unlike your computer, your Pocket PC doesn't need to have the Terminal Services client installed. The Terminal Services client is part of the Pocket PC 2002 package and is already installed on your Pocket PC. To find the client, on the Start menu, point to Programs, and tap Terminal Services Client. Tapping the application icon with your stylus launches the application. The Terminal Services Client dialog box, which is similar to the connection dialog box, appears when the Terminal Services client starts, as shown in Figure 15-8.

In the Server box, type the name of the server to which you want to connect, or select one of the servers listed in the Recent Servers box. If you select the Limit Size Of Server Desktop To Fit On This Screen check box, the Terminal Services client will provide a window the same size as your screen—in other words, 320 by 240. This size is very different from the 640 by 480 that it generally uses as a minimum size. If you do not select this check box, you might see some strange side effects, such as the User Name box getting cut off, as shown in Figure 15-9.

Figure 15-8 *The Pocket PC Terminal Services Client dialog box is not hard to use.*

Figure 15-9 *If you don't have enough room, things get chopped off.*

If you leave the screen at the 640 by 480 size, you will have to scroll around to control which part of the screen you're looking at, as shown in Figure 15-10. This isn't impossible to deal with, but it can be awkward.

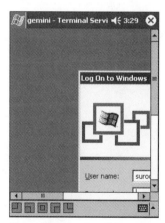

Figure 15-10 *Scroll bars are workable, but somewhat less than ideal.*

Because the navigation system on the Pocket PC is different from the one on the Terminal Services client, it's easier to figure out which controls go with the local device and which ones go with the Terminal Services client. When you're done, log off using the Start menu.

Summary

In this chapter, I explained some of the uses for Terminal Server in the corporate environment and how it can be used as a transition tool to corporate applications developed for a wireless platform.

I also covered the basics of installing and using the Terminal Services client on both your personal computer and your Pocket PC. The most difficult thing about using a Terminal Server on the computer is determining which computer you're working on. On the Pocket PC, the most difficult thing is scrolling around the screen, or getting everything to fit on the smaller screen. Despite these difficulties, a Terminal Server and the Terminal Services client are a great tool for many environments.

As always, I leave you with some food for thought:

- Do you need a wireless application but find that your internal IT department does not have the skills to develop one for the Pocket PC?

- Do you need features from your desktop computer software while you're on the road?

- Do you ever sit in a meeting and wish you could verify or dispute the facts that others are discussing? Could you find that information if you had access to your Enterprise Resource Planning (ERP) system?

- Could you use a Terminal Server to run month-end processing for the accounting package, or long sales reports, or any other processes that seem to take too long?

Applying Mobile Technology to Your Enterprise

Over 300 pages ago, we started a journey together. You've seen a lot of technologies and ways to use them to meet your business needs. In this chapter, I will show you how you can use mobile technologies to make your enterprise work better and more efficiently. I'll point out three different types of applications your enterprise already uses and show you how to apply mobile technologies to improve them.

For the most part, I've tried to shy away from suggesting big, sweeping changes that your entire enterprise would have to implement to receive a benefit. I've also avoided those technologies that require much more than your own ingenuity to get started. This chapter is different because, in most cases, the level of organizational change required to make the technology useful is much more corporate and much less personal.

This chapter is also different because it is designed to address many different kinds of organizations, situations, and solutions, not all of which will apply directly to your situation. I hope that while you read this chapter, you will ask yourself how you might apply the technologies and techniques that are being used in different industries to your situation.

The first area I'll focus on is Sales Force Automation (SFA). I'll explain how mobile technologies can be used to link a sales force to its corporation for an easy flow of information.

The second area I'll focus on is a category of applications known as Enterprise Resource Planning (ERP). These applications help to control inventory, manufacturing, and a broad class of issues known as logistics. If your organization offers services and not products, you might want to skip over this section.

Finally, I'll focus on what I call "specialized applications"—those targeted to specific industries. The selections here are designed to give you a broad overview of applications you might use.

Sales Force Automation

There are two main challenges to successfully managing a sales force. First, an organization must get the necessary information to its salespeople in the field. Without the necessary information, salespeople can't be effective. Second, the sales force must be able to compile their information and return it to the organization. Without information from its sales staff, the organization can't plan. Let's take a look at each of these challenges in turn.

Getting Information to the Sales Force

Clearly, a sales force must know what products its company sells and how much the products cost. However, salespeople must know more than this basic information to be able to sell effectively.

A sales force needs three basic types of information:

- Product information
- Customer service information
- Competitive information

Product Information

Supplying a sales force with product information is important; if they don't know what they're selling, they can't sell it. However, saying that they have to know about the products is quite an understatement.

To be able to sell a product effectively, they must understand its features and benefits. They must also understand the problem that the product solves. People will not buy a product that doesn't solve some problem or open up some new opportunity for them. Of course, salespeople attend classes to learn this information. They are taught about the products they sell and how they work.

Even with extensive training, it's impossible to know everything about the products a company produces. That is why it's important for an organization to support its sales staff with ways to reference product information conveniently. Historically, this has been done by assigning technical staff to provide detailed technical information to the sales staff.

An automated system can't replace technical assistance, but it can provide the sales staff with more complete product information. An automated system can minimize how much the sales staff must lean on the technical staff.

In many organizations, the complexity of the products dictates a complicated configuration process. Incorrect configuration can be costly in terms of production problems, customer satisfaction issues, and lost sales due to unnecessary and expensive options that make the quote too expensive.

Many organizations today still use standard configurations that can be tailored to fit individual corporate needs and that rely on technical support staff for confirmation. Other organizations have PC-based configuration software that builds the configuration of their products and ensures that the product is configured correctly. This software greatly reduces the complexity of configuring a product by either prompting the user through the process of creating a configuration or preventing incorrect configurations.

As organizations move to a more mobile work force, configuration software is becoming available for mobile devices. The Microsoft Pocket PC platform has enough processing capacity to run this software if careful attention is paid to the storage space required by the data for the configuration. Pocket PCs can store a library of information about each product. The configuration program itself usually occupies very little additional space. The trick is storing the product information library in a format that can be used for both the salesperson's review and for the configuration program. For instance, the power requirements of a module might be stored on the product information sheet—and also be necessary to determine how large a power supply is required in the solution.

Of course, there is one other key piece of information for many sales professionals—information that frequently determines whether the sale will be made or not. That is the availability of the product. Before a customer places an order, the salesperson needs to know whether the company can ship the product to the customer within the requested time frame; this is sometimes critical to the success of the sale. More importantly, not overcommitting to a customer (by promising that the product can ship when it can't), might make future sales to that customer easier.

Most organizations don't provide up-to-the-minute inventory information to their entire sales force, but some are developing strategies to help sales professionals know how much inventory is available for a customer—before the order is placed. The solutions can come in the form of downloadable inventory information that's just a few hours old, or it can come in the form of interactive voice response (IVR) systems that the sales staff can dial into. However, in some cases, the sales staff use wireless cards in their Pocket PCs and notebooks to download the latest information. Some organizations use an extranet that enables customers to check the availability of a potential order themselves.

Both the IVR systems and extranet solutions have the advantage of providing completely accurate inventories, so there is no chance that someone else has ordered the same product the salesperson is trying to sell. But they have the disadvantage of not fitting well within the sales cycle. They make the salesperson or customer break off negotiations to verify availability.

In many organizations, having an inventory that is a few hours old is sufficient, because orders don't happen often enough to make it likely that the inventory that a customer wants will have been ordered by someone else in a few short hours. This does, however, create the chance of setting the wrong expectation with the customer.

The final, and best, solution outfits sales professionals with wireless network cards that enable them to check the inventory while sitting with the customer. This option doesn't disrupt the negotiation process and provides accurate-to-the-minute inventories, but it comes at a cost. To work, it requires that each salesperson be equipped with a wireless card and monthly service. In many organizations, the $75 monthly fee for wireless service might not be justifiable. It also suffers from the potential problem of being unable to get coverage in the customer's office.

Customer Service Information

Whether a salesperson sells products, services, or a combination, it's his or her goal to keep customers happy. Salespeople need information so that they can answer their customers' questions about delivery or service. Otherwise, there is little chance of making repeat sales.

There are several aspects to keeping a customer happy, including the following:

- Managing orders
- Preventing service problems
- Knowing service status

Many organizations are realizing the need for salespeople to have access to this information and are implementing systems to make the information available. The first step is, of course, making the information available on the salespeople's notebooks. The information also needs to be made available to the salespeople when they are disconnected from the corporate network.

With the current state of the technology, it's possible for salespeople to review information about their customers offline. However, the next steps aren't far off. Automated systems are being tested today that review salespeople's calendars and download information to them about the customers they are scheduled to see. The salespeople can then review that information on route to their customers so that they will be familiar with the customers' recent interactions with the company.

Competitive Information

One key to successful selling is understanding the unique features and benefits that the company's products have over competitors' products. This understanding helps salespeople present the products to customers with the greatest chance of success. Many organizations have employees who collect and disseminate information on competitors' products and how they are marketed.

This is the most difficult kind of information to provide to the salesperson in the field. It is difficult to organize it into the neat little categories necessary for creating a database.

However, there are tools that help make this information accessible to the traveling salesperson. There are databases designed for the storage of free text information, like the kind of information captured about competitors.

By and large, these database applications are available only for notebooks, because of the large volume of information and because the search tools exist only for notebooks. It's unlikely that these tools will move to a Pocket PC format soon because of their complexity. However, much of the information available in these databases is available directly from the Web sites of the competitors. Even if a corporation doesn't have a solution in place, its salespeople can peruse competitors' Web sites to better understand their products and learn what their own products' unique benefits are.

Note The necessity for these applications to be on notebooks is changing as CompactFlash-sized MicroDrives reach for 6 GB capacities and CompactFlash memory cards have hit 1 GB, making the idea of storing all of this information on a Pocket PC an imminent reality.

Getting Information from the Salespeople

An organization needs three basic types of information from its salespeople:

- Quote status
- Orders
- Forecasts

Quote Status

The first step in the sales process for most sales staff is meeting with customers and discussing their needs. Frequently, the next step is providing a quote to the customer. In some industries, quotes are given verbally. However, in other industries, quotes are formal documents that respond to a Request for Proposal (RFP) that customers give to a small number of potential vendors.

Salespeople don't usually create quotes in front of the customer; they generally create them at night in the hotel, on the airplane, or back in the office. This allows the salesperson to access the sales system and record all the details of the quote as it is created. These details might include the quote amount, the date of the quote, the expiration date of the quote, and other specifics. A salesperson equipped with a cellular modem card and the appropriate software could enter the quote into a Pocket PC after leaving the customer's office; the sales system could then fax a copy of the quote to the customer for the salesperson.

What is far more likely, however, is that the salesperson will use the tools on a Pocket PC to update the status of a previous quote that he or she sent to the customer. After having met with the customer, the salesperson should be able to update the status of the order. He or she can find out whether the customer has decided to put the order on hold or has decided to order the items on the quote. The Pocket PC is an ideal way to send all the order information back to the office so that it can be synchronized to the corporate network.

Often, if order information is updated only at the office, it can be forgotten until a few moments before a sales staff meeting. Providing a tool to make it easy to update quote status is critical to ensuring that the organization has a grasp of the overall quote picture.

Orders

In some industries, it's important to get orders into the order system as soon as possible so that the product can be shipped immediately. In industries that sell perishable products, such as the food service industry, it's very important to get orders entered into the system as soon as possible. Most food orders are entered on paper by the restaurant manager or the head chef, but there are organizations in which salespeople visit frequently so that they can enter an order while at the customer's site. Those organizations can equip their salespeople with mobile devices from which to enter the customer's order.

Restaurants still typically fax their orders, or give their orders for the next day to the driver who delivers their food for the current day. In either case, these orders must be manually entered by data-entry personnel. There's always a risk that people will key in the wrong item or the wrong amount. Giving the salesperson or the delivery driver the ability to enter orders with the customer means that the orders can be confirmed before being placed.

Note Ultimately, situations like these require a much broader set of solutions. In many cases, a fax server and optical character recognition (OCR) software are appropriate. An extranet Web site designed for customers to log in and verify or change their orders would also be helpful. Having salespeople use mobile devices to enter orders is just the beginning of the solution to this problem.

Forecasts

Pending quotes are often used to determine a service-driven organization's upcoming workflow. They are probably the best short-term indicator of the business that can be expected. Unfortunately, this doesn't work in a lot of other types of organizations. Production lines can't be shifted quickly enough to fill a customer's order, at least not in the amount of time it typically takes to ship. That's why a more traditional forecasting method is necessary.

Often, the sales staff is asked to forecast what and how much their customers will order. Forecasting is kind of like predicting what the weather will be like in a few weeks. The forecast will be wrong—it's just a matter of how wrong it is going to be. Similarly, you have to decide what margin of error you're going to build into the sales forecast to make sure that you can meet a customer's needs.

Predicting the Weather

As a private pilot, I've been required by the Federal Aviation Administration (FAA) to learn more about weather systems than most people have to. I have learned how difficult weather forecasting is. But accurate weather forecasting is very important. Most people are unhappy if the meteorologist on their local TV station cannot accurately predict the weather for the next five days. In aviation I've learned that weather predictions are good for about six hours—and sometimes not even for that long. I'm not just referring to the complexities of knowing where the clouds will be. I'm referring to knowing what hour of the day those thunderstorms will be rumbling through.

I believe that this analogy provides a unique perspective on the idea that you can forecast product-by-product activity six months into the future. I've run into a few professionals in my career who want business forecasts to be very accurate. Some have even suggested they should be within 10 percent of the actual numbers. I believe that this is ludicrous.

Mobile technology can facilitate the transfer of forecast information back to the organization by making it easy to update while on the road. A Pocket PC application that shows the last period's sales to the customer and allows the salesperson to quickly enter the new projection could be used easily on a plane ride home.

Forecasting in an Import Business

Many import businesses have to deal with long lead times to receive their products—up to six months. A typical struggle is forecasting what will need to be ordered from overseas. Sometimes, sophisticated forecasting software will help create an accurate forecast.

The use of mobile technology can help importers get more frequent and more accurate forecasts from their sales staff, even if it probably can't prevent all instances of over-ordering a product. Excess inventory is a substantial expense for these organizations, because it fills warehouse space that is needed for other products and it means cash is expended for items that cannot return value for a long time.

In an import business, bad forecasting isn't just an annoyance. If left unchecked, it can quickly devour an organization. The better information an organization puts into the forecasting system the better forecasts it will get out. This means continuously updating the forecast system, which can be facilitated by mobile technology.

ERP Applications

Enterprise Resource Planning (ERP) applications have been used with mobile technology for years. In large distribution centers, mobile barcode scanners can speed up distribution by helping workers find the products that need to be shipped and get them to the right truck. That's not the only application for mobile technology in the world of ERP systems; it's just one example of how mobile technology is used. Let's visit a few others.

Note The devices discussed here are Pocket PC based, but they aren't the same kind of devices you give to the office staff, for three reasons. First, it's likely that you'll need a keyboard for these applications. Second, most of these applications need a barcode reader to be effective. Finally, the devices must be much more rugged than the devices used by the office staff—because when they are dropped, it's likely to be on a concrete floor.

Manufacturing Line

In some kinds of manufacturing, tracking each operation that happens to a part of an assembly is a must. One such industry is the aerospace repair industry. Because the tolerances in the aerospace industry are so small, and because there are documentation requirements for the FAA, it is important to ensure that every operation is signed off and checked.

Historically, each part is followed by a packet of papers called a *traveler* or a *work order*. These documents are designed to show each step the part goes through from the moment it enters the shop to the moment it leaves. The information in these travelers is entered into the manufacturing control or ERP system when the parts are completed.

Today, these documents can be replaced with mobile barcode scanners and workstations at the equipment locations. At the beginning of the day, machine operators log on to mobile workstations next to their computers. The workstation shows which parts are ready to be machined.

The terminal provides the operator with information about where to get the appropriate part and displays an overall view of what the part looks like. The operator scans the barcode attached to the part, and the terminal displays a schematic of the part and describes the operation or operations to be performed. This dramatically improves the turnaround time between parts. Because all the information the operator needs is readily available, the operator saves valuable time and increases accuracy and production.

When the part is finished, the operator enters the amount of time spent on the part into the terminal. The operator takes his or her mobile terminal and the part to the location where he or she is placing the part; the location barcode and the barcode on the part are scanned to confirm the move.

Supervisors and shop floor controllers can use mobile terminals to see what machines are currently operating and what jobs they are performing. The same applies to quality assurance checks. This can help identify gaps in the production line, such as machines that might become idle because of the way that materials are flowing through the plant. Perhaps more importantly, mobile terminals can call attention to parts awaiting final quality control checks, documentation, and shipping. This enables the shop floor controller to keep materials moving out the door so that they can be invoiced.

> **Note** In some parts of the aerospace industry, a single part can be worth hundreds of thousands of dollars. Shipping parts even a day earlier can create a substantial shift in the cash flow of an organization.

Mobile computers can also be used to call for assistance. If a machine operator indicates on his or her computer that a supervisor's assistance with a part is needed, the message is sent out to all the shop floor controllers and supervisors. An available supervisor can signal that he or she will handle the need. This sends the operator a message that a supervisor is on the way. The message is cancelled on the other shop floor controllers' and supervisors' mobile computers.

One might initially think that a simple paging system would be much easier to use; however, most paging systems would require that the operators have a mechanism to send and receive messages from their work area, something that isn't practical for most paging systems.

Turning Pocket PCs into Walkie-Talkies

BInTouch is a unique application by bSquare (*http://www.bsquare.com*). The application enables you to use your Pocket PC just like a walkie-talkie over your local network. Unfortunately, at this time the application is being sold only to enterprises that can purchase 100 or more licenses of the product.

However, the product is ideal for large manufacturing environments where you need to have a mobile computer but might not want to carry a separate radio. This is particularly true if the radio isn't needed frequently, but might be beneficial from time to time.

Obviously, for this to work, there must be a wireless infrastructure in place to support the data moving across the line. For most organizations, this will be the 802.11b wireless LAN I covered in Chapter 2.

> **Tip** Ruksun offers a product, Voice Messenger Force, that allows you to use MSN Messenger as a conduit for initiating voice communications. This isn't exactly as easy as a dedicated voice application, but it certainly allows voice communications to work on your Pocket PC. You can find out more at *http://www.ruksun.com/mobile_computing/windowsce/products /voice_messengerforce/*.

Statistical Quality Control

In some manufacturing operations, there aren't single parts that move from machine to machine; there are hundreds or thousands of parts moving through an automated production line. Think of nuts or washers flowing out of machines on an assembly line, or if you've ever seen the opening to the 1970s TV show *Laverne and Shirley*, think of the beer bottles flowing past them.

To provide a reasonable assurance of product quality without the cost of inspecting every part, manufacturing organizations use statistical process control. Essentially, this means sampling the production at regular intervals to ensure that the parts meet specifications.

Note I've greatly oversimplified this section because the mathematical mechanics relating to statistics are not necessary to the understanding of how mobile technology is being used.

Mobile technology is now used in some organizations so that quality engineers can quickly enter the dimensions of parts that they pull off the line. The software in the system calculates the variance, when the next part should be checked from the line, and when the line should be taken down for recalibration. This information is processed largely by servers on the network that are connected to Pocket PCs. The servers keep a database of the quality engineers' work, as well as detailed records on each machine and the process, so that the number of samples that need to be taken, as well as machine maintenance, is optimized. After receiving a result from the server, the quality engineer can proceed to the next machine to test its parts.

Distribution Center

The old saying "the devil is in the details" was never more true than in a distribution center. With distribution centers generally measuring hundreds of thousands of square feet, and many of them with three or more levels of pallet racking, it's easy to see how there might be a few details to keep track of.

Distribution centers were among the first business environments to use wireless technology. Specialized barcode readers were developed that contained not only barcode readers but wireless radios as well. These devices historically required special programming languages and tools, so they were limited to core logistic functions such as locating products—a process called picking.

As the devices evolved, they moved to an MS-DOS–based environment on handheld scanners. This meant that organizations could develop applications that would run on the scanner devices with tools that were familiar. Programming these devices took some getting used to, because the screens were generally only 4 lines high and 20 characters wide. The devices also didn't have much memory.

Today, you can still get MS-DOS-based mobile devices to run in a corporate environment, but there's been a shift toward PDA operating systems like the Palm and Microsoft Windows CE/Pocket PC operating systems. The scanner devices of today are rugged and have keyboards, onboard wireless LAN connectivity, and, of course, barcode scanners. They are, however, internally very similar to a regular PDA.

The tools used to develop applications for these mobile platforms are the same as those used to create applications for the associated PDA platforms. There is no difference in the software development tools, except that the hardware is designed specifically for ERP applications.

Moving to PDA platforms might not seem like much of an advance in terms of technology, but it can provide a better user interface. PDA platforms support touch screens, enabling users to work with soft buttons on the screen. Soft buttons enable users to select a task without hunting for the right key on the keypad and without having to decipher complex statements. For instance, employees who float between different roles might need to periodically change their operation mode. On MS-DOS–based systems, those employees must access a menu in which numbers are associated with the different kinds of tasks. In a PDA environment, the employees simply press soft buttons on the screen for each of the different tasks. Similarly, the system doesn't need to ask questions that can be answered by a single key press. In an MS-DOS environment, the system might provide the following prompt:

```
Incorrect serial number. Press Y to override and use this item, or N to exit and
try again.
```

In a graphic environment, the same problem might be addressed by providing the following prompt:

```
Serial # XYZ is incorrect. Please select action.
```

followed by two buttons: "Accept new serial number" and "Try again."

These mobile terminals are now used for almost every aspect of operations in a distribution center. In the warehouse, the staff uses them to locate and organize all the products that need to be shipped. If a package isn't available where the system indicates it should be, the employee records that package as missing. The system locates more of the same product and updates the records to indicate that a new package is being sent to the customer. Typically, the system flags the location where the first package was supposed to be so that an inventory control person can review that location.

Mobile technology is also used in the shipping process. As items are placed on a pallet, they are scanned to confirm that they were loaded on the truck. In some organizations, pallets themselves get bar codes, indicating the products that are on that pallet.

Note Symbol Technologies (*http://www.symbol.com*), a developer of wireless applications, is pushing for support of a two-dimensional barcode that can be used to store information in a small space. Ideally, this information could be used to store what products are on a pallet.

Incoming products go through a similar process. If the products are already barcoded when they arrive, they are scanned and sent to a specific location determined by the system. If a problem occurs, the receiver records it and the system finds a new location for the material.

Mobile devices can also facilitate inventory control. They are used to ensure that the products are in their proper location and in the proper amount. This process, called cycle-counting, helps to ensure that the warehouse inventory remains accurate.

Specialized Applications

In the next few sections, I will explore a slightly wider set of applications. Some of these applications are somewhat mainstream, but they're very different from the applications that I have already explained.

Field Service

It's important for field service representatives to have access to the same kinds of service information as the salespeople. However, field service reps often need more detailed information, because they will ultimately be responsible for resolving the customer's problem.

Salespeople typically have a schedule that determines which customers they will see, but field service reps go where the customer's needs are most urgent. When there are dozens—or hundreds—of service reps in a region, just deciding whom to send to a customer can be a challenging process by itself.

The pagers that most field service reps carry are used to dispatch them to customer sites. However, mobile devices can improve the dispatching process by enabling the dispatcher to see the exact location of each field service rep.

Today, organizations use mobile solutions that enable customers to know where their service rep is, and enable field service representatives to record notes about the customer service call. Devices that store information about complete inventories and availability are used to simplify the process of ordering a replacement part for the customer or to replenish the field service representative's stock. If a field service representative records in the morning that he or she had to replace a customer's hard disk, the system can automatically ship a replacement hard disk the same day. This keeps the field service rep stocked, in case another customer needs the same part the next day.

Health Care

The health care industry implements information systems differently than most other industries. Because the process of caring for patients doesn't always fit into specifically defined categories, health care systems struggle to collect all the various kinds of information about a patient and keep it accessible to the health care providers.

Because of the challenges inherent to health care information systems, the industry is often willing to try new ideas and new technologies. Many health care organizations are starting to use handheld devices to gather complete patient medical records. With these devices, doctors can see a patient's medical history at a glance, rather than having to sift through reams of paper in the patient's file.

Note These concepts apply equally well to keeping information about customers or students.

Handheld devices also enable doctors to see a list of the patients who are waiting for them, so they know to keep moving. In a hospital, mobile systems help doctors access more information about a patient's status than ever before.

Another way that the health care industry uses mobile technology is in the collection of information at an accident scene. In Sweden, ambulance crews have mobile computers that are connected by a wireless LAN to systems in the ambulance. The technicians collect information about the patient's injuries and current condition, and record this information on the mobile computers. The information is then relayed from the ambulance's onboard systems to the hospital so that the emergency staff has the information they need to make life-saving decisions.

Transportation

Trucking companies are installing systems that enable drivers to check on the status of pending loads and bid on those loads. In addition, the systems also report the exact location of the truck based on the GPS receiver integrated into these systems. Businesses that receive freight usually depend on the timely delivery of merchandise, so they can check the location of a truck at any given moment. These systems can sometimes give the recipient a notification before delivery as well.

The next step is to automate the rest of the paperwork required in the transportation industry. You might have already seen this technology in use by United Parcel Service; they've been using tablets for some time now. These tablets can record the signature of the recipient directly—no more paper. By accepting the signature digitally, organizations can provide delivery confirmation, with signature, quickly and easily.

Hospitality

The hotel industry faces a very difficult problem: controlling access to the rooms. Traditional locks need to be changed frequently to prevent people from entering the rooms with copied keys. Many hotels have been using electronic locks for more than 10 years, but until recently, programming and monitoring them required a notebook computer.

Today, a hotel can use a Pocket PC's infrared port to communicate with the computers in the room locks. This way, the operator can determine how much battery life is left in the lock and review the last 200 accesses to the room.

This technology has also made it possible for hotels to confirm who entered a room and when. Because a hotel employee's unique card number is logged into each lock he or she opens, hotels can reduce their losses caused by employee theft.

Some hotels are also beginning to use wireless technology to get their managers out from behind the desk and mingling with the guests of the hotel. This helps them to make guests feel more welcome and at home without compromising their managerial duties.

Through the use of wireless LAN technology and Pocket PCs, managers can now keep tabs on their vacancy rates, and even adjust room rates on the fly. This in turn helps the hotel become more profitable by renting out more rooms at higher rates.

Summary

This chapter took a whirlwind tour through different scenarios in different industries. Most of these scenarios might not apply directly to your organization and your business, but it's worth examining the ways that wireless and portable solutions are being used. My goal here was to expose you to some of the uses of mobile technology so that you can find commonality in the kinds of problems that your organization or department faces. You can then take pieces of the solutions and apply them to your needs.

As mobile technology becomes easier to afford, simpler to use, and more powerful, the number of processes that could be augmented by mobile system support will grow as well. Frankly, in today's world of high-speed wireless LANs, mobile computers can be used for almost any process that is currently confined within the walls of the corporation.

It has been my habit throughout this book to leave you with a series of questions to help you think about how you can use the information. As the book comes to a close, I leave you with one fundamental question that I hope the information I have provided will help you answer:

- How can you use mobile technology in your daily work, in your organization's processes, or in your daily life to improve your productivity and reduce your frustrations?

Index

Numerics

3G wireless services, 53
802.11b standard, 45

A

Access, synchronizing
databases, 114
access control lists, 64
accessibility of Pocket PCs, 18, 20
accessing
e-mail messages, 139
information from
anywhere, 26–33
ACLs, 64
Acrobat, 246
activating
conduits, 114
Microsoft Reader, 246
ActiveSync, 109–15
backing up with, 123
conduits (*see* conduits)
conflicts, resolving, 124
connectivity problems, 125
failure to recognize device, 125
file conversion, 119–20
Mobile Explorer, 117–18
adapters, DC to AC, 92
addresses, finding in Pocket
Streets, 218
Adobe Acrobat, 246
agents, 250–51
gatherers (*see* gatherers)
saved searches (*see* saved
searches)
search engines (*see* search
engines)
AIM. *See* AOL Instant Messenger
airplane power adapters, 92

airports, theft prevention and
recovery, 73–74
alert sounds, 235
algorithms for message digests, 68
aligning
Bluetooth, ease of, 42
infrared ports, 41
text, in Pocket Word, 191
analyzing projects, in cyProj, 200
annotating documents in Pocket
Word, 194–95
annotations
in eBooks, 244
in Palm Reader, 246
anonymous e-mail. *See* Hotmail
accounts
AOL Instant Messenger, 185
applications, 305
on Pocket PCs, 306
resource-intensive, 308
on Terminal Server, 306, 308
on Windows-based notebooks, 5,
7
arcade games for Pocket PCs, 81
asymmetric key systems. *See* public/
private keys
attachments, e-mail, 140–41
file conversion, 133
in OWA, 157
synchronizing, 132
Audible.com, 249
audio books, 249
auditing, 65
authentication, 58–63
for authorization, 65
biometric, 60–62
signatures (*see* signature
authentication)
smart cards (*see* smart cards)
tokens (*see* tokens)
Web (*see* Passport)
authorization, 58, 64–65

auditing, 65
automatic device detection, 38
AvantGo, 260
Axis cameras, 290–300. *See also*
network-attached cameras

B

backing up
notebooks, 83–84
Pocket PCs, 123–24
backlight, PDA, 23
BackupExec, 84
bags for notebooks, 88–89
bandwidth, shared over local area
networks, 43
bar code readers, 86–87
base mapping GPS display, 207
batch processes on Terminal
Server, 308
batteries
disposable zinc air-
powered, 92–93
extending life of, 13
extra, 93
in notebooks, lifespan, 10
in PDAs, lifespan, 23
infrared, lifespan, 41
lithium ion, 11
micro drives, consumption of, 91
in Pocket PCs, 22
weight, 93
Bcc lines, displaying in e-mail
messages, 135
biometric authentication, 60–62
blind carbon copies, 135
blocking users
on AOL Instant Messenger, 185
on MSN Messenger, 177
Bluetooth, 42–43
boats, connecting from, 51

About the Author   Robert L. Bogue (Rob.Bogue@ThorProjects.com) is a Microsoft Certified Systems Engineer and owns Thor Projects (*http://www.ThorProjects.com*), a technology consultancy in Carmel, Indiana. He has contributed to over a hundred book projects and written countless magazine articles and reviews. It is Rob's firsthand experience as a mobile professional; his extensive research into the types, practicalities, and pitfalls of all the aspects of mobile technology; and his straightforward approach that make this book so timely and essential.

Get a **Free**
e-mail newsletter, updates,
special offers, links to related books,
and more when you

register on line!

Register your Microsoft Press® title on our Web site and you'll get
a FREE subscription to our e-mail newsletter, *Microsoft Press
Book Connections.* You'll find out about newly released and upcoming
books and learning tools, online events, software downloads, special
offers and coupons for Microsoft Press customers, and information
about major Microsoft® product releases. You can also read useful
additional information about all the titles we publish, such as detailed book descriptions, tables of contents and indexes, sample
chapters, links to related books and book series, author biographies,
and reviews by other customers.

Registration is easy. Just visit this Web page and fill in your information:

http://www.microsoft.com/mspress/register

Microsoft

Proof of Purchase

Use this page as proof of purchase if participating in a promotion or rebate offer on
this title. Proof of purchase must be used in conjunction with other proof(s) of
payment such as your dated sales receipt—see offer details.

Mobilize Yourself!: The Microsoft® Guide to Mobile Technology
0-7356-1502-0

CUSTOMER NAME

Microsoft Press, PO Box 97017, Redmond, WA 98073-9830